"I'm proud to be part of a book that inspires and obviously really cares about teenagers. No preaching, no telling teens what not to do. Everyone should read this book."

Jennifer Love Hewitt
singer and actress, *Party of Five*

"What a wonderful gift this book is for teenagers. These stories will make you laugh, make you cry, and inspire you to feel better about life, love and learning."

Barbara DeAngelis
bestselling author, *Real Moments*

"I love this book. It picks you up and shows you how to get the most out of life through the stories of other people"

Janet, age 15

"I will read this book over and over again. It does more than just entertain you, it actually changes the way you feel inside . . . in a good way."

Jennifer, age 16

"I liked reading about how girls feel in relationship to guys. That was the best part."

Michael, age 16

"I realized after reading this that I can do more than I thought. I play sports and sometimes, if I have a bad game, I think I'm finished. After reading these stories, I feel differently."

Daniel, age 15

CHICKEN SOUP FOR THE TEENAGE SOUL

101 Stories of Life, Love and Learning

Jack Canfield
Mark Victor Hansen
Kimberly Kirberger

Health Communications, Inc.
Deerfield Beach, Florida

www.hci-online.com

We would like to acknowledge the many publishers and individuals who granted us permission to reprint the cited material. (Note: The stories that were penned anonymously, that are in the public domain, or, that were written by Jack Canfield, Mark Victor Hansen or Kimberly Kirberger are not included in this listing.)

After an exhaustive search, we were unable to find the authors or copyright holders of the following stories that we have included in the book:

First Kiss—First Lesson, by Jennifer Braunschweiger

Passing the Dream, by Penny Caldwell

The Most Mature Thing I've Ever Seen, by Susan Doenim

Mason-Dixon Memory, by Clifton Davis

Please Listen

The Gossiper

The Bible

Please Hear What I'm Not Saying

The Oyster

Wild Thing, by Jennifer Philbin

If you are, or if you know, the authors or copyright holders, please contact us and we will properly credit you and reimburse you for your contribution.

(Continued on page 351)

Library of Congress Cataloging-in-Publication Data

Canfield, Jack, date.
Chicken soup for the teenage soul: 101 stories of life, love, and learning / Jack Canfield, Mark Victor Hansen, Kimberly Kirberger.
p. cm.
ISBN 1-55874-468-1 (hardcover). — ISBN 1-55874-463-0 (trade paper)
1. Teenagers—Conduct of life. I. Hansen, Mark Victor. II. Kirberger, Kimberly, date.
BJ1661.C17 1997 97-5378
158.1'28'0835—dc21 CIP

ISBN 1-55874-463-0 (trade paper)—ISBN 1-55874-468-1 (hardcover)

Publisher: Health Communications, Inc.
3201 S.W. 15th Street
Deerfield Beach, FL 33442-8190

Cover artwork by Fred Babb
Cover re-design by Andrea Perrine Brower

Dedication

With love we dedicate this book to
all the teenagers who have become our friends
and who have taught us through their friendship
that we all have something important
to offer each other.

We also dedicate this book to
John and Jesse, two perennial teenagers
who gave Kim the time and space to
work on this book for two years
to Lia, who first opened our minds to the
possibility of creating this book,
to Oran and Kyle, who taught their
dad a lot during their teenage years,
and to our younger children,
Christopher, Elisabeth and Melanie,
who will soon enter their teenage years,
and all of whom we love very much.

Contents

3. ON FAMILY

4. ON LOVE AND KINDNESS

5. ON LEARNING

6. TOUGH STUFF

7. MAKING A DIFFERENCE

8. GOING FOR IT!

Acknowledgments

It takes a thousand voices to tell a single story.

Native American Saying

This book took two years to write, compile and edit. It has been a true labor of love for all of us. One of the greatest joys in creating this book has been working with hundreds of teenagers and adults who gave this project not just their time and attention, but their hearts and souls as well. We would like to thank the following people for their dedication and contributions, without which this book could not have been created:

Our family members—Georgia, Christopher, Oran, Kyle, Patty, Elisabeth, Melanie, John and Jesse—for once again sharing with us the incredibly time-consuming process of creating a book. Thanks again for giving us the space, time and emotional support we needed to follow our passion and complete what must have seemed like an endless task. We love you all more than words can ever express.

We would like to extend a very special thanks to a group of teens who worked with us to ensure this book would be about issues that truly concern teenagers. To Lisa Gumenick whose enthusiasm for this project inspired the entire group, to Lisa Rothbard whose honesty and kindness touched us all, to Bree Abel for her incredible spirit and her contagious confidence, to Hana Ivanhoe for her depth of character and for sharing so openly with us. To Jamie Yellin for her big heart and smile and to Lia Gay for always being so generous with your wisdom. You guys are the heart of this book and we thank you and love you. We'd also like to thank your parents for acknowledging the importance of these meetings and making sure you got there.

Heather McNamara, for editing and preparing the final manuscript with such ease, talent and clarity. We deeply appreciate your incredible ability to take everything in the roughest of form and make it all work.You are truly a master at what you do.

Patty Aubrey, for all that you do to make our lives work easier and better. Thank you for the countless ways you make a significant difference. You are the best!

Nancy Mitchell, for the hundreds of hours spent obtaining permissions for the stories, and for your keen sense of what works and what doesn't. Your commitment and dedication—as well as your detective skills on the Internet—are amazing!

Jessie Braun, who read every story (and there were lots), and who kindly told us which ones didn't work by simply refusing to type them. At 18, you are more together than most grownups. This book could not have happened without you.

The students at John F. Kennedy High School in Granada Hills, California, for giving us extensive feedback and invaluable suggestions for improving the first draft of the manuscript. We especially want to thank Willy Ackerman for organizing this huge project.

Kim Foley, whose dedication and hard work supporting Kimberly Kirberger never ceases to fill our hearts with gratitude. You are an amazing person.

All those who read the original manuscript, helped us make the final selections and made invaluable comments on how to improve the book: Bree Abel, Christine Belleris, Jessie Braun, Morgan Brown, Kyle Canfield, Taycora Canfield, Matthew Diener, Pegine Echivaria, Kim Foley, Sima Freed, Steve Freedman, Lia Gay, Jessica Ghaemmaghami, Randee Goldsmith, Lisa Gumenick, Alejandra Hernandez, Hana Ivanhoe, Ben Kay, Lauren Leb, Katy Leicht, James Malinchak, Maggie McQuisten, Dave Murcott, Lisa Rothbard, Hilary Russell, Alyson Sena, Ben Watkins and Linda Zehr.

Pegine Echivaria, Jim Hullihan, James Malinchak and Jack Schlatter, for all your important work with teens and for being there on the phone for countless hours when we needed support and expert advice about the world of today's teenagers.

Peter Vegso and Gary Seidler at Health Communications, Inc., for believing in this book and for working hard to get it into the hands of millions of readers. Thank you, Peter and Gary!

Christine Belleris, Matthew Diener and Mark Colucci, our editors at Health Communications, Inc., for your generous efforts in bringing this book to its high state of excellence.

Fred Babb, for your creative efforts in contributing to the cover design of the book.

Kim Weiss and Arielle Ford, for letting people know the book exists through your brilliant public relations efforts.

Teresa Spohn, Veronica Romero, Rosalie Miller, Lisa Williams, Julie Barnes and Kathleen Long, for handling everything else in our offices so that we could concentrate on completing this book.

To Terri Andruk and Clay White for nourishing us with your delicious food and your kind hearts.

To Leigh Taylor, Jessie Braun and Trudy Klefstad whose

excellent typing skills helped us get this project completed on time.

Dale Lindholm and Brad Frye for your continuing support. You guys are the best!

Nancy Berg, Eileen Lawrence, Sharon Linnéa Scott, Dave Murcott and Jane Watkins, who edited some of the more difficult pieces into wonderfully moving stories.Thanks for being so talented and so fast at what you do!

The more than 1,500 people who submitted stories, poems and other pieces for our consideration. You all know who you are. While many of the pieces you submitted were wonderful, they just didn't fit into the overall structure of this book. Nevertheless, you provided us with hundreds of hours of enjoyable and inspiring reading. Thank you.

Because of the enormity of this project we are sure we have left out the names of some of the people who helped us. For that we are sorry but nonetheless grateful for the many hands that made this book possible. Thank you all for your vision, your caring, your commitment and your heartfelt actions. We love you all!

Introduction

Dear Teenager,

Finally, a book for you. REALLY. This book is filled with stories that will make you laugh and make you cry. It will act as a best friend, there for you when you need it, always ready to tell you a story that will indeed make you feel better. When you are lonely it will keep you company, and when you are thinking of your future it will tell you, "YES, you can do it, whatever you set your mind to." There are stories in here about dreams realized and loves lost; about overcoming shyness and surviving a suicide. There are stories of triumph and stories so sad that you will definitely cry. And each one speaks *to* you, not *at* you.

How to Read This Book

Read this book however you want to, from beginning to end or jumping around. If there is a particular subject that concerns you or that you have a special interest in, go there first. Latina Johnson, a high school student, wrote to us after reading the chapter on relationships:

> *I loved reading "Losing the 'Us.'" It described everything I was going through with this boy. I definitely still have feelings for him, though.*

Stephanie Chitaca wrote:

> *I have to say that "A Famous Father" was my favorite one. It made me realize just how meaningless our (my father's and mine) arguments are. My father's well-being is very important to me.*

Diana Verdigan had a special connection to the story "Tigress":

> *I felt the same when I had to leave my cat. No rage, no denial, no hysteria, just acceptance of the inevitable, and it cost me a lot, too. It is possible that the boy won't have any more pets.*

This is a book you never finish. It is our hope that you read it over and over, referring to it when you have a problem, or turning to it for some inspiration or guidance.

Kara Salsburg, a teenager, wrote to us about the other *Chicken Soup* books, "I read them over and over again. *Chicken Soup for the Soul* has been my most enjoyable reading experience."

"I enjoy reading [the stories in *Chicken Soup*]," wrote Shannon Richard, age 14, "and I find I have a new sense of life after reading them."

Share These Stories

We had a panel of readers grade these stories. One of them told us that by the end, she had friends come over every day after school, and they took turns reading to each other from the book.

You will find as you read this book that you just can't keep some of these stories to yourself. You will want to share them with a friend. We have had countless reports of teenagers reading stories to each other on the phone, or staying up late with a friend "reading just one more."

A.J. Langer, who played Rayanne on *My So-Called Life*, told us that she took the book with her on a camping trip, and she and her friends sat around the campfire reading to each other their favorite stories. They were so inspired (and creative) that they then wrote their own stories, which they read to each other the following night.

Teens have also told us that these stories are good at saying things that they have trouble expressing. One teen (who prefers not to be named) said:

> *"Please Listen" was exactly what my friend Karen needed to hear. She is my best friend, but she never listens to me, so I wrote it out and gave it to her. I just said that it was one of my favorites. I think she got the message 'cause she started listening to me more.*

This Is *Your* Book

It was very important to us that this book be about what *you* are really about. We went to great lengths to ensure that it dealt with the issues that concern you, and that it addressed those issues in an open-minded and caring way. If we felt a story was preachy or too corny we took it out.

After the students at John F. Kennedy High School helped grade the stories, we received literally hundreds of letters. It thrilled us to see that we had accomplished our goal.

> *This book is definitely a book I would get, not only for myself, but for my friends as well.*
>
> —Jason Martinson

If ever I would buy a book, this is the book I would buy.

—Regina Funtanilla

What I liked best were the poems. They really had a lot of meaning.

—Richard Nino

I really appreciate that you care what we [high school students] think.

—Edward Zubyk

Share with Us

We would love to hear what you think. Please let us know how these stories affected you and which ones were your favorites.

Also, please send us any stories you would like to submit for consideration in our upcoming *2nd Helping of Chicken Soup for the Teenage Soul.* You can send us either stories and poems that you have written or ones that you have read and liked.

We hope you enjoy reading this book as much as we enjoyed compiling, editing and writing it. Making this *Chicken Soup* has truly been a labor of love.

Send these stories to:

Kimberly Kirberger
P.O. Box 936
Pacific Palisades, CA 90272
e-mail: Jewels24@aol.com

1

ON RELATIONSHIPS

Relationships—of all kinds—are like sand held in your hand. Held loosely, with an open hand, the sand remains where it is. The minute you close your hand and squeeze tightly to hold on, the sand trickles through your fingers. You may hold on to some of it, but most will be spilled. A relationship is like that. Held loosely, with respect and freedom for the other person, it is likely to remain intact. But hold too tightly, too possessively, and the relationship slips away and is lost.

Kaleel Jamison, *The Nibble Theory*

"Brian promised to love me forever. Then he told me about a Star Trek episode where they scientifically proved the possibility that forever might actually last only a few days."

Losing the "Us"

When an emotional injury takes place,
the body begins a process
as natural as the healing
of a physical wound.

Let the process happen.
Trust that nature
will do the healing.

Know that the pain will pass,
and, when it passes,
you will be stronger,
happier, more sensitive and aware.

Mel Colgrove
from *How to Survive the Loss of a Love*

"So does this mean you want to break up?" I asked softly, hoping my question would go unanswered. That is how it all began, or I guess, ended. The months the two of us had shared were some of the happiest, hardest and most educational months I ever experienced. It seemed impossible that this was the last conversation we would have as Ben and Lia, the couple.

I had ignored the fact that the majority of high-school relationships do not last. I guess, in the back of my mind, I always thought that Ben was the only boy I would ever have these feelings for, that he was the only boy who would ever understand me. I never took into account that the last month of our relationship was one of the hardest times I had ever gone through. It just stopped being fun. It stopped being about us and started to be about everything that surrounded him and me.

The next day at school I tried looking great to make him see what he had given up. I even tried to talk to him like my heart wasn't aching, like I was better off and even happier. But inside I looked at him and could only see all the love and time I had given and all the hurt I had received. I walked around school in a complete daze and cried myself to sleep every night. He was the only thing I thought about, dreamt about and talked about. I drove my friends crazy by constantly analyzing the situation. *How could it have ended?* I found my other half when I was with him. I felt like something had been torn from me, like I was no longer whole.

One night, I couldn't stand it. I gave up and called him. I didn't last five minutes before I broke down and started crying. I told him I had forgotten how to be by myself, and that I needed him. I didn't know how to be Lia without Ben. We had been through so much together that I could not imagine getting through this on my own. He told me that he would always care for me, but that it had become impossible to love me.

For weeks I couldn't see him with other girls without thinking that they were dating. I threw myself at different guys.

I don't know at exactly what point things started to change. I began spending time with my friends. I joined clubs and made after-school plans. I was doing all I could to stay busy.

Slowly I began to have fun by myself, without Ben. Beyond that, I discovered things I liked doing, ways I could be of help. I lent a sympathetic ear to others who were hurting.

I began to smile and, finally, to laugh again. Whole days would pass without a thought of Ben. I would see him at school and wave. I was not ready to be friends with him. I was still healing. But I know I didn't cover a big wound with a Band-Aid and forget about it. I let the wound heal itself and felt enough pain to know that I had truly cared for him.

In my rebound stage, I pursued a lot of guys. Once I healed, they pursued me. The wonderful thing that happened was that I learned how to be a whole person, not half a couple. I'm in a new relationship now, and eventually we will probably break up, and it will be hard, and I will cry and feel just as much, if not more, pain. But I had to ask myself if never caring for someone so that I wouldn't feel that hurt was worth it. I know now that the famous quote is true. "Better to have loved and lost than never to have loved at all." Because no matter what, loving yourself can heal anything.

Lia Gay, 16

"This is the 90s. You can't just dump your boyfriend anymore. You have to recycle him."

Reprinted by permission of Randy Glasbergen.

After a While

After a while you learn the subtle difference between
holding a hand and chaining a soul,
And you learn that love doesn't mean leaning and
company doesn't mean security,
And you begin to learn that kisses aren't contracts
and presents aren't promises,
And you begin to accept your defeats with your head
up and your eyes open, with the grace of an adult,
not the grief of a child,
And you learn to build all your roads on today
because tomorrow's ground is too uncertain for
plans.
After a while you learn that even sunshine burns if
you get too much.
So plant your own garden and decorate your own
soul, instead of waiting for someone to bring you
flowers.
And you learn that you really can endure . . .
That you really are strong,
And you really do have worth.

Veronica A. Shoffstall
written at age 19

Soul Mates

I have often told my daughter, Lauren, the story of how her father and I met and of our courtship. Now that she is 16 years old, she is concerned because she realizes that her soul mate might be sitting next to her in a class or might even ask her for a date, and she is not quite ready to make the same commitment her parents made years ago.

I met Mike on October 9, 1964. Our shy eyes met from across the patio at our friend Andrea's party. We smiled and eventually found ourselves in a conversation that lasted the entire evening, to the exclusion of everyone else. I was 11 and he was 12. We went steady three days later, which ended after a somewhat tumultuous month.

Months later, Mike still invited me to his lavish bar mitzvah and even asked me to dance. (Years later he told me that despite my braces, my skinny legs and my flipped hair, he thought I was beautiful.)

Mike and I had many mutual friends and were in the same social group at school, so our paths constantly crossed throughout the next few years. Every time I broke up with a boyfriend or had my heart broken by another, my mother would say, "Don't worry, you're going to end up with Mike Leb." I would shriek, "Never! Why would you think such a thing?" She would remind me how his name often came up in my conversations and what a nice guy he was.

Finally, I was in high school, and it was packed with new cute guys. I was ready. What did I care if Mike started dating my best friend? Why, I wondered, was this slowly driving me crazy? Why did we find ourselves talking while waiting for our buses? I will never forget the navy blue penny loafers he wore. Nobody else I knew had such great shoes. My mother's words often came to my mind, but I still wanted to erase them.

By the summer after tenth grade, Mike and I had spent more time together—in the company of his girlfriend, also known as my best friend, and others. That summer Mike left for a Spanish program in Mexico. I found I really missed seeing him. When he returned in August, he called and came by my home. He was so adorable with his tan skin and worldly demeanor. He still couldn't speak a word of Spanish but he looked so good. It was August 19, 1968, when we looked at each other outside my home and realized we had to be together. Of course, we had to wait until after the date I had that night with another guy. I told my date that I was going to start dating Mike so I had to be home early. Mike then told his on-again, off-again girlfriend it was off again for good.

We kept our relationship our little secret until we could proudly announce it at the next party. We walked in late and boldly told all of our friends that we were officially a couple. Not a soul seemed surprised as they uttered "finally."

After graduation from high school, I went away to college. I lasted 10 weeks before I transferred to a closer college to be near Mike. On June 18, 1972, we were wed.

I was 19, and Mike was 20. We set up our love nest in married housing while we both finished our college degrees. I became a special-education teacher while Mike went on to medical school.

Now, 25 years later, I smile at our beautiful daughter, Lauren, and our handsome son, Alex. Although their parents' legacy causes them to look at high school relationships a bit differently, they will never have to worry about their parents saying "Don't take it so seriously; it's only puppy love."

Fran Leb

The Miss of a Great "Miss"

You never lose by loving. You always lose by holding back.

Barbara De Angelis

I'll never forget the day I first saw "a dream walking." Her name was Susie Summers (name changed to protect the fantastic). Her smile, which sparkled beneath two twinkling eyes, was electric and made people who received it (especially guy people) feel very special.

While her physical beauty was astounding, it was her invisible beauty I shall always remember. She really cared about other people and was an extremely talented listener. Her sense of humor could brighten your entire day and her wise words were always exactly what you needed to hear. She was not only admired but also genuinely respected by members of both sexes. With everything in the world to be conceited about, she was extremely humble.

Needless to say, she was every guy's dream. Especially mine. I got to walk her to class once a day, and once I even got to eat lunch with her all by myself. I felt on the top of the world.

I would think, "If only I could have a girlfriend like Susie Summers, I'd never even look at another female." But I figured that someone this outstanding was probably dating someone far better than myself. Even though I was president of the student body, I just knew I didn't stand a ghost of a chance.

So at graduation, I said farewell to my first big crush.

A year later, I met her best friend in a shopping center and we had lunch together. With a lump in my throat, I asked how Susie was.

"Well, she got over you," was the reply.

"What are you talking about?" I asked.

"You were really cruel to her the way you led her on, always walking her to class and making her think you were interested. Do you remember the time you had lunch with her? Well, she stayed by the phone the entire weekend. She was sure you were going to call and ask her out."

I was so afraid of rejection, I never risked letting her know how I felt. Suppose I had asked her out and she'd said no? What's the worst thing that could have happened? I wouldn't have had a date with her. Well, guess what? I DIDN'T HAVE A DATE WITH HER ANYHOW! What makes it worse is that I probably could have.

Jack Schlatter

CLOSE TO HOME ©John McPherson/Dist. of UNIVERSAL PRESS SYNDICATE.

My First Kiss, and Then Some

I was a very shy teenager, and so was my first boyfriend. We were high school sophomores in a small town. We had been dating for about six months. A lot of sweaty hand-holding, actually *watching* movies, and talking about nothing in particular. We often came close to kissing—we both knew that we wanted to be kissed—but neither of us had the courage to make the first move.

Finally, while sitting on my living room couch, he decided to go for it. We talked about the weather (really), then he leaned forward. I put a pillow up to my face to block him! He kissed the pillow.

I wanted to be kissed sooooo badly, but I was too nervous to let him get close. So I moved away, down the couch. He moved closer. We talked about the movie (who cared!), he leaned forward again. I blocked him again.

I moved to the end of the couch. He followed, we talked. He leaned . . . I stood up! (I must have had a spasm in my legs.) I walked over near the front door and stood there, leaning against the wall with my arms crossed, and said impatiently, "Well, are you going to kiss me or not?"

"Yes", he said. So I stood tall, closed my eyes tight, puckered my lips and faced upwards. I waited . . . and waited. (Why wasn't he kissing me?) I opened my eyes; he was coming right at me. I smiled.

HE KISSED MY TEETH!

I could have died.

He left.

I wondered if he had told anyone about my clumsy behavior. Since I was so extremely and painfully shy, I practically hid for the next two years, causing me to never have another date all through high school. As a matter of fact, when I walked down the hallway at school, if I saw him or any other great guy walking toward me, I quickly stepped into the nearest room until he passed. And these were boys I had known since kindergarten.

The first year at college, I was determined not to be shy any longer. I wanted to learn how to kiss with confidence and grace. I did.

In the spring, I went home. I walked into the latest hangout, and who do you suppose I see sitting at the bar, but my old kissing partner. I walked over to his bar stool and tapped him on the shoulder. Without hesitation, I took him in my arms, dipped him back over his stool, and kissed him with my most assertive kiss. I sat him up, looked at him victoriously, and said, "So there!"

He pointed to the lady next to him and said to me, "Mary Jane, I'd like you to meet my wife."

Mary Jane West-Delgado

LUANN By Greg Evans

LUANN reprinted by permission of United Feature Syndicate, Inc.

First Kiss—First Lesson

It's all right letting yourself go, as long as you can get yourself back.

Mick Jagger

The night of my first real kiss was also the night of the worst fight I ever had with my mother. I'd had my eye on Jon Glass forever, and suddenly out of nowhere I spied him at the party that my best friend, Lara, and I had finally gathered the courage to stop by. The guy throwing the party lived in a skinny brick house on a crazy steep hill in San Francisco. Light from the kitchen and a streetlight down the block spilled into the little backyard garden, not quite reaching the corner where Jon was standing in a cluster of people. I was wearing my favorite pink shirt and Levi's with patches I'd sewn onto the knees. Lara smoothed my hair and told me to smile and pushed me out the door of the kitchen and into the garden. The next thing I knew, Jon and I were talking and then we were the only people still in the garden and then we were leaving the party together and walking hand in hand up and up the steep street and then we kissed and I felt like I was living someone else's life, I was so happy.

The party was only a couple of blocks from my school, so I knew the streets we walked along as well as I knew the ones in my own neighborhood. But as I held Jon's hand and we walked and stopped and kissed, I felt like I was seeing the houses and the trees and the world for the first time. In a way I felt as if I were seeing Jon for the first time. Like, before he was just this guy—okay, a very nice guy with amazing pale blue eyes who helped me with my calculus homework and played soccer as if he were born with cleats on his feet—but now here he was picking me a flower off a tree in someone's front yard. We meandered to a nearby park and sat on the swings and looked at the stars. Of course I lost track of time as we roamed around, and when Jon finally dropped me off at my house, the sky was starting to turn light blue and pink with the dawn.

My key had barely hit the lock on the front door when my mother pulled it open and said in her most dangerous and quiet voice, "Where is he?" Just like that—deadpan. Each word equally weighted, equally heavy: "Where is he?" I stood on the stoop in the early-morning spring cold, yearning to bolt the 10 feet—so close, so far—between me and the safety of my room.

I tried to play dumb. "Who are you talking about, Mom?"

But she just stood there blocking the doorway—hands on hips, face contorted with anger—and said; "You're untrustworthy, you're irresponsible, and you're a disappointment."

Later that day, Lara told me my mom had freaked out and called her at home in the middle of the night. Lara didn't have any idea where I'd gone after I left the party, but she tried to cover for me by saying she was sure I was fine; after all, I was just hanging out with Jon. But that just made my mother worry more ("Jon? Who is Jon?"), and by the time I got home, her worry and stress and churning imagination—combined with her fatigue and relief that I was home safely (no longer wandering the streets in the middle of the night with some strange boy)—finally boiled over, and she exploded at me. I was so shocked at her harsh reaction—shouldn't she be happy that I was actually safe and would no longer have to cope with the shame of never having kissed a boy?—that I screamed right back at her and, after she let me in off the stoop, I slammed my door and flung myself face down on my bed and cried and cried at the grand injustice that was my life.

The next morning at breakfast, I could barely eat. My mom didn't yell anymore—she just told me I couldn't go to the formal citywide dance I'd been looking forward to for months. So I didn't yell anymore, either. I just got up from the table and went to my room and called Lara and made plans to have her pick me up for the dance at 7 P.M. that Friday. I didn't care what my mother said. I was going anyway.

The week passed perfectly pleasantly. I went to school, I raced home in time to see *Days of Our Lives,* I fussed around pretending to study, my mom got home late from work, we ate spaghetti and salad, and I silently cleared the table without her asking. When Friday night rolled around, I gathered my formal dress and my favorite heels and my stockings and shoved them into a bag. Then, as soon as the headlights from Lara's car swept into my window as she swung into the driveway, I slipped out the front door and softly pulled it closed behind me. Free.

Jon didn't show up at the dance but some other cute boys did, and a couple of them talked to me and I was complimented on my purple silk dress and my purple suede shoes and I made sure to stand next to Lara, who looked stunning in something backless and red and short. But I was so racked with guilt for having taken it out on my mother that I just couldn't have the time of my life like I'd anticipated. Afterward, I was scared to go home and face the music, so Lara and I just drove the dark streets of San Francisco aimlessly, with the radio on way too loud, and ended up eating slightly stale muffins at Dunkin' Donuts with a couple of worn-out cops who looked at us like we were crazy delinquents for not being home in bed at such a late hour.

I finally went home and crept under the covers, and in the morning my mother looked upset and didn't really talk to me. In fact, she hadn't really talked to me since our big fight. I guess she didn't know what to do, so she put me on the phone with my father, who was living in Los Angeles at the time. He didn't lose his temper. He just asked, "Why didn't you talk to her about it? Ask her again if you could go to the dance? Tell her you were sorry you were late? Call when you knew you'd be out with Jon?" In other words, why didn't I just think about what I was doing and realize my actions affected other people?

Uh, good question. And I wish I could say that I had a big talk with my mother right after I got off the phone with my father, but I didn't. And the situation got worse before it got better.

The next time I saw Jon outside of school was when I walked into a party just in time to see him disappear into a bedroom with another girl. Her name was Michele, and she was a year younger than me and had a reputation for going too far with too many people. Standing there in the middle of some stranger's sunken living room where people were dancing. I started crying. In a burst of boldness, Lara tried the door of the room Jon and Michele occupied ("I'll interrupt them, and then he'll feel bad and come out," she promised)—but the door was locked. I had lost him. I had never had him.

While I sat in another bedroom and cried and imagined what the two of them were doing together, girls from the party came in and sat with me and told me raunchy men-are-jerks jokes. ("A man asked a genie to make him a billion times smarter than any other man on earth. The genie turned him into a woman.") Eventually, after Jon had finally emerged from the locked bedroom, I confronted him by a swing set in the backyard and made him tell me to my face that he was sorry.

I listened to him say that he didn't want a girlfriend and had a problem with commitment, and I listened to the litany of crimes against his soul: his parents' divorce, the death of his dog, the difficulty of his chemistry class, living in the shadow of his older brother. All the excuses he used to forgive himself for harming me. Everything he said seemed pretty lame and beside the point, to tell the truth. In fact, what he offered wasn't an apology at all, and it didn't make me feel any better because nothing really could. (Although, I must admit, I was not unhappy the next week at school when all the girls snubbed Jon because they knew everything that had happened. And I was willing to listen when his cousin cornered me in an empty classroom and told me that she thought I was too cool for him anyway.)

So things with Jon obviously didn't end perfectly or even anywhere near how I would have liked, but at least I tried to settle things with him and gave him the benefit of listening to his side of the story. It kills me that I cornered Jon—who had betrayed me—and made him talk to me, but I never even gave my mom that chance. So how could I expect her to understand what was at stake for me in staying out late that night, in going to the dance? I owed her—and she owed me—a conversation. But that meant we each would have to articulate what we wanted, we each would have to deal with the other person's needs, and at the time I thought I couldn't deal.

A conversation is a slippery creature. A conversation is a risk. A real conversation changes the people who have it. It's about exchanging ideas, considering other opinions, shifting positions. That's why conversations are so difficult: You risk changing yourself, admitting you were wrong, coming to appreciate the other person's perspective. My mother and I were afraid to have an honest conversation because then she would have to admit her daughter was no longer a baby, was old enough to kiss a boy, wanted to kiss boys. And I would have to admit I was wrong not to call. That I was way later coming home than I'd ever been before. That even though I wanted to kiss boys, I still needed my mom.

Sometimes the whole story replays in my mind like a movie, and I know exactly what to do. Outside by the swing set, I calmly tell Jon how hurt I am, how I feel that he misled and betrayed me, and that I'm sorry about all the stuff he's been through in his life, but it's really no excuse for the way he acted. And instead of being silent at breakfast, I tell my mom how sorry I am to make her worry, but I also tell her why I like Jon so much. I describe how he sits next to me in history class and leans over and doodles on the edge of my notebook and how his shoes are always scuffed and his socks almost never match, and my mom and I laugh together. I mean, what mom's heart isn't going to melt when you tell her about a guy who saves you a seat in class and waves as the boys' soccer team runs by the girls' practice field? And in the new movie, I listen to my mom's side of the story and try to see the situation from her point of view.

It's not like I just settle for everything she tells me, either. When she says that I can't go to the dance, I persist. Ask again. Think about why she says I can't go, reevaluate the situation using my new understanding of where she's coming from, revise my approach and ask again. When it comes out in our conversation that she doesn't think I deserve to go out because I rarely help out around the house, I do extra chores and ask again. Bring home an A on a tough test and ask again.

What I really wanted in the end wasn't Jon, specifically—obviously, he turned out to be a jerk—but the kind of life where Jon was possible, where my mom wouldn't freak out when I missed curfew, where I could go out with boys without causing a major crisis. And what my mother ultimately wanted wasn't a slave daughter who blindly obeyed her every rule, but a daughter she could rely on and trust and not stay up half the night worrying about. And what I know now is this: If my mom and I had done that deceptively simple thing, talking, negotiating, compromising until we agreed on a set of privileges, then we both would have gotten something we wanted.

Jennifer Braunschweiger

"Oh, look at this! Our little girl coming home from her first date! You kids just go ahead and say good night as though we're not even here!"

Changes in Life

I was 16 years old and a junior in high school, and the worst possible thing that could happen to me did. My parents decided to move our family from our Texas home to Arizona. I had two weeks to wrap up all of my "business" and move before school began. I had to leave my first job, my boyfriend and my best friend behind, and try to start a new life. I despised my parents for ruining my life.

I told everyone that I did not want to live in Arizona and would be returning to Texas the first chance I had. When I arrived in Arizona, I made sure everyone knew that I had a boyfriend and best friend waiting for me in Texas. I was determined to keep my distance from everyone; I would just be leaving soon anyway.

The first day of school came, and I was miserable. I could only think of my friends in Texas and how I wished I could be with them. For a while, I felt that my life was over. Eventually though, things got a little better.

It was in my second period accounting class where I first saw him. He was tall, trim and really good looking. He had the most beautiful blue eyes I had ever seen. He was sitting just three seats away from me in the same front row of class. Feeling I had nothing to lose, I decided to talk to him.

"Hi, my name is Sheila; what's yours?" I asked with a Texas drawl.

The guy next to him thought that I was asking *him*. "Mike."

"Oh, hi, Mike," I humored him. "What's your name?" I asked again, focusing my attention on this blue-eyed boy.

He looked behind him, not believing that I could be asking him for his name. "Chris," he responded quietly.

"Hi, Chris!" I smiled. Then I went about my work.

Chris and I became friends. We enjoyed talking to each other in class. Chris was a jock, and I was in the school band; in high school, peer pressure demanded that the two groups did not mix socially. Our paths crossed occasionally at school functions; but for the most part, our friendship remained within the four classroom walls of accounting class.

Chris graduated that year, and we went our separate ways for a while. Then one day, he came to see me while I was working in a store in the mall. I was very happy to see him. He went on my breaks with me, and we started talking again. The pressure from his jock friends had subsided, and we became very close friends. My relationship with my boyfriend in Texas had become less important to me. I felt my bond with Chris growing stronger, taking the place of my relationship in Texas.

It had been a year since I moved from Texas, and Arizona was starting to feel like home. Chris escorted me to my senior prom; we triple-dated with two of his jock friends and their dates. The night of my prom changed our relationship forever; I was accepted by his friends, and that made Chris feel more comfortable. Finally, our relationship was in the open.

Chris was a very special person to me during such a difficult time in my life. Our relationship eventually blossomed into a very powerful love. I now understand that my parents did not move the family to Arizona to hurt me, although at the time, it sure felt as though they had. I now firmly believe that everything happens for a reason. For had I not moved to Arizona, I never would have met the man of my dreams.

Sheila K. Reyman

First Love

Truly loving another means letting go of all expectations. It means full acceptance, even celebration of another's personhood.

Karen Casey

Michael and I were never really boyfriend and girlfriend. He was three-and-a-half years older than I, which was a lot when I still didn't need to wear a bathing suit top. We grew up around the pool and tennis courts of a country club. He was an excellent tennis player with sure, calm strides and a powerful stroke. When I had to take time out from swimming and diving because my lips had turned blue, I sat on the grass wrapped in a towel and watched the tennis matches. Later in the day, the guys would come to the pool and hoist the girls on their shoulders for water fights. I liked it best on Michael's shoulders, which were broad. I felt safe.

At 16 his parents allowed him to drive during the day, and he often brought me home in his gray Dodge. The autumn after I turned 14, he started asking if I wanted to go to a late-afternoon movie with him. I wanted to say yes, but then I would get this jumpy feeling in my stomach and always change my mind. His dark eyes looked into mine, both pleasing and frightening me.

Gradually I stayed longer in his car, talking about things that troubled me. My older sister had lots of boyfriends, and although I worshipped her, she mostly didn't want anything to do with me. Then there were the intrigues around who was dating whom and which friends I trusted and why. A lot of my pain centered around my relationship with my parents, who had divorced when I was 11 and remarried when I was 13. I didn't know anyone else with a broken family, and I felt ashamed and unsure of myself, like I wasn't as good as the other kids. I could talk with Michael about all this. He was reassuring, and I began to trust him.

As time passed, I was ready to go to the movies with him. We also enjoyed hanging out at my house, where we would go down to the television room in the basement. I loved to watch TV with Michael so that I could cuddle with him on the couch. We were a strange pair. He loved sports, while I loved the arts. My sister and others made fun of his sports obsession. I guess I would have preferred it if everyone thought he was cool or if he'd been more artistic, but no one else cared about me the way he did. When he kissed me for the first time, we were at his house during a thunderstorm, watching a baseball game on television. I ran up to my sister's room when I got home. I must have looked goofy as I stood in her doorway and announced, "Michael kissed me."

"So?" she said. "Was that the first time?"

"Yeah," I nodded.

"What have you guys been doing all this time?" she demanded.

Michael dated other girls, and I went out with other boys. But I hated their sweaty palms and was horrified when a blind date tried to put his tongue in my mouth.

Only Michael understood that I needed to move slowly, and he was always very patient with me. Even though Michael reassured me many times that our relationship was special by saying, "It doesn't matter whether or not I have a girlfriend or you have a boyfriend; I will always be there for you," I still got jealous when I saw him interested in someone else.

Michael got engaged to a girl from out of town when I was 19. I was the only unmarried, unrelated girl at the wedding. As the bride and groom said good-bye to everyone, Michael came over to me and kissed me on the cheek. "I love you," he said.

He remained true to his word. When I needed to talk to someone, he was there. I got jealous sometimes when I thought of him loving and being romantic with his wife, but that changed as she and I became friends. I moved across the country and only saw Michael occasionally, at the club when I returned to visit my family. Now we sat at the pool and watched his kids swimming. Our lives were very different. I thought I probably wouldn't have much more than a half hour's worth of conversation to share with him, but I always felt a current of love go through me when I saw him.

When I was 38, my father died. The morning before his funeral, I thought to myself, *I wonder if Michael knows.* We hadn't seen each other or spoken for years. After the service the next day, as I was talking with the many friends and family who had come for the funeral, I felt a hand on my shoulder. I turned and saw those dark eyes.

"Are you all right?" he asked. I nodded. Putting both hands on my shoulders, he held me, looking into my eyes.

No one had ever understood the bond between us. I'm not sure that we did. But it was, and will always be, there.

Mary Ellen Klee

A High School Love Not Forgotten

When they saw him walking across our high school campus, most students couldn't help but notice Bruce. Tall and lanky, he was a thinner replica of James Dean, his hair flipped back above his forehead, and his eyebrows always cocked upward when he was in deep conversation. He was tender, thoughtful and profound. He would never hurt anyone.

I was scared of him.

I was just breaking up with my not-so-smart boyfriend, the one you stayed with and went back to 30 times out of bad habit, when Bruce headed me off at a campus pass one morning to walk with me. He helped me carry my books and made me laugh a dozen times with giddiness. I liked him. I really liked him.

He scared me because he was brilliant. But in the end, I realized I was more scared of myself than of him.

We started to walk together more at school. I would peer up at him from my stuffed locker, my heart beating rapidly, wondering if he would ever kiss me. We'd been seeing each other for several weeks and he still hadn't tried to kiss me.

Instead, he'd hold my hand, put his arm around me and send me off with one of my books to class. When I opened it, a handwritten note in his highly stylized writing would be there, speaking of love and passion in a deeper sense than I could understand at 17.

He would send me books, cards, notes, and would sit with me at my house for hours listening to music. He especially liked me to listen to the song, "You Brought Some Joy Inside My Tears," by Stevie Wonder.

At work one day I received a card from him that said, "I miss you when I'm sad. I miss you when I'm lonely. But most of all, I miss you when I'm happy."

I remember walking down the street of our small village, cars honking, the warm lights from stores beckoning strollers to come in from the cold, and all I could think about was, "Bruce misses me most when he's happy. What a strange thing."

I felt deeply uncomfortable to have such a romantic spirit by my side, a boy—really a man at 17—who thought his words out wisely, listened to every side of an argument, read poetry deep into the night and weighed his decisions carefully. I sensed a deep sadness in him but couldn't understand it. Looking back, I now think the sadness stemmed from being a person who really didn't fit into the high school plan.

Our relationship was so different from the one I'd had with my prior boyfriend. Our lives had been mostly movies and popcorn and gossip. We broke up routinely and dated other people. At times, it seemed like the whole campus was focused on the drama of our breakups, which were always intense and grand entertainment for our friends to discuss. A good soap opera.

I talked to Bruce about these things and with each story, he'd respond by putting his arm around me and telling me he'd wait while I sorted things out. And then he would read to me. He gave me the book *The Little Prince,* with the words underlined, "It's only in thy mind's eye that one can see rightly."

In response—the only way I knew how—I wrote passionate letters of love and poetry to him with an intensity I never knew before. But still I kept my walls up, keeping him at bay because I was always afraid that he'd discover I was fake, not nearly as intelligent or as deep a thinker as I found him to be.

I wanted the old habits of popcorn, movies and gossip back. It was so much easier. I remember well the day when Bruce and I stood outside in the cold and I told him I was going back to my old boyfriend. "He needs me more," I said in my girlish voice. "Old habits die hard."

Bruce looked at me with sadness, more for me than himself. He knew, and I knew then, I was making a mistake.

Years went by. Bruce went off to college first; then I did. Every time I came home for Christmas, I looked him up and went over for a visit with him and his family. I always loved his family—the warm greetings they gave me when they ushered me into their house, always happy to see me. I knew just by the way his family behaved that Bruce had forgiven me for my mistake.

One Christmas, Bruce said to me: "You were always a good writer. You were so good."

"Yes." His mother nodded in agreement. "You wrote beautifully. I hope you'll never give up your writing."

"But how do you know my writing?" I asked his mom.

"Oh, Bruce shared all the letters you wrote him with me," she said. "He and I could never get over how beautifully you wrote."

Then I saw his father's head nod, too. I sank back in my chair and blushed deeply. What exactly had I written in those letters?

I never knew Bruce had admired my writing as much as I had his intelligence.

Over the years, we lost touch. The last I heard from his father, Bruce had gone off to San Francisco and was thinking about becoming a chef. I went through dozens of bad relationships until I finally married a wonderful man—also very smart. I was more mature by then and could handle my husband's intelligence—especially when he'd remind me I had my own.

There's not one other boyfriend I ever think about with any interest, except for Bruce. Most of all, I hope he is happy. He deserves it. In many ways, I think he helped shape me, helped me learn how to accept the side of myself I refused to see amid movies, popcorn and gossip. He taught me how to see my spirit and my writer inside.

Diana L. Chapman

2

ON FRIENDSHIP

Some people come into our lives and quickly go. Some stay for a while and leave footprints on our hearts. And we are never, ever the same.

Source Unknown

Betty Ann

If you judge people, you have no time to love them.

Mother Teresa

Mistakes.

We all make them. Sometimes, if we're lucky, an eraser will do the trick, and we can rub it across the page, wipe away the dust, and all that's left of our careless mess is a hardly noticeable smudge.

But some mistakes can't be erased. No matter how old or young we are.

I was in the ninth grade the first time I really thought about all this. That year, I learned to diagram sentences on the blackboard, got my learner's permit, wore my first strapless bra, wrote poetry I never read to my parents—but by far, the toughest lesson I learned was that life doesn't come with erasers. I couldn't make something that had happened, not happen. Even imagination is powerless. There are no erasers. I was 14, and I wished then, and I wish now, that I could erase or imagine away what I did, what we all did, to Betty Ann.

She came to our school from Cleveland, Ohio, and to our ninth-grade class in Richmond, Virginia, Cleveland was on another planet.

"Oh, hi! Ohhooo . . ." whispered Margie under her breath, as Mrs. Johnson introduced Betty Ann in homeroom that first day. Margie could be real snooty sometimes. Nobody took her too seriously when she got into her rich-kid, old-money mood. She'd entertain us with cruise stories and New York gossip every afternoon as we sat on the front steps after lunch, licking the icing off Oreos and begging quarters for a Dr. Pepper from the drink machine in the gym. Margie would try to impress us, in her high-pitched, bragging voice, with the Vogue models she knew and how they shampooed their hair with beer, that people who ate their whole dinner with their salad fork were not the kind of people her family wanted her to marry into.

Actually, Margie was as insecure and as homely as the rest of us, and her life was about as exciting as the metric system, but we all knew Margie. We all knew everybody. Except Betty Ann. Most of us had been in the same class since kindergarten.

Then came Betty Ann of Cleveland, in her peasant blouses, rolled-down socks, and strange ideas.

If it had been just Margie who dug into Betty Ann, it wouldn't have turned out the way it did; she probably could have handled that. But we all were in on it.

I guess what started us off was when Betty Ann wrote a better English composition than Susan Henderson. Susan was the writer of the class, and we were very proud of her. Her weekly story was always so good, Miss Moon usually chose it to read aloud to the class every Friday. Susan would sit back in her desk, a pencil stuck behind her ear, looking to all of us just like a promising young literary genius we could say we once knew.

The Friday after Betty Ann arrived on the scene, Susan twirled her pencil, leaned back in her desk, and waited for the best composition of the week to be read. Hers, of course.

Only it wasn't. It was Betty Ann's, and it was about a black poet named Langston Hughes and how he had become a spokesman for his people. Susan's stories were always about horse shows or opening nights.

We'd never heard of Langston Hughes. Besides, this was an all-white private school. Martin Luther King was being nailed by most of the adults we knew. All in all, it was a real bomb to have Betty Ann go on about Langston Hughes's "Black Nativity" and his description of the "maple-sugar child" and how he thought Carl Sandburg's poems fall on the page like blood clots of song from the wounds of humanity.

In Susan's stories, the "telephone jangled" and "the rainbow painted the sky." Stuff like that. Betty Ann was writing about the civil war in Spain and the black ghettos of Harlem. Langston Hughes was from Cleveland. We might have guessed.

Mrs. Johnson came to the part in Betty Ann's composition where Langston Hughes writes a poem about how he likes watermelon so much that if he should meet the queen of England, he'd be proud to offer her a piece. That was when Agnes Matherson's eyes caught mine (or was it the other way around?) and we started imitating the queen of England eating a piece of watermelon. The whole class burst out laughing. The rest of the story was never read, and everybody but Betty Ann had to stay after school and clean blackboards. The next day at lunch, Betty Ann found a note under her lettuce saying we were sorry, but the cafeteria was sho' nuf out of watermelon.

After that, she became the class joke. What she wore, what she said, what she ate somehow always gave one of us an idea for a wisecrack. There was a kind of one-upmanship about getting Betty Ann that had less to do with Betty Ann than with our own jungle mentality. I know that now, but I didn't think about it then. She became a pawn.

She started getting sick a lot. There'd be whole weeks when she'd miss school, but the Betty Ann stories went on even without her. She came to our school from another planet. She was our little moron, our Polack, our village idiot.

Then one day, Betty Ann and I were assigned a project together. Everyone had selected a partner, and I was out of town at a school swimming meet the day the assignment was given, so I got stuck with Betty Ann. Everyone kidded me, and I laughed with them. The day before the project was due, I had to go over to her house after school to work on it with her. Her mother fixed a plate of cookies and kept coming into the room to see if I wanted more Coke or anything. She said I was the only one of Betty Ann's friends who had come over after school, and she was glad to meet me.

The phone rang while I was there, and it was for me. Betty Ann's mother was in the kitchen when I heard Margie giggling at the other end of the line: "Have you eaten any maple sugar candy or watermelon, kiddo?"

She waited for me to snicker an undercover laugh.

I saw Betty Ann's mother just standing in the kitchen with her back to me, pretending not to be listening. It was as if she had heard everything. I hung up. I think it was at that moment when I began to see what we had been doing.

"Why don't you girls like Betty Ann? She likes you . . ."

Nobody had ever asked me a question before or since that made me feel so stupid.

If kindness could kill, Betty Ann would have been dead in a week. But it was too late. Her parents moved her to another school, then we heard later that she'd had a nervous breakdown.

Once, years later when I was home from college, I saw Betty Ann in the doctor's office. She didn't even recognize me.

Sticks and stones only break bones. Words can shatter the soul. A little, quiet, picked-on 10-year-old runs away because kids on the bus laugh at him. A sensitive ninth-grader flips out because a group of self-rising girls decide to throw her to the wolves. We tell ourselves it takes more than that to send someone over the edge. Maybe so, maybe not.

But there are no erasers.

Ina Hughs

The Gossiper

A woman repeated a bit of gossip about a neighbor. Within a few days the whole community knew the story. The person it concerned was deeply hurt and offended. Later, the woman responsible for spreading the rumor learned that it was completely untrue. She was very sorry and went to a wise old sage to find out what she could do to repair the damage.

"Go to the marketplace." he said, "and purchase a chicken, and have it killed. Then on your way home, pluck its feathers and drop them one by one along the road." Although surprised by this advice, the woman did what she was told.

The next day the wise man said, "Now, go and collect all those feathers you dropped yesterday and bring them back to me."

The woman followed the same road, but to her dismay the wind had blown all the feathers away. After searching for hours, she returned with only three in her hand. "You see," said the old sage, "it's easy to drop them, but it's impossible to get them back. So it is with gossip. It doesn't take much to spread a rumor, but once you do, you can never completely undo the wrong."

Author Unknown
Submitted by Helen Hazinski

A Simple Christmas Card

A friend is a gift you give yourself.

Robert Louis Stevenson

Abbie, shy and reserved, started ninth grade in the big-city high school in the center of town. It never occurred to her that she would be lonely. But soon she found herself dreaming of her old eighth-grade class. It had been small and friendly. This new school was much too cold and unfriendly.

No one at this school seemed to care if Abbie felt welcome or not. She was a very caring person, but her shyness interfered with making friends. Oh, she had those occasional buddies—you know, the kind that took advantage of her kindness by cheating off her.

She walked the halls every day almost invisible; no one spoke to her, so her voice was never heard. It reached the point where she believed that her thoughts weren't good enough to be heard. So she continued to stay quiet, almost mute.

Her parents were very worried about her, for they feared she'd never make friends. And since they were divorced, she probably needed to talk with a friend very badly. Her parents tried everything they could to help her fit in. They bought her the clothes and the CDs, but it still didn't work.

Unfortunately, Abbie's parents didn't know Abbie was thinking of ending her life. She often cried herself to sleep, believing that no one would ever love her enough to be her real friend.

Her new pal Tammy used her to do her homework by pretending to need help. Even worse, Tammy was leaving Abbie out of the fun she was having. This only pushed Abbie closer to the edge.

Things worsened over the summer; Abbie was all alone with nothing to do but let her mind run wild. She let herself believe that this was all that life was cracked up to be. From Abbie's point of view, it wasn't worth living.

She started the tenth grade and joined a Christian youth group at a local church, hoping to make friends. She met people who on the outside seemed to welcome her, but who on the inside wished she'd stay out of their group.

By Christmastime Abbie was so upset that she was taking sleeping pills to help her sleep. It seemed as though she was slipping away from the world.

Finally, she decided that she would jump off the local bridge on Christmas Eve, while her parents were at a party. As she left her warm house for the long walk to the bridge, she decided to leave her parents a note in the mailbox. When she pulled down the door to the mailbox, she found letters already there.

She pulled the letters out to see who they were from. There was one from Grandma and Grandpa Knight, a couple from the neighbors . . . and then she saw one addressed to her. She tore it open. It was a card from one of the guys in the youth group.

Dear Abbie,

I want to apologize for not talking with you sooner, but my parents are in the middle of a divorce, so I didn't have a chance to talk with anyone. I was hoping you could help me with some questions I have about divorced kids. I think we could become friends and help each other. See you at Youth Group on Sunday!

Sincerely your friend,
Wesley Hill

She stared at the card for a while, reading it over and over again. "Become friends," she smiled, realizing that someone cared about her life and wanted plain, quiet Abbie Knight as a friend. She felt so special.

She turned around and went back to her house. As soon as she walked in the door, she called Wesley. I guess you could say he was a Christmas miracle, because friendship is the best gift you can give anyone.

Theresa Peterson

Please Listen

When I ask you to listen to me
and you start giving me advice,
you have not done what I asked.
When I ask you to listen to me
and you begin to tell my why
I shouldn't feel that way,
you are trampling on my feelings.
When I ask you to listen to me
and you feel you have to do something
to solve my problem,
you have failed me,
strange as that may seem.
Listen! All I ask is that you listen.
Don't talk or do—just hear me.
Advice is cheap; 20 cents will get
you both Dear Abby and Billy Graham
in the same newspaper.
And I can do for myself; I am not helpless.
Maybe discouraged and faltering,
but not helpless.
When you do something for me that I can

and need to do for myself,
you contribute to my fear and
inadequacy.
But when you accept as a simple fact
that I feel what I feel,
no matter how irrational,
then I can stop trying to convince
you and get about this business
of understanding what's behind
this irrational feeling.
And when that's clear, the answers are
obvious and I don't need advice.
Irrational feelings make sense when
we understand what's behind them.
Perhaps that's why prayer works, sometimes,
for some people—because God is mute,
and he doesn't give advice or try
to fix things.
God just listens and lets you work
it out for yourself.
So please listen, and just hear me.
And if you want to talk, wait a minute
for your turn—and I will listen to you.

Author Unknown

She Told Me It Was Okay to Cry

It takes a lot of understanding, time and trust to gain a close friendship with someone. As I approach a time of my life of complete uncertainty, my friends are my most precious asset.

Erynn Miller, age 18

I saw her last night for the first time in years. She was miserable. She had bleached her hair, trying to hide its true color, just as her rough front hid her deep unhappiness. She needed to talk, so we went for a walk. While I thought about my future, the college applications that had recently arrived, she thought about her past, the home she had recently left. Then she spoke. She told me about her love—and I saw a dependent relationship with a dominating man. She told me about the drugs—and I saw that they were her escape. She told me about her goals—and I saw unrealistic material dreams. She told me she needed a friend—and I saw hope, because at least I could give her that.

We had met in the second grade. She was missing a tooth, I was missing my friends. I had just moved across the continent to find cold metal swings and cold smirking faces outside the foreboding doors of P.S. 174, my new school. I asked her if I could see her Archie comic book, even though I didn't really like comics; she said yes, even though she didn't really like to share. Maybe we were both looking for a smile. And we found it. We found someone to giggle with late at night, someone to slurp hot chocolate with on the cold winter days when school was canceled and we would sit together by the bay window, watching the snow endlessly falling.

In the summer, at the pool, I got stung by a bee. She held my hand and told me that she was there and that it was okay to cry—so I did. In the fall, we raked the leaves into piles and took turns jumping, never afraid because we knew that the multicolored bed would break our fall.

Only now, she had fallen and there was no one to catch her. We hadn't spoken in months, we hadn't seen each other in years. I had moved to California, she had moved out of the house. Our experiences were miles apart, making our hearts much farther away from each other than the continent she had just traversed. Through her words I was alienated, but through her eyes I felt her yearning. She needed support in her search for strength and a new start. She needed my friendship now more than ever. So I took her hand and told her that I was there and that it was okay to cry—so she did.

Daphna Renan

Lessons in Friendship

". . . There's the people you've known forever. Who like . . . know you . . . in this way. That other people can't. Because they've seen you change. They've let you change."

This is a quote from an episode of *My So-Called Life,* one of the many subtly profound quotes characteristic of the show. This one in particular refers to an aspect of a certain kind of friendship, a very special kind of friendship, that I have and cherish. Let me explain.

Throughout my experience on the show, there were many character concepts and story lines from *My So-Called Life* that touched me. In portraying Rayanne I was most deeply affected by the dynamic of her friendship with Angela.

Being Rayanne's friend was getting harder and harder for Angela. Rayanne was being knocked off, or was knocking herself off, the pedestal new friends have a tendency to put each other on. This awesome new friend, who lived life on the edge, actually fell over the side every once in a while, and fair or not, Angela was disappointed.

This happens. As Rayanne, I didn't have to go far to feel the frustration, the disappointment a situation like this causes because I've been there. I've been through the turn of events that sneak up on a friendship forcing it in another direction, the closeness suddenly gone and replaced by questions and doubts. This is that point many relationships come to where a decision has to be made: to stay in or bail out, to decide what it's worth.

I had a best friend from third grade through seventh grade. We were practically inseparable for those years. Then I changed.

After growing up with the same group of kids from age 5 to age 12, I hit Jr. High and a whole new world opened up to me. It seemed everyone was there, the boys from the Little League where I played ball, friends from the Pop Warner football teams I cheered for (and my brother played for), as well as a number of people from the summer drama workshop. Not to mention my big bro, who was a ninth-grader, and all of his friends who adopted me as their own lil' sis. The "in" crowd welcomed me, figuring that I had to be cool to know so many people, and life was good. Always someone to pass notes to, always someone to gossip about, always someone else to call, always about something really important.

I was a different person with each new group of friends. I wanted to be everything to everyone, and I became so wrapped up in not only all of that, but so wrapped up in myself that I couldn't see what was really going on. I was just too busy to realize that I had gotten a little lost. My best friend started to distance herself from me. I don't think she liked what I was becoming. But I didn't see that then; I just felt her lose faith in me. It hurt so much, and I didn't understand. To keep from dealing with it I threw myself even further into my new life. It wasn't long before I made a few mistakes, some worse than others, and the "in" crowd got a peek at the real me. Or at least someone other than who they thought I was, and they were disappointed. That's when it got ugly.

These so-called friends (no pun intended) turned fast. In a melodrama of gossip and rumors, I was banished. I had been part of this "in" crowd until they found out I really wasn't cool enough to be there.

The time had come to step back and take a look around. This was one of the hardest times in my life. I felt alone and was very disappointed in myself. My first step was to go back to my old best friend. I tried so hard to show her that I was sorry for messing up, that I still loved her and missed her incredibly . . . that I needed her. In return, I received blank stares and emotionless responses. So I tried harder. Still, barely a trace of that sisterhood she once shared with me. It took me a long time to realize that I had lost her, that she had changed, too. And our best-friendship was gone.

At school, I found myself wandering around at nutrition and lunch, no longer floating from group to group being the social butterfly. It was then, when I thought I had nowhere else to go, that I rediscovered the "kindergarten group." This group had a base of five or six of us who had actually gone to kindergarten together, along with a few additions welcomed in throughout elementary school. We had all grown up in the same community, shared the same schools, classes, birthday parties, and all the ups and downs of our pre-pubescent lives.

The group was even bigger now. They had all made new friends, but instead of choosing one over the other, as I had done, they simply included them. At my lowest, I had gone so far as to not invite them to my bat mitzvah. I can still hear my mom asking, "What about Susie and Greg and the rest of the 'kindergarten group'?" as she shook her head at my invite list. "*Mom,* I don't hang out with them anymore," I'd said. "They don't even know my new friends . . . besides, if I invite one, I have to invite them all." I received invitations to every one of their birthday parties and bar or bat mitzvahs that year.

I tried to inconspicuously make my way back into this circle of friends, not expecting it to be easy. I assumed I was going to get what I deserved which was for them to be cold and exclude me as I had done to them. I had to take that chance.

I was completely caught off guard by how little effort was needed to feel welcomed again. There was absolutely no resentment, only comfort and an unexpected sense of belonging. It was incredible, as though there were no time lapse. We just picked up right where we left off. Over the next months I realized the more I hung out with them, the less insecure I became. I was a new person with them . . . one I liked.

But, there was something that I didn't get, something about it being too easy. I mean, weren't they hurt when I had so obviously chosen these other friends over them? Didn't they lose faith in me, or resent the fact that I had taken their friendship for granted? I just didn't feel I could truly fit in again until these issues were dealt with. I needed answers.

They came a few months later at a camp-out I organized just for the kindergarten group (we joked that it was a makeup for not inviting them to the bat mitzvah). When the sun went down we huddled up around the campfire. All night we laughed, roasted marshmallows (and old teachers), counted shooting stars and talked. I finally felt safe enough to bring up my questions. I stumbled through them and waited. After a moment, only awkward for me, one of them said, "Yeah, maybe it hurt a little, but . . ." he shrugged, "I don't know, I guess . . . we just understood." And that was that. They just understood.

They saw me change. They gave me room, freedom to screw up, to grow and learn my own lessons, my own way, in my own time. Through the years, we've *all* had our phases, our ups and downs, and I expect we'll continue because that's the way it goes. We know we will be each other's constant from now on. We will all continue to grow separately together, all the while providing the unconditional love, understanding and support only friends like these are capable of.

"There's the people you've known forever. Who like . . . know you . . . in this way. That other people can't. Because they've seen you change. They've let you change."

I might never have understood the true magnitude of this seemingly simple concept without having experienced those defining years. From the kindergarten group, the best friend and the cool crowd, I had learned two things: the type of friends I wanted, and the type of friend I wanted to be.

A. J. Langer

Always Return Your Phone Calls

All you need is love.

John Lennon

[EDITORS' NOTE: *We received this story from a young reader who wanted her story told but wishes to remain anonymous.*]

Angela knew that Charlotte, her best friend, was having a rough time. Charlotte was moody and depressed. She was withdrawn around everyone except for Angela. She instigated arguments with her mom and had violent confrontations with her sister. Most of all, Charlotte's bleak and desperate poetry worried Angela.

No one was on particularly good speaking terms with Charlotte that summer. For most of her friends, Charlotte had become too difficult. They had no interest in hanging out with someone who was so bleak and in so much pain. Their attempts to "be a friend" were met with angry accusations or depressed indifference.

Angela was the only one who could reach her. Although she would have liked to be outside, Angela spent most of her time inside with her troubled friend. Then a day came when Angela had to move. She was going just across town, but Charlotte would no longer be her neighbor, and they would be spending far less time together.

The first day in her new neighborhood, out playing with her new neighbors, Angela wondered how Charlotte was doing. When she got home, shortly before twilight, her mother told her Charlotte had called.

Angela went to the phone to return the call. No answer. She left a message on Charlotte's machine. "Hi Charlotte, it's Angela. Call me back."

About half an hour later Charlotte called. "Angela, I have to tell you something. When you called, I was in the basement. I had a gun to my head. I was about to kill myself, but then I heard your voice on the machine upstairs."

Angela collapsed into her chair.

"When I heard your voice I realized someone loves me, and I am so lucky that it is you. I'm going to get help, because I love you, too."

Charlotte hung up the phone. Angela went right over to Charlotte's house, and they sat on the porch swing and cried.

Anonymous

My New Best Friend

Today I met a great new friend
Who knew me right away
It was funny how she understood
All I had to say

She listened to my problems
She listened to my dreams
We talked about love and life
She'd been there, too, it seems

I never once felt judged by her
She knew just how I felt
She seemed to just accept me
And all the problems I'd been dealt

She didn't interrupt me
Or need to have her say
She just listened very patiently
And didn't go away

I wanted her to understand
How much this meant to me
But as I went to hug her
Something startled me

I put my arms in front of me
And went to pull her nearer
And realized that my new best friend
Was nothing but a mirror

Retold by Kimberly Kirberger

The Days of Cardboard Boxes

Enjoy yourself. These are the good old days you're going to miss in the years ahead.

Anonymous

Cardboard boxes played a significant role in my childhood days. Don't get me wrong; toys were wonderful, too, but nothing could out-do a cardboard box and a few kids to go along with it—especially my two best neighborhood friends, Chris and Nick, brothers who lived three blocks away.

Summer was always the perfect time to have a cardboard box. The long, lazy days offered sufficient time to experience the true essence of a box and to truly bond with it. However, in order to bond with a box, we first had to find one. The three of us would pile into the back of my parents' truck, briefly jockeying for the coveted wheel seats, then sing the "Na Na Na" song (any song we only knew some of the words to but sang anyway) while we waited for my mom to find her keys. None of us dared to suggest that we ride in the front of the truck; that was for sissies.

Finally, after an infinite number of "Na Na Na" songs, Mom drove us to a box place, and there it was! The most beautiful box we had ever seen. It was a refrigerator box, most definitely the best kind to have. Refrigerator boxes could journey to far better places than any other box, and their ability to be anything was simply phenomenal. The furniture warehouse/showroom had thrown this glorious bounty out the back door like it was useless. We had arrived in time to rescue it from the nefarious jaws of a trash truck.

We watched with anticipation as Mom slid the box to the back of the truck. We crawled into the box for the ride home, sheltered from the wind and the bugs that seemed to aim right for the tonsils during mid-"Na."

Arriving back in the neighborhood was an experience that made our heads swell. Everyone who was outdoors could see us, and word would soon spread that Nick, Chris and Eva possessed a refrigerator box. You see, anyone who owned a refrigerator box held an esteemed position. We would be legends. We would take our box where no kids had ever gone before.

We unloaded our treasure and carried it with great care into the back yard. Chris said we should spend a few minutes of quiet time to gather our thoughts, and then we could discuss our ideas for this magnificent being. We did so for about five seconds. Then suddenly, as if an unknown force opened our voice boxes, we broke into song:

Na na na na
Our box is groovy
Na Na Na
And so are we!

Okay, it was a short song. But it was beautiful. And I'm sure it would have touched the hearts of those fortunate enough to hear it.

It was time to make our decision. "Let's go to Zo in our box," I said.

"Who?" Nick and Chris gave me one of their looks.

"Where to go or where not to go, that is the question," I retorted.

Nick told me I didn't make any sense, and I explained that it was all very simple, that he and Chris just needed to learn how to think backwards. Chris decided Nick was right—I didn't make any sense.

"Zo is Oz backwards, you ignorant little twerps! We wanna go to Zo and do everything Dorothy does in Oz, but backwards." I was hollering at them because I knew they had better sense than they were using.

Chris looked first at me and then at the box as he contemplated my bright idea. I wondered if Chris and Nick were seriously ill because they should have known by then, from all our past experiences, that boxes (especially this one) could take us anywhere. We could be or do anything we wanted because of the power of the almighty refrigerator box. And we could be backwards about it too.

"You know, Eva is right," Chris said. "We have never done anything backwards before, so let's make this the first time. But we can go *anywhere* backwards, not just Zo."

At that moment in our young lives we understood clearly that we were going to go down in history. People all over the world would be talking about "The Three Backwards Box Kids." Other children would attempt to go where we had gone, but none of them could ever be like us because their imaginations were inferior to ours.

We made a solemn declaration that our box would be a time machine. We swore on chocolate peanut butter cups that this backward idea was here to stay (at least until the next box). And anyone who broke a promise made over chocolate peanut butter cups was basically considered immoral.

After we had traveled several years back in time, we were faced with a dilemma. We were visiting with a singer named Elvis who inquired about how we got to Graceland. We told him about our time machine, the backwards idea, the chocolate-peanut-butter-cup promise, and how we were going to go down in history. Elvis was all shook up about us, and he said that we were pretty neat kids . . . but . . .

"But what?" we pressed.

He wanted to know how we were eventually going to get home again if we could only go backwards.

In all our days, we had never been faced with a predicament such as this. We had also never broken a chocolate-peanut-butter-cup promise. We were, you know, up a creek. We could not capitulate. Life always had its ups and downs—this was just one of the very big downs that would take a long night of pondering. Luckily, our parents would not let us stay out all night to play our make-believe games.

Soon my mom called out the back door, breaking us out of our imaginary world and landing us abruptly in the backyard again. It was time for Nick and Chris to go home. The three of us quickly made plans to meet at eight o'clock the next morning to discuss solutions to get us out of the disaster we were in. As I ran the few feet to my back door, Nick and Chris took off running the three blocks toward their home. Time could not be squandered. We only had until morning before we would be back in the reality of our imaginary world again.

At 7:33 the next morning, the phone broke the silence, and I stumbled out of bed with a hangover from thinking too much. When I answered the phone, Nick demanded to know if I had covered the box with plastic the night before like we were supposed to do, in case of rain. I looked out the window to see that it had rained, a very hard and drenching rain. With deep regret in my heart, I told Nick I hadn't, but the responsibility belonged to all of us, so it wasn't completely my fault.

Nick and Chris came over, and silence replaced our usual banter. Our box had only been with us for one day. Now we were stuck in the real world because our box was dead.

The soggy cardboard couldn't just be left out in the yard to rot away. It had been a good box while it lasted, and it deserved proper respect. So we dragged it to the side of the street where the garbage was picked up. The day before we had saved it from a trash truck that would have taken its life too early; now it was time for our box to go. Although it was a natural death, it could have been prevented. This reality would be a weight we would carry for all our childhood days.

The three of us sat next to our dead box so we could be there when the trash truck came. We even made up a "Na Na Na" requiem, and we sang with all our might as the truck hauled our box away. No one could have put more sincerity or emotion into a song than we did that day. Although we were mourning our box, we knew we must go on. We must find another box, and we must build another imaginary world with it.

I miss the cardboard-box days. However, just as we had to go on after the demise of our box, I had to go on and grow up. But my childhood imagination will always be a part of me. I will always believe in cardboard boxes.

Eva Burke

3

ON FAMILY

The family—that dear octopus from whose tentacles we never quite escape nor, in our inmost hearts, ever quite wish to.

Dodie Smith

Reprinted by permission of Dave Carpenter.

She Didn't Give Up on Me

She never once gave up. My mom is my hero.

Kimberly Anne Brand

I lay on the floor, furiously kicking my legs and screaming until my throat felt raw—all because my foster mother had asked me to put my toys away.

"I hate you," I shrieked. I was six years old and didn't understand why I felt so angry all the time.

I'd been living in foster care since I was two. My real mom couldn't give my five sisters and me the care we needed. Since we didn't have a dad or anyone else to care for us, we were put in different foster homes. I felt lonely and confused. I didn't know how to tell people that I hurt inside. Throwing a tantrum was the only way I knew to express my feelings.

Because I acted up, eventually my current foster mom sent me back to the adoption agency, just as the mom before had. I thought I was the most unlovable girl in the world.

Then I met Kate McCann. I was seven by that time and living with my third foster family when she came to visit.

When my foster mother told me that Kate was single and wanted to adopt a child, I didn't think she'd choose me. I couldn't imagine anyone would want me to live with them forever.

That day, Kate took me to a pumpkin farm. We had fun, but I didn't think I'd see her again.

A few days later, a social worker came to the house to say that Kate wanted to adopt me. Then she asked me if I'd mind living with one parent instead of two.

"All I want is someone who loves me," I said.

Kate visited the next day. She explained that it would take a year for the adoption to be finalized, but I could move in with her soon. I was excited but afraid, too. Kate and I were total strangers. I wondered if she'd change her mind once she got to know me.

Kate sensed my fear. "I know you've been hurt," she said, hugging me. "I know you're scared. But I promise I'll never send you away. We're a family now."

To my surprise, her eyes were filled with tears. Suddenly I realized that she was as lonely as I was!

"Okay . . . Mom, " I said.

The following week I met my new grandparents, aunt, uncle and cousins. It felt funny—but good—to be with strangers who hugged me as though they already loved me.

When I moved in with Mom, I had my own room for the first time. It had wallpaper and a matching bedspread, an antique dresser and a big closet. I had only a few clothes I'd brought with me in a brown paper bag. "Don't worry," Mom said. "I'll buy you lots of pretty new things."

I went to sleep that night feeling safe. I prayed I wouldn't have to leave.

Mom did lots of nice things for me. She took me to church. She let me have pets and gave me horseback riding and piano lessons. Every day, she told me she loved me. But love wasn't enough to heal the hurt inside me. I kept waiting for her to change her mind. I thought, "If I act bad enough, she'll leave me like the others."

So I tried to hurt her before she could hurt me. I picked fights over little things and threw tantrums when I didn't get my way. I slammed doors. If Mom tried to stop me, I'd hit her. But she never lost patience. She'd hug me and say she loved me anyway. When I got mad, she made me jump on a trampoline.

Because I was failing in school when I came to live with her, Mom was very strict about my homework. One day when I was watching TV, she came in and turned it off. "You can watch it after you finish your homework," she said. I blew up. I picked up my books and threw them across the room. "I hate you and I don't want to live here anymore!" I screamed.

I waited for her to tell me to start packing. When she didn't, I asked, "Aren't you going to send me back?"

"I don't like the way you're behaving," she said, "but I'll never send you back. We're a family, and families don't give up on each other."

Then it hit me. This mom was different; she wasn't going to get rid of me. She really did love me. And I realized I loved her, too. I cried and hugged her.

In 1985, when Mom formally adopted me, our whole family celebrated at a restaurant. It felt good belonging to someone. But I was still scared. Could a mom really love me forever? My tantrums didn't disappear immediately, but as months passed, they happened less often.

Today I'm 16. I have a 3.4 grade point average, a horse named Dagger's Point, four cats, a dog, six doves and a bullfrog that lives in our backyard pond. And I have a dream: I want to be a veterinarian.

Mom and I like to do things together, like shopping and horseback riding. We smile when people say how much we look alike. They don't believe she's not my real mom.

I'm happier now than I ever imagined I could be. When I'm older, I'd like to get married and have kids, but if that doesn't work out, I'll adopt like Mom did. I'll pick a scared and lonely kid and then never, ever give up on her. I'm so glad Mom didn't give up on me.

Sharon Whitley
excerpted from Woman's World *magazine*

Reprinted by permission of Randy Glasbergen.

Mama's Hands

I saw you hide your hands in line,
behind that lady fair,
I noticed too, hers soft and white—
immaculate from care.
But Ma, I say, it's no disgrace
to have workin' hands like you,
and had she lived the life you have,
she'd have hands just like it too.

But her hands have never hauled in wood,
or worked in God's good earth.
They've never felt the bitter cold,
or chopped ice for waitin' stock,
they've never doctored sick ones,
or dressed a horse's hock.
They've never pulled a hip-locked calf,
or packed water to the barn.
They've probably never patched blue jeans,
or had worn ol' socks to darn.

They've never touched a young'n,
or caressed a fevered head,

with hands so gently folded,
all night beside his bed.

They've never scrubbed a kitchen floor,
or done dishes every day.
They've never guided with those hands
a child who's lost the way.

They've never made a Christmas gift,
shaped by a lovin' hand.
They've never peeled apples,
nor vegetables they've canned.
They've never worn a blister,
or had calluses to show,
for all they've done for others,
and the kindnesses I know.

So you see, my dearest Mama—
yours are hands of love.
And I bet the Lord will notice
when he greets you from above.

Tommi Jo Casteel

Unconditional Mom

My mother had a great deal of trouble with me, but I think she enjoyed it.

Mark Twain

I was a rotten teenager. Not your average spoiled, know-it-all, not-going-to-clean-my-room, getting-an-attitude-because-I'm-15 teenager. No, I was a manipulative, lying, acid-tongued monster, who realized early on that I could make things go my way with just a few minor adjustments. The writers for today's hottest soap opera could not have created a worse "villainess." A few nasty comments here, a lie or two there, maybe an evil glare for a finishing touch, and things would be grand. Or so I thought.

For the most part, and on the outside, I was a good kid. A giggly, pug-nose tomboy who liked to play sports and who thrived on competition (a nice way of saying: somewhat pushy and demanding). Which is probably why most people allowed me to squeak by using what I now call "bulldozer behavior tactics," with no regard for anyone I felt to be of value. For a while, anyway.

Since I was perceptive enough to get some people to

bend my way, it amazes me how long it took to realize how I was hurting so many others. Not only did I succeed in pushing away many of my closest friends by trying to control them; I also managed to sabotage, time and time again, the most precious relationship in my life: my relationship with my mother.

Even today, almost 10 years since the birth of the new me, my former behavior astonishes me each time I reach into my memories. Hurtful comments that cut and stung the people I cared most about. Acts of confusion and anger that seemed to rule my every move—all to make sure that things went my way.

My mother, who gave birth to me at age 38 against her doctor's wishes, would cry to me, "I waited so long for you, please don't push me away. I want to help you!"

I would reply with my best face of stone, "I didn't ask for you! I never wanted you to care about me! Leave me alone and forget I ever lived!"

My mother began to believe I really meant it. My actions proved nothing less.

I was mean and manipulative, trying to get my way at any cost. Like many young girls in high school, the boys whom I knew were off limits were always the first ones I had to date. Sneaking out of the house at all hours of the night just to prove I could do it. Juggling complex lies that were always on the verge of blowing up in my face. Finding any way to draw attention to myself while simultaneously trying to be invisible.

Ironically, I wish I could say I had been heavy into drugs during that period of my life, swallowing mind-altering pills and smoking things that changed my personality, thus accounting for the terrible, razor-sharp words that came flying from my mouth. However, that was not the case. My only addiction was hatred; my only high was inflicting pain.

But then I asked myself why. Why the need to hurt? And why the people I cared about the most? Why the need for all the lies? Why the attacks on my mother? I would drive myself mad with all the why's until one day, it all exploded in a suicidal rage.

Lying awake the following night at the "resort" (my pet name for the hospital), after an unsuccessful, gutless attempt to jump from a vehicle moving at 80 miles per hour, one thing stood out more than my Keds with no shoe laces. I didn't want to die.

And I did not want to inflict any more pain on people to cover up what I was truly trying to hide myself: self-hatred. Self-hatred unleashed on everyone else.

I saw my mother's pained face for the first time in years—warm, tired brown eyes filled with nothing but thanks for her daughter's new lease on life and love for the child she waited 38 years to bear.

My first encounter with unconditional love. What a powerful feeling.

Despite all the lies I had told her, she still loved me. I cried on her lap for hours one afternoon and asked why she still loved me after all the horrible things I did to her. She just looked down at me, brushed the hair out of my face and said frankly, "I don't know."

A kind of smile penetrated her tears as the lines in her tested face told me all that I needed to know. I was her daughter, but more important, she was my mother. Not every rotten child is so lucky. Not every mother can be pushed to the limits I explored time and time again, and venture back with feelings of love.

Unconditional love is the most precious gift we can give. Being forgiven for the past is the most precious gift we can receive. I dare not say we could experience this pure love twice in one lifetime.

I was one of the lucky ones. I know that. I want to

extend the gift my mother gave me to all the "rotten teenagers" in the world who are confused.

It's okay to feel pain, to need help, to feel love—just feel it without hiding. Come out from under the protective covers, from behind the rigid walls and the suffocating personas, and take a breath of life.

Sarah J. Vogt

The Bible

Dear Abby:

A young man from a wealthy family was about to graduate from high school. It was the custom in that affluent neighborhood for the parents to give the graduate an automobile. Bill and his father had spent months looking at cars, and the week before graduation they found the perfect car. Bill was certain that the car would be his on graduation night.

Imagine his disappointment when, on the eve of his graduation, Bill's father handed him a gift-wrapped Bible! Bill was so angry, he threw the Bible down and stormed out of the house. He and his father never saw each other again. It was the news of his father's death that brought Bill home again.

As he sat one night, going through his father's possessions that he was to inherit, he came across the Bible his father had given him. He brushed away the dust and opened it to find a cashier's check, dated the day of his graduation, in the exact amount of the car they had chosen.

Author Unknown

"Someday, son, you'll finally be old enough to do anything you want to do . . . but your son will have the car, so you'll have to stay home and watch television."

The Birthday

As I sat in the chair by the window and felt the warm June sunshine on my arm, I had to remind myself where I was. It was hard to believe that behind the nicely finished oak cabinets hid various medical equipment, and that in a moment's notice the ceiling tiles could be removed to reveal surgical lights. Except for the few instruments and the IV cart next to the bed, it barely looked like a hospital room. While looking at the carefully selected wallpaper and furnishings, I remembered back to that day, not so long before, when this adventure first began.

It was a crisp October day. Our field hockey team had just won a 2-1 victory over Saratoga. I dropped, exhausted but excited, into the passenger side of our car. While leaving the school my mother mentioned that she had gone to the doctor that day. "For what?" I asked, becoming nervous as I ran through all the ailments my mother could possible have.

"Well . . ." She hesitated and my worry increased. "I'm pregnant."

"You're what?" I exclaimed.

"Pregnant," she repeated.

I was speechless to say the least. I sat in the car and all I could think was that these things do not happen to your parents when you are a sophomore in high school. Then the realization that I was going to have to share my mother hit me. The mother who had been all my own for 16 years. I was overcome with resentment and confusion over a tiny person nesting inside my mom. I had never wanted my mother to have another child after she remarried. This was a selfish feeling, but when it came to my mom, I was reluctant to share the smallest bit of her.

When I saw the shock and joy in my stepfather's eyes when he was told of the impending arrival of his first child, I could not help but feel excited. I could hardly wait to tell everyone and my joy showed on the outside. On the inside, though, I was trying to deal with my fear and anger.

My parents involved me in all the preparations, from decorating the nursery to picking out names to going to Lamaze classes and deciding that I could be present for the baby's birth. But despite all the excitement and happiness this pregnancy brought, it was hard to hear my friends and relatives constantly talk about the new baby. I feared that I would be pushed back into the woodwork when the baby came. Sometimes when I was alone, all the resentment for what this child was going to take from me would overcome the joy.

Sitting in the delivery room that June 17, knowing that the baby would soon be here, I began to feel all my insecurities surface. What was my life going to be like? Would it be one endless baby-sitting job? What would I have to give up? Most important, would I lose my mother? The time to ponder and worry was rapidly melting away. The baby was coming.

It was the most incredible experience of my life, being in the delivery room that day, for birth is truly a miracle.

When the doctor announced that it was a girl, I cried. I had a baby sister.

All my fears and insecurities have passed now, with the help of a warm and understanding family. I cannot explain how special it is to have a tiny person who waits with me every morning until my ride to school comes and then, as Mom holds her in the window, waves her little hand good-bye. It is so wonderful to come home and not even have a chance to take off my coat before she is tugging at me to come play with her.

I realize now that there is plenty of love in my home for Emma. My resentment for what I thought she would take away had been erased with the realization that she took away nothing and instead brought so much to my life. I never thought I could love a baby this much, and I would not trade the joy I get from being her big sister for anything.

Melissa Esposito

The Home Run

On June 18th, I went to my little brother's baseball game as I always did. Cory was 12 years old at the time and had been playing baseball for a couple of years. When I saw that he was warming up to be next at bat, I decided to head over to the dugout to give him a few pointers. But when I got there, I simply said, "I love you."

In return, he asked, "Does this mean you want me to hit a home run?"

I smiled and said, "Do your best."

As he walked up to the plate, there was a certain aura about him. He looked so confident and so sure about what he was going to do. One swing was all he took and, wouldn't you know, he hit his first home run! He ran around those bases with such pride—his eyes sparkled and his face was lit up. But what touched my heart the most was when he walked back over to the dugout. He looked over at me with the biggest smile I've ever seen and said, "I love you too, Ter."

I don't remember if his team won or lost that game. On that special summer day in June, it simply didn't matter.

Terri Vandermark

My Big Brother

First say to yourself what you would be; and then do what you have to do.

Epictetus

I never thought that the absence of smelly socks and loud music would make my heart ache. But my brother is off at college, and at age 14, I miss him terribly. We share a rare kind of closeness for siblings, but then, my brother is a rare kind of guy. Of course he's smart and kind, plus my friends say he is gorgeous and all that. But it's more how he handles things, how he treats his friends and his family, how he cares about people that makes me so proud. That's the stuff that I aspire to be. If it's okay with you, I would like to show you what I mean . . .

He applied to 14 colleges. He was accepted to all but one, the one he wanted, Brown University. So he opted for his second choice, and off he went to a fine though uneventful first year. When he came home for summer vacation, he informed us that he had come up with a plan. He was going to do whatever it took to get into

Brown. Would we support him?

His plan was to move to Rhode Island near Brown, find a job, and do whatever he could to become known in the area. He'd work his heart out, he said, and do the very best at everything. Someone, he was sure, would notice. This was a big deal for my parents because it meant agreeing to a year without college, a scary thing for them. But they trusted him and encouraged him to do whatever he thought it would take to achieve his dream.

It wasn't long before he was hired to produce the plays at—yes, you guessed it—Brown. Now was his chance to shine, and shine he did. No task was too big or too small. He put every bit of himself into the job. He met teachers and administrators, talked to everyone about his dream and never hesitated to tell them what he was after.

And sure enough, at the end of the year, when he reapplied to Brown, he was accepted.

We were all really happy, but for me the happiness went very deep. I had learned an important lesson—a lesson no one could have taught me with words, a lesson I had to see with my own eyes. If I work hard for what I want, if I keep trying after I've been turned away, my dreams also can come true. This is a gift I still hold in my heart. Because of my brother, I trust life.

Recently, I flew to Rhode Island all by myself to visit him, and I had a blast hanging out for a week in an apartment without parents. The night before I left, we were talking about all kinds of stuff like boyfriends, girlfriends, peer pressure and school. At one point, my brother looked me right in the eye and said he loved me. He told me to remember to never do anything that I feel isn't right, no matter what, and never to forget that I can always trust my heart.

I cried all the way home, knowing that my brother and I will always be close, and realizing how lucky I am to have him. Something was different: I didn't feel like a little girl anymore. Part of me had grown up on this trip, and for the first time I thought about the important job that I had waiting for me at home. You see, I have a 10-year-old little sister. It looks as though I've got my work cut out for me. But you know, I had a great teacher.

Lisa Gumenick

A Brother's Voice

Most people have an inspiration in their life. Maybe it's a talk with someone you respect or an experience. Whatever the inspiration, it tends to make you look at life from a different perspective. My inspiration came from my sister Vicki, a kind and caring person. She didn't care about accolades or being written about in newspapers. All she wanted was to share her love with the people she cared about, her family and friends.

The summer before my junior year of college, I received a phone call from my father saying that Vicki was rushed to the hospital. She had collapsed and the right side of her body was paralyzed. The preliminary indications were that she suffered a stroke. However, test results confirmed it was much more serious. There was a malignant brain tumor causing her paralysis. Her doctors didn't give her more than three months to live. I remember wondering how this could happen? The day before Vicki was perfectly fine. Now, her life was coming to an end at such a young age.

After overcoming the initial shock and feeling of emptiness, I decided that Vicki needed hope and encouragement. She needed someone to make her believe that she would overcome this obstacle. I became Vicki's coach. Everyday we would visualize the tumor shrinking and everything that we talked about was positive. I even posted a sign on her hospital room door that read, "If you have any negative thoughts, leave them at the door." I was determined to help Vicki beat the tumor. She and I made a deal that was called 50-50. I would do 50% of the fighting and Vicki would do the other 50%.

The month of August arrived and it was time to begin my junior year of college 3,000 miles away. I was unsure whether I should leave or stay with Vicki. I made the mistake of telling her that I might not leave for school. She became angry and said not to worry because she would be fine. There was Vicki lying ill in a hospital bed telling me not to worry. I realized that if I stayed it might send a message that she was dying and I didn't want her believing that. Vicki needed to believe that she could win against the tumor.

Leaving that night feeling it might be the last time I would ever see Vicki alive was the most difficult thing I have ever done. While at school, I never stopped fighting my 50% for her. Every night before falling asleep I would talk to Vicki, hoping that there was some way she could hear me. I would say, "Vicki I'm fighting for you and I will never quit. As long as you never quit fighting we will beat this."

A few months had passed and she was still holding on. I was talking with an elderly friend and she asked about Vicki's situation. I told her that she was getting worse but that she wasn't quitting. My friend asked a question that really made me think. She said, "Do you think the reason she hasn't let go is because she doesn't want to let you down?"

Maybe she was right? Maybe I was selfish for encouraging Vicki to keep fighting? That night before falling asleep, I said to her, "Vicki, I understand that you're in a lot of pain and that you might like to let go. If you do, then I want you to. We didn't lose because you never quit fighting. If you want to go on to a better place then I understand. We will be together again. I love you and I'll always be with you wherever you are."

Early the next morning, my mother called to tell me that Vicki had passed away.

James Malinchak

Daddy Weirdest

My dad just called. He's going to be in the city tonight and wants me to meet him for dinner. Nice, right? Maybe for a child of a normal parent, which I am not. Here's the scenario: Dad's traveling on business from upstate New York to Washington, D.C. While a lot of people would just hop on a plane, he will take the evening train from Syracuse, arrive in New York at 10:00 P.M., and check into a sleeper car of the D.C.-bound train, which will leave New York at 5:00 A.M. And if you think that means dinner at a swanky late-night bistro, you're wrong. There's really no place my dad would rather be than Penn Station. So if I want to see him, I get to hang out there in the late evening with the heroin addicts until his train pulls in. We'll have chicken sandwiches and a cup of instant hot cocoa at Roy Rogers, after which he will kiss me good-bye and go find his sleeper car.

The man loves trains—riding them, photographing them, even listening to them. When I was little, I thought it was normal to take Amtrak everywhere; I truly believed that only the filthy rich took domestic flights. I also didn't find it odd that if we had to drive—say, to visit my grandparents—the route was carefully plotted near a railroad track so that somewhere along the way, Dad could stop and take pictures.

By the time I reached middle school, I realized that my dad was a freak. By the eighth grade I was the only kid who had never been on an airplane. And it got worse. No other parents played albums with titles like "Sounds of Steam," live recordings of steam engines that sent the dog and cats running for cover. Other parents also weren't teased by neighbors and friends about having memorized all the train schedules in the northeast corridor. But Dad remained oblivious and blithely continued to entertain company with his uncanny imitation of an oncoming train that made the dog howl.

In ninth grade, the coolest girl in my class, Krista Marshall, decided I was her new best friend, and my father almost ruined my life. Hoping to cement the friendship, I invited Krista on a vacation with my family. In my effort to please, I had forgotten that Dad's definition of vacation is different from most people's. Other families go to Disneyland or to the beach, or at least get to stay in a motel. But Frank Barry believes in self-sufficiency, so we ended up in a tent in the woods in the Adirondacks. As was our luck with camping trips, it rained from the first night on, which wouldn't have been a problem if my father wasn't such a fix-it-yourself type of guy and hadn't duct-taped our old canvas tent together. But he is, and he had, and the tent leaked. After four days of waking up sopping wet, going for 5- to 10-mile hikes (on which we saw lots of endangered plants but not one cute boy) and living off Dinty Moore beef stew, we finally piled back into the car for the four-hour drive home.

Poor Krista, bug-bitten and sneezing, could no longer contain herself when my father pulled off the road in what seemed like the middle of nowhere, got out of the car, and disappeared into the woods.

"Why are we stopping?" she asked, a note of panic rising in her voice, probably fearing that we were going to set up camp again.

My mother smiled as if everything and everyone were normal, and said, "Frank is just going to take some pictures." To my horror, there was my dad, some 20 feet above the ground, leaning out precariously from a railroad bridge to get just the right angle to photograph the train when it came along. The train was late and we ended up waiting in the car for 45 minutes. Krista tried not to cry, and I miserably wondered how a man who didn't look malevolent could single-handedly destroy his own flesh and blood's chances at ever being hip.

I have to admit that my father never really ruined my life. It turned out that Krista's parents have a piece of paper strategically placed over a hole in their living room that says in bold red letters, "What in the hell are you looking up here for?!" Krista always tried to remove it before friends or boyfriends came over, but somehow it always reappeared in all its defensive glory. With our socially challenged progenitors in common, we became and remain great friends.

I also should admit that when not humiliated by my dad's bizarre behavior, I have to love and admire that he's a free spirit. The truth is, he simply doesn't worry about what other people think. How many other girls have a dad who hitchhiked all over Latin America to photograph trains his first year out of college? Or whose spare time is devoted to the worthy cause of educating the world about the environmental correctness of taking the train? He's a maverick. That's cool because I'm kind of like that, too. I don't care if my socks don't match, or if people laugh at me because I obstinately still believe that life should be fair. Maybe I got it from him, but I definitely make my own choices, regardless of other people's opinions.

So I guess it's better to have an embarrassing father than one who is busy trying to impress other people. Sometimes I even love my dad all the more for his quirkiness, like his love for Penn Station. And at least now I have some ammunition when he starts to scold me about being careful in Manhattan. I mean, I appreciate his concern and everything, but he's the one sleeping in the train station, not me.

Rebecca Barry

"Are you trying to destroy my social life?! I know people around here, Dad! Please take off that stupid hat!"

A Famous Father

A great man died today. He wasn't a world leader or a famous doctor or a war hero or a sports figure. He was no business tycoon, and you will never see his name in the financial pages. But he was one of the greatest men who ever lived. He was my father.

I guess you might say he was a person who was never interested in getting credit or receiving honors. He did corny things like pay his bills on time, go to church on Sunday and serve as an officer in the P.T.A. He helped his kids with their homework and drove his wife to do the grocery shopping on Thursday nights. He got a great kick out of hauling his teenagers and their friends to and from football games.

Tonight is my first night without him. I don't know what to do with myself. I am sorry now for the times I didn't show him the proper respect. But I am grateful for a lot of other things.

I am thankful that God let me have my father for 15 years. And I am happy that I was able to let him know how much I loved him. That wonderful man died with a smile on his face and fulfillment in his heart. He knew that he was a great success as a husband and a father, a brother, a son and a friend. I wonder how many millionaires can say that.

Author Unknown

Lessons in Baseball

There are always two choices, two paths to take. One is easy. And its only reward is that it's easy.

Unknown

As an 11-year-old, I was addicted to baseball. I listened to baseball games on the radio. I watched them on TV. The books I read were about baseball. I took baseball cards to church in hopes of trading with other baseball card junkies. My fantasies? All about baseball.

I played baseball whenever and wherever I could. I played organized or sandlot. I played catch with my brother, with my father, with friends. If all else failed, I bounced a rubber ball off the porch stairs, imagining all kinds of wonderful things happening to me and my team.

It was with this attitude that I entered the 1956 Little League season. I was a shortstop. Not good, not bad. Just addicted.

Gordon was not addicted. Nor was he good. He moved into our neighborhood that year and signed up to play baseball. The kindest way of describing Gordon's baseball skills is to say that he didn't have any. He couldn't catch. He couldn't hit. He couldn't throw. He couldn't run.

In fact, Gordon was afraid of the ball.

I was relieved when the final selections were made and Gordon was assigned to another team. Everyone had to play at least half of each game, and I couldn't see Gordon improving my team's chances in any way. Too bad for the other team.

After two weeks of practice, Gordon dropped out. My friends on his team laughed when they told me how their coach directed two of the team's better players to walk Gordon into the woods and have a chat with him. "Get lost" was the message that was delivered, and "get lost" was the one that was heard.

Gordon got lost.

That scenario violated my 11-year-old sense of justice, so I did what any indignant shortstop would do. I tattled. I told my coach the whole story. I shared the episode in full detail, figuring my coach would complain to the League office and have Gordon returned to his original team. Justice and my team's chances of winning would both be served.

I was wrong. My coach decided that Gordon needed to be on a team that wanted him—one that treated him with respect, one that gave everyone a fair chance to contribute according to their own ability.

Gordon became my team member.

I wish I could say Gordon got the big hit in the big game with two outs in the final inning, but it didn't happen. I don't think Gordon even hit a foul ball the entire season. Baseballs hit in his direction (right field) went over him, by him, through him, or off him.

It wasn't that Gordon didn't get help. The coach gave him extra batting practice and worked with him on his fielding, all without much improvement.

I'm not sure if Gordon learned anything from my coach that year. I know I did. I learned to bunt without tipping off my intention. I learned to tag up on a fly if there were less than two outs. I learned to make a smoother pivot around second base on a double play.

I learned a lot from my coach that summer, but my most important lessons weren't about baseball. They were about character and integrity. I learned that everyone has worth, whether they can hit .300 or .030. I learned that we all have value, whether we can stop the ball or have to turn and chase it. I learned that doing what is right, fair and honorable is more important than winning or losing.

It felt good to be on that team that year. I'm grateful that man was my coach. I was proud to be his shortstop and his son.

Chick Moorman

The Champ

He had a featherweight build, but what this 15-year-old lacked in strength and speed, he made up for in attitude. Jason never missed a practice, even though he rarely got playing time, and then only in the fourth quarter when our team outdistanced the opponent by at least three touchdowns. Even so, number 37 never so much as frowned, let alone complained, and always put forth his best effort—even if it amounted to very little.

One day he didn't come to practice. When he didn't show up on the second day, as his concerned coach, I telephoned his home to check on him. The out-of-town relative I spoke with informed me that Jason's father had passed away and the family was making funeral arrangements.

Two weeks later, my faithful number 37 was again in the lineup, ready for practice. Only three days of practice remained before our next game. This was an important game because it was against our most fierce opponent and late in the season, and we only had a one-game lead over them. This was a critical game at a pivotal point in the season.

When the big day rolled around, my top players were ready to bolt onto the field. All the familiar faces were there but one—Jason. But suddenly, Jason appeared at my side and with a totally uncharacteristic look and manner said, "I'm going to be a starter today. I'm ready now." He left no room for refusal or argument. When the game began, he was in position on the field. The regular starter whom he replaced sat awestruck on the bench.

Jason played like a first-stringer that day. He was in every respect equal if not better than the best player on the team. He ran fast, found every open hole in the line, and jumped up after every tackle as if he had never been hit. By the third quarter he had run for three touchdowns. As a grand finale, as if to remove even the slightest doubt in anyone's mind, he scored another touchdown in the last seconds of the fourth quarter.

As he ran off the field with his teammates, Jason received a volley of body slaps and body slams against the backdrop of thunderous applause from the crowd. Despite all the adulation, Jason managed to maintain his characteristic humble, low-key manner. Puzzled by Jason's sudden transformation, I approached him and said, "Jason, you played an extraordinary game today. By the second touchdown, I had to wipe my eyes and pinch myself. But by the time the clock ran out in the fourth quarter, my curiosity got the best of me. What happened to you?"

Jason, hesitating at first, said, "Well, Coach Williams, as you know, my father recently died. When my dad was alive he was blind, so he couldn't see me play. But now that he has gone to heaven, this is the first time he has been able to see me play. I wanted to make him proud."

As told by Nailah Malik, the "Vela Storyteller"

I Love You, Dad

If God can work through me, he can work through anyone.

St. Francis of Assisi

I met a man who came to Tampa for his father's funeral. Father and son hadn't seen each other in years. In fact, according to the son, his father had left when he was a boy, and they had had little contact until about a year ago, when his father had sent him a birthday card with a note saying he'd like to see his son again.

After discussing a trip to Florida with his wife and children and consulting his busy schedule at his office, the son tentatively set a date to visit his father two months later. He would drive his family down when school was out for vacation. He scribbled a note and with mixed emotions, dropped it in the mail.

He heard back immediately. Written on lined paper torn from a spiral notebook, such as a schoolboy would use, were words of excitement penned in a barely legible scrawl. Misspelled words, poor grammar and incorrect punctuation bounced off the page. The man was embarrassed for his father. He thought twice about the upcoming visit.

It just so happened that the man's daughter made the cheerleading squad at her school and had to go to a camp conducted for cheering techniques. Coincidentally, it started the week after school was out. The trip to Florida would have to be postponed.

His father said he understood, but the son didn't hear from him again for some time. A note here or there, an occasional call. They didn't say much—muttered sentences, comments about "your mother," a couple of clouded stories about the man's childhood—but it was enough to put together a few of the missing pieces.

In November the son received a call from his father's neighbor. His father had been taken to the hospital with heart problems. The son spoke with the charge nurse, who assured him his father was doing well following a heart attack. The doctor could provide details.

His father said, "I'm fine. You don't have to make a trip out here. The doctor says there was minor damage, and I can go home day after tomorrow."

He called his father every few days after that. They chatted and laughed and talked about getting together "soon." He sent money for Christmas. His father sent small gifts for his children and a pen and pencil set for his son. It was a cheap set, probably purchased at a discount pharmacy or variety-type store, and the kids tossed their tokens from Grandpa aside without much notice. But his wife received a precious music box made of crystal. Overwhelmed, she expressed her gratitude to the old man when they called him on Christmas Day. "It was my mother's," the old man explained. "I wanted you to have it."

The man's wife told her husband that they should have invited the old man for the holidays. As an excuse for not having done so, she added, "But it probably would be too cold for him here, anyway."

In February, the man decided to visit his father. As luck would have it, however, his boss's wife had to have an operation, and the man had to fill in and work a few extra hours. He called his father to tell him he'd probably get to Florida in March or April.

I met the man on Friday. He had finally come to Tampa. He was here to bury his father.

He was waiting when I arrived to open the door that morning. He sat in the chapel next to his father's body, which had been dressed in a handsome, new, navy blue pinstriped suit and laid out in a dark blue metal casket. "Going Home" was scripted inside the lid.

I offered the man a glass of water. He cried. I put my arm around his shoulder and he collapsed in my arms, sobbing. "I should have come sooner. He shouldn't have had to die alone." We sat together until late afternoon. He asked if I had something else to do that day. I told him no.

I didn't choose the act, but I knew it was kind. No one else came to honor the life of the man's father, not even the neighbor he spoke of. It cost nothing but a few hours of my time. I told him I was a student, that I wanted to be a professional golfer, and that my parents owned the funeral home. He was an attorney and lived in Denver. He plays golf whenever he can. He told me about his father.

That night, I asked my dad to play golf with me the next day. And before I went to bed, I told him, "I love you, Dad."

Nick Curry III, age 19

I Am Home

Peace, like charity, begins at home.

Source Unknown

You know how some people say that they never realized how much they loved their childhood until after they grew up? Well, I always knew that I was having a great childhood while it was happening. It wasn't until later on, when things weren't going so well, that I clung to the memories of that happiness and used them to find a way back home.

I grew up on a farm with a huge family. There was lots of love, lots of space and lots to do. From gardening to cutting hay, from working the horses to doing household chores, the word "bored" never found its way into my vocabulary—I loved it all and none of it seemed like work to me. Peer pressure was nonexistent, since the only "gang" I ran around with was the gang of animals on the ranch. My family and I were very close, and living so far out in the country kept us all at home most nights. After supper, my brothers and sisters and I would play games or tell stories, laughing and having fun until it was time to go to bed. Falling asleep was never a problem for me. I just listened to the sounds of chirping crickets and dreamed of another day on the farm. This was my life, and I knew I was lucky.

When I was 12, something tragic happened that would change my life forever. My father suffered a severe heart attack and underwent a triple bypass. He was diagnosed with hereditary heart disease, and it became a terrifying time for all of us. The doctors informed my dad that he would need to drastically change his lifestyle, which meant no more horse training, no more tractor driving . . . no more ranch life. Realizing that we couldn't keep up the place without him, we were forced to sell our home and move west, leaving behind family and friends and the only life that I knew.

The dry Arizona air was healing for my father, and I was adjusting to a new school, new friends and a new way of living. Suddenly I was going on dates, "cruising the mall" and dealing with the pressures of being a teenager. While things were different and strange, they were also exciting and fun. I learned that change, even when it is unexpected, can be a good thing. Little did I know that my life would be changing again, and in a very big way.

I was approached by a personal manager from Los Angeles who asked me if I had ever thought about acting. The idea had never crossed my mind, but now that it did, my interest was sparked. After giving it some thought and talking it over with my mom and dad, we decided that my mother and I would move to L.A. for a while and give it a shot. I had no idea what I was getting myself into!

Thank goodness my mother was right by my side from the very start. Together, we approached it like an adventure, and as my career grew, so did I. By the time that *Beverly Hills, 90210* had become successful, my mom and I both decided that it was time for her to return to Arizona and the rest of the family. The little girl from the farm was disappearing and being replaced by the grown-up woman in the big city.

I truly loved my job and my success was more than I could have ever dreamed of. And yet . . . something was missing. Slowly a dark void found its way into my heart and began to eat away at my happiness.

I tried to figure out what was missing. I tried working harder, then working less. I made new friends and lost touch with old ones. Nothing I did seemed to fill the void. I realized that I wasn't going to find the solution to the problem while going to clubs and endless parties, and living in the fast lane. I tried to remember when I was happiest, when the things in my life mattered most. I asked myself what was important to me. Finally, I had the answer. I knew what I had to do to be happy. Once again, my life was about to change.

I called my mom and dad and said, "I miss you too much. I need my parents back. I'm buying a place out here and I want you to move to California." My father wasn't too keen on the idea of being back in the rat race, but I assured him that this time, it would be nothing like that. So we began looking for a place outside of the city—a place complete with animals running all around and a garden full of vegetables just waiting to be picked for the supper table. A place that could be the family home where everyone could visit. A gathering place for the holidays. A haven, safe from the outside world. A place just like I remember growing up in.

Then one day we found it: the perfect ranch, nestled in a warm and sunny valley. My dream had become reality. The dark void that gnawed inside me began to fade, and a sense of balance and serenity returned to my soul. I was home.

Jennie Garth
actress, Beverly Hills, 90210

4

ON LOVE AND KINDNESS

Kindness in words creates confidence
Kindness in thinking creates profoundness
Kindness in giving creates love.

Lao-tzu

Tigress

Be kind, for everyone you meet is fighting a harder battle.

Plato

I'm not sure how Jesse got to my clinic. He didn't look old enough to drive, although his body had begun to broaden and he moved with the grace of young manhood. His face was direct and open.

When I walked into the waiting room, Jesse was lovingly petting his cat through the open door of the carrier on his lap. With a schoolboy's faith in me, he had brought his sick cat in for me to mend.

The cat was a tiny thing, exquisitely formed, with a delicate skull and beautiful markings. She looked like she was about 15 years old, give or take a year. I could see how her spots and stripes and her fierce, bright face had evoked the image of a tiger in a child's mind, and Tigress she had become.

Age had dimmed the bright green fire of her eyes and there was a dullness there now, but she was still elegant and self-possessed. She greeted me with a friendly rub against my hand.

I began to ask questions to determine what had brought these two to see me. Unlike most adults, the young man answered simply and directly. Tigress had had a normal appetite until recently, when she'd begun to vomit a couple of times a day. Now she was not eating at all and was withdrawn and sullen. She had also lost a pound, which is a lot when you weigh only six.

Stroking Tigress, I told her how beautiful she was while I examined her eyes and mouth, listened to her heart and lungs, and felt her stomach. And then I found it: a tubular mass in mid-abdomen. Tigress politely tried to slip away. She did not like the mass being handled.

I looked at the fresh-faced teen and back at the cat he had probably had all his life. I was going to have to tell him that his beloved companion had a tumor. Even if it were surgically removed, she probably would survive less than a year, and might need weekly chemotherapy to last that long.

It would all be very difficult and expensive. So I was going to have to tell him that his cat was likely to die. And there he was, all alone.

It seemed he was about to learn one of life's toughest lessons: that death is something that happens to every living thing. It is an omnipresent part of life. How death is first experienced can be life-forming, and it seemed that I was going to be the one to guide him through his first. I did not want to make any mistakes. It had to be done perfectly, or he might end up emotionally scarred.

It would have been easy to shirk this task and summon a parent. But when I looked at his face, I could not do it. He knew something was wrong. I could not just ignore him. So I talked to Jesse as Tigress's rightful owner and told him as gently as I could what I had found, and what it meant.

As I spoke, Jesse jerked convulsively away from me, probably so I could not see his face, but I had seen it begin to twist as he turned. I sat down and turned to Tigress, to give Jesse some privacy, and stroked her beautiful old face while I discussed the alternatives with him: I could do a biopsy of the mass, let her fade away at home, or give her an injection and put her to sleep.

Jesse listened carefully and nodded. He said he didn't think she was very comfortable anymore, and he didn't want her to suffer. He was trying very hard. The pair of them broke my heart. I offered to call a parent to explain what was going on.

Jesse gave me his father's number. I went over everything again with the father while Jesse listened and petted his cat. Then I let the father speak to his son. Jesse paced and gestured and his voice broke a few times, but when he hung up, he turned to me with dry eyes and said they had decided to put her to sleep.

No arguing, no denial, no hysteria, just acceptance of the inevitable. I could see, though, how much it was costing him. I asked if he wanted to take her home overnight to say good-bye. But he said no. He just wanted to be alone with her for a few minutes.

I left them and went to sign out the barbiturate I would use to ease her into a painless sleep. I could not control the tears streaming down my face, or the grief I felt welling up inside for Jesse, who had to become a man so quickly and so alone.

I waited outside the exam room. In a few minutes he came out and said that he was ready. I asked if he wanted to stay with her. He looked surprised, but I explained that it was often easier to observe how peaceful it was than forever to wonder how it actually happened.

Immediately seeing the logic of that, Jesse held her head and reassured her while I administered the injection.

She drifted off to sleep, her head cradled in his hand.

The animal looked quiet and at rest. The owner now bore all the suffering. This was the finest gift you could give, I said, to assume another's pain so that a loved one might rest.

He nodded. He understood.

Something was missing, though. I did not feel I had completed my task. It came to me suddenly that though I had asked him to become a man instantly, and he had done so with grace and strength, he was still a young man.

I held out my arms and asked him if he needed a hug. He did indeed, and in truth, so did I.

Judith S. Johnessee

Bright Heart

The greatest gift is a portion of thyself.

Ralph Waldo Emerson

Last year around Halloween, I was invited to participate in a carnival for Tuesday's Child, an organization that helps children with the AIDS virus. I was asked to attend because I'm on a television show; I went because I care. I don't think that most of the kids recognized me as a celebrity. They just thought of me as a big kid who came to play with them for the day. I think I liked it better that way.

At the carnival they had all kinds of booths. I was drawn to one in particular because of all the children that had gathered there. At this booth, anyone who wanted to could paint a square. Later that square was going to be sewn together with the others, to make a quilt. The quilt would be presented to a man who had dedicated much of his life to this organization and would soon be retiring.

They gave everyone fabric paints in bright, beautiful colors and asked the kids to paint something that would make the quilt beautiful. As I looked around at all the squares, I saw pink hearts and bright blue clouds, beautiful orange sunrises and green and purple flowers. The pictures were all bright, positive and uplifting. All except for one.

The boy sitting next to me was painting a heart, but it was dark, empty, lifeless. It lacked the bright, vibrant colors that his fellow artists had used.

At first I thought maybe he took the only paint that was left and it just happened to be dark. But when I asked him about it, he said his heart was that color because his own heart felt dark. I asked him why and he told me that he was very sick. Not only was he very sick, but his mom was very sick also. He said that his sickness was not ever going to get better and neither was his mom's. He looked straight into my eyes and said, "There is nothing anyone can do that will help."

I told him I was sorry that he was sick and I could certainly understand why he was so sad. I could even understand why he had made his heart a dark color. But . . . I told him that it isn't true that there is nothing anyone can do to help. Other people may not be able to make him or his mom better . . . but we can do things like give bear hugs, which in my experience can really help when you are feeling sad. I told him that if he would like, I would be happy to give him one so he could see what I meant. He instantly crawled into my lap and I thought my own heart would burst with the love I felt for this sweet little boy.

He sat there for a long time and when he had had enough, he jumped down to finish his coloring. I asked him if he felt any better and he said that he did, but he was still sick and nothing would change that. I told him I understood. I walked away feeling sad, but recommitted to this cause. I would do whatever I could to help.

As the day was coming to an end and I was getting ready to head home, I felt a tug on my jacket. I turned around and standing there with a smile on his face was the little boy. He said, "My heart is changing colors. It is getting brighter . . . I think those bear hugs really do work."

On my way home I felt my own heart and realized it, too, had changed to a brighter color.

Jennifer Love Hewitt
actress, Party of Five

The Secret of Happiness

If you would be loved, love and be lovable.

Benjamin Franklin

There is a wonderful fable about a young orphan girl who had no family and no one to love her. One day, feeling exceptionally sad and lonely, she was walking through a meadow when she noticed a small butterfly caught unmercifully in a thornbush. The more the butterfly struggled to free itself, the deeper the thorns cut into its fragile body. The young orphan girl carefully released the butterfly from its captivity. Instead of flying away, the little butterfly changed into a beautiful fairy. The young girl rubbed her eyes in disbelief.

"For your wonderful kindness," the good fairy said to the girl, "I will grant you any wish you would like."

The little girl thought for a moment and then replied, "I want to be happy!"

The fairy said, "Very well," and leaned toward her and whispered in her ear. Then the good fairy vanished.

As the little girl grew up, there was no one in the land

as happy as she. Everyone asked her the secret of her happiness. She would only smile and answer, "The secret of my happiness is that I listened to a good fairy when I was a little girl."

When she was very old and on her deathbed, the neighbors all rallied around her, afraid that her fabulous secret of happiness would die with her. "Tell us, please," they begged. "Tell us what the good fairy said."

The lovely old woman simply smiled and said, "She told me that everyone, no matter how secure they seemed, no matter how old or young, how rich or poor, had need of me."

The Speaker's Sourcebook

Reaching Out to a Stranger

To give pleasure to a single heart by a single act is better than a thousand heads bowing in prayer.

Gandhi

Frank Daily stared down at the frozen ground. He kicked chunks of snow, blackened with car exhaust, to the side. He only pretended to listen to the chatter of his friends, Norm and Ed, as they all clambered aboard the number 10 bus after school. He spouted out automatic answers to their questions: "Yeah, I aced the Milton test . . . No, I can't tonight. I've got to hit the books."

Frank and his friends flopped down in the back of the Milwaukee city bus along with several other high school boys, some from other schools. The bus belched a gray cloud out the back and headed west on Blue Mound Road.

Frank slouched into his seat. His hands hung from his two thumbs stuffed in the center of his belt. It had been another cold, gray day just a month ago in November when his world had come crashing down around him. He knew that his basketball skills were as good as the other boys'. His mom used to call him "the athlete of the season." When he was smaller, she had nicknamed him "Search and Destroy." He smiled at the memory.

The bus lurched away from a curb, and Frank instinctively braced his Nikes against the floor. *It must have been my size,* he thought. *That had to be it. Five-feet-four. Since I'm new at Marquette High and only a freshman, the coach must have taken one look at me and decided I was too small to make the basketball team.*

It wasn't easy starting a new school, especially an all-boys Catholic school. The older boys tended to be a bit clannish. It was especially hard for Frank because he had been a star athlete in all the sports in elementary school. Now, it seemed, he was a nothing.

Not only had he excelled in athletics before arriving at Marquette; he had also come alive to politics and history in the fifth and sixth grades. He recalled the advice his teacher, Don Anderson, had given him: "Look, Frank, if you'd put as much time into books as you do into basketball, you could do great in both."

Well, Frank thought, *Anderson was right about the books, at least. My grades have been A's and B's ever since. Basketball is another story.*

A loud horn and a screech of brakes somewhere behind the bus startled Frank. He looked at Norm and Ed. Norm was leaning his head against the window with half-shut eyes, his warm breath creating a circle of fog on the glass.

Frank rubbed his own eyes. He still remembered his stomach chilling into a frozen knot as he approached the locker room last month. He had read the team list posted on the locker room door, hoping, searching frantically for his name. It hadn't been there. It was missing. No name. He had felt suddenly as if he had ceased to exist. Become invisible.

The bus jerked to a stop at the County Institutions grounds. The bus driver called to some noisy boys at the back to settle down. Frank glanced up at the driver, who had been dubbed "Kojak" because of his bald head.

A very pregnant woman hung onto the silver handrail and slowly pulled herself onto the bus. As she fell backward into the seat behind the bus driver, her feet kicked up, and Frank saw that she was in stocking feet.

As Kojak steered the bus back into traffic, he yelled over his shoulder, "Where are your shoes, lady? It ain't more than 10 degrees out there."

"I can't afford shoes," the woman answered. She pulled her fraying coat collar around her neck. Some of the boys at the back exchanged glances and smirked. "I got on the bus just to get my feet warm," the woman continued. "If you don't mind, I'll just ride around with you for a bit."

Kojak scratched his bald head and shouted, "Now just tell me how come you can't afford shoes?"

"I got eight kids. They all got shoes. There's not enough left for me. But it's okay, the Lord will take care of me."

Frank looked down at his new Nike basketball shoes. His feet were warm and snug, always had been. And then he looked back at the woman. Her socks were ripped. Her coat, missing buttons, hung open around her stomach, as swollen as a basketball and covered by a smudgy dress.

Frank didn't hear anything around him after that. He wasn't aware of Norm or Ed. He just felt a warm thawing in his gut. The word "invisible" popped into his mind again. *An invisible person, marginal, forgotten by society, but for a different reason,* he thought.

He would probably always be able to afford shoes. She probably never would. Under his seat, he pried the toe of one shoe into the heel of the other and slipped it off. Then the other shoe. He looked around. Nobody had noticed. He would have to walk three blocks in the snow. But the cold had never bothered him much. When the bus stopped at the end of the line, Frank waited until everyone else had emptied off. Then he reached under his seat and picked up his basketball shoes. He walked quickly up to the woman and handed them to her, looking down and saying, "Here, lady, you need these more than I do."

And then Frank hurried to the door and stepped down. He managed to land in a puddle. It didn't matter. He wasn't at all cold. He heard the woman exclaim, "Look, they fit me just perfect!"

Then he heard Kojak call, "Hey, come back here, kid! What's your name?"

Frank turned around to face Kojak. At the same time, Norm and Ed asked where his shoes were.

Frank's cheeks burned in confusion at Kojak, his friends and the woman. "Frank Daily," he said quietly. "My name is Frank Daily."

"Well, Frank," Kojak said, "I've never seen anything like that in the 20 years I've been driving this bus."

The woman was crying. "Thank you, young man," she said. She turned to Kojak. "See, I told you the Lord would take care of me."

Frank mumbled, "You're welcome." He smiled at the woman. "It's no big deal. Besides, it's Christmas."

He hurried off after Norm and Ed. It seemed to him that the grayness had lifted. On the way home, he hardly felt the cold beneath his feet at all.

Barbara A. Lewis

Smile

She smiled at a sorrowful stranger.
The smile seemed to make him feel better.
He remembered past kindnesses of a friend
and wrote him a thank-you letter.
The friend was so pleased with the thank-you
that he left a large tip after lunch.
The waitress, surprised by the size of the tip,
bet the whole thing on a hunch.
The next day she picked up her winnings,
and gave part to a man on the street.
The man on the street was grateful;
for two days he'd had nothing to eat.
After he finished his dinner,
he left for his small dingy room.
(He didn't know at that moment
that he might be facing his doom.)
On the way he picked up a shivering puppy
and took him home to get warm.
The puppy was very grateful
to be in out of the storm.
That night the house caught on fire.

The puppy barked the alarm.
He barked 'til he woke the whole household
and saved everybody from harm.
One of the boys that he rescued
grew up to be President.
All this because of a simple smile
that hadn't cost a cent.

Barbara Hauck, age 13

Mrs. Link

I was 18, about to start college and broke. To make some money, I plodded down a quiet street of older homes, selling books door-to-door. As I approached one gate, a tall, handsome woman in her 80s came to the gate in her bath robe. "There you are darling! I've been waiting for you! God told me you'd be coming today." Mrs. Link needed help around her yard and house, and, apparently, I was the one for the job. Who was I to argue with God?

The next day I worked for six hours, harder than I had ever worked before. Mrs. Link showed me how to plant bulbs, what flowers and weeds to pull up, and where to haul the wilted plants. I finished off the day by mowing the lawn with a mower that looked like an antique. When I had finished, Mrs. Link complimented me on my work and looked under the mower at the blade. "Looks like you hit a stone. I'll get the file." I soon learned why everything Mrs. Link owned looked like an antique, but worked like brand-new. For six hours of work she gave me a check for three dollars. It was 1978. God's funny sometimes, isn't he?

The next week I cleaned Mrs. Link's house. She showed me exactly how to vacuum her antique Persian rug with her antique-looking vacuum. As I dusted her beautiful treasures, she told me where she had acquired them while she traveled the world. For lunch she sautéed fresh vegetables from her garden. We shared a delicious meal and a lovely day.

Some weeks I got to be a chauffeur. The last gift to Mrs. Link from Mr. Link was a glorious new car. By the time I met Mrs. Link, the car was 30 years old, but still glorious. Mrs. Link was never able to have children, but her sister, nieces and nephews lived nearby. Her neighbors also were fond of her, and she was active in civic affairs.

A year and a half passed since I met Mrs. Link. School, work and church were taking up more of my time, and I saw Mrs. Link less and less. I found another girl to help her around the house.

Valentine's Day was coming, and being very undemonstrative and very broke, I was compiling a very short list of my valentines. Mom glanced at my list and said, "You need to get Mrs. Link a valentine."

I incredulously asked, "Why? Mrs. Link has a lot of family, friends and neighbors. She's active in the community. I don't even spend a lot of time with her anymore. Why would Mrs. Link want a valentine from me?"

Mom was unimpressed. "Get Mrs. Link a valentine," she insisted.

On Valentine's Day I self-consciously presented Mrs. Link a small bouquet, which she graciously accepted.

A couple of months later, I visited Mrs. Link again. Centered on her mantle, in her living room full of beautiful things, stood my wilted and faded Valentine's Day bouquet—the only valentine Mrs. Link received that year.

Susan Daniels Adams

A Mason-Dixon Memory

Dondre Green glanced uneasily at the civic leaders and sports figures filling the hotel ballroom in Cleveland. They had come from across the nation to attend a fund-raiser for the National Minority College Golf Scholarship Foundation. I was the banquet's featured entertainer. Dondre, an 18-year-old high-school senior from Monroe, Louisiana, was the evening's honored guest.

"Nervous?" I asked the handsome young man in his starched white shirt and rented tuxedo.

"A little," he whispered, grinning.

One month earlier, Dondre had been just one more black student attending a predominantly white Southern school. Although most of his friends and classmates were white, Dondre's race had never been an issue. Then, on April 17, 1991, Dondre's black skin provoked an incident that made nationwide news.

"Ladies and gentlemen," the emcee said, "our special guest, Dondre Green."

As the audience stood applauding, Dondre walked to the microphone and began his story. "I love golf," he said quietly. "For the past two years, I've been a member of the

St. Frederick High School golf team. And though I was the only black member, I've always felt at home playing at mostly white country clubs across Louisiana."

The audience leaned forward; even the waiters and busboys stopped to listen. As I listened, a memory buried in my heart since childhood began fighting its way to life.

"Our team had driven from Monroe," Dondre continued. "When we arrived at the Caldwell Parish Country Club in Columbia, we walked to the putting green."

Dondre and his teammates were too absorbed to notice the conversation between a man and St. Frederick athletic director James Murphy. After disappearing into the clubhouse, Murphy returned to his players.

"I want to see the seniors," he said. "On the double!" His face seemed strained as he gathered the four students, including Dondre.

"I don't know how to tell you this," he said, "but the Caldwell Parish Country Club is reserved for whites only." Murphy paused and looked at Dondre. His teammates glanced at each other in disbelief. "I want you seniors to decide what our response should be," Murphy continued. "If we leave, we forfeit this tournament. If we stay, Dondre can't play."

As I listened, my own childhood memory from 32 years ago broke free.

In 1959, I was 13 years old, a poor black kid living with my mother and stepfather in a small black ghetto on Long Island, New York. My mother worked nights in a hospital, and my stepfather drove a coal truck. Needless to say, our standard of living was somewhat short of the American dream.

Nevertheless, when my eighth-grade teacher announced a graduation trip to Washington, D.C., it never crossed my mind that I would be left behind. Besides a complete tour of the nation's capital, we would visit Glen Echo Amusement Park in Maryland. In my imagination, Glen Echo was Disneyland, Knott's Berry Farm and Magic Mountain rolled into one.

My heart beating wildly, I raced home to deliver the mimeographed letter describing the journey. But when my mother saw how much the trip would cost, she just shook her head. We couldn't afford it.

After feeling sad for 10 seconds, I decided to try to fund the trip myself. For the next eight weeks, I sold candy bars door-to-door, delivered newspapers and mowed lawns. Three days before the deadline, I'd made just barely enough. I was going!

The day of the trip, trembling with excitement, I climbed onto the train. I was the only nonwhite in our section.

Our hotel was not far from the White House. My roommate was Frank Miller, the son of a businessman. Leaning together out of our window and dropping water balloons on tourists quickly cemented our new friendship.

Every morning, almost a hundred of us loaded noisily onto our bus for another adventure. We sang our school fight song dozens of times—en route to Arlington National Cemetery, and even on an afternoon cruise down the Potomac River.

We visited the Lincoln Memorial twice, once in daylight, the second time at dusk. My classmates and I fell silent as we walked in the shadows of those 36 marble columns, one for every state in the Union that Lincoln labored to preserve. I stood next to Frank at the base of the 19-foot seated statue. Spotlights made the white Georgian marble seem to glow. Together, we read those famous words from Lincoln's speech at Gettysburg remembering the most bloody battle in the War between the States: " . . . *we here highly resolve that these dead shall not have died in vain—that this nation, under God, shall have a new birth of freedom . . .* "

As Frank motioned me into place to take my picture, I took one last look at Lincoln's face. He seemed alive and so terribly sad.

The next morning I understood a little better why he wasn't smiling. "Clifton," a chaperone said, "could I see you for a moment?"

The other guys at my table, especially Frank, turned pale. We had been joking about the previous night's direct water balloon hit on a fat lady and her poodle. It was a stupid, dangerous act, but luckily nobody got hurt. We were celebrating our escape from punishment when the chaperone asked to see me.

"Clifton," she began, "do you know about the Mason-Dixon line?"

"No," I said, wondering what this had to do with drenching fat ladies.

"Before the Civil War," she explained, "the Mason-Dixon line was originally the boundary between Maryland and Pennsylvania—the dividing line between the slave and free states." Having escaped one disaster, I could feel another brewing. I noticed that her eyes were damp and her hands were shaking.

"Today," she continued, "the Mason-Dixon line is a kind of invisible border between the North and the South. When you cross that invisible line out of Washington, D.C., into Maryland, things change."

There was an ominous drift to this conversation, but I wasn't following it. Why did she look and sound so nervous?

"Glen Echo Amusement Park is in Maryland," she said at last, "and the management doesn't allow Negroes inside." She stared at me in silence.

I was still grinning and nodding when the meaning finally sank in.

"You mean I can't go to the park," I stuttered, "because I'm a Negro?"

She nodded slowly. "I'm sorry, Clifton," she said, taking my hand. "You'll have to stay in the hotel tonight. Why don't you and I watch a movie on television?"

I walked to the elevators feeling confusion, disbelief, anger and a deep sadness. "What happened, Clifton?" Frank said when I got back to the room. "Did the fat lady tell on us?"

Without saying a word, I walked over to my bed, lay down and began to cry. Frank was stunned to silence. Junior-high boys didn't cry, at least not in front of each other.

It wasn't just missing the class adventure that made me feel so sad. For the first time in my life, I was learning what it felt like to be a "nigger."

Of course there was discrimination in the North, but the color of my skin had never officially kept me out of a coffee shop, a church—or an amusement park.

"Clifton," Frank whispered, "what is the matter?"

"They won't let me go to Glen Echo Park tonight," I sobbed.

"Because of the water balloon?" he asked.

"No," I answered, "because I'm a Negro."

"Well, that's a relief!" Frank said, and then he laughed, obviously relieved to have escaped punishment for our caper with the balloons. "I thought it was serious."

Wiping away the tears with my sleeve, I stared at him. "It *is* serious. They don't let Negroes into the park. I can't go with you!" I shouted. "That's pretty damn serious to me."

I was about to wipe the silly grin off Frank's face with a blow to his jaw when I heard him say, "Then I won't go either."

For an instant we just froze. Then Frank grinned. I will never forget that moment. Frank was just a kid. He wanted to go to that amusement park as much as I did, but there was something even more important than the class night out. Still, he didn't explain or expand.

The next thing I knew, the room was filled with kids listening to Frank. "They don't allow Negroes in the park," he said, "so I'm staying with Clifton."

"Me too," a second boy said.

"Those jerks," a third muttered. "I'm with you, Clifton." My heart began to race. Suddenly, I was not alone. A pint-sized revolution had been born. The "water balloon brigade," 11 white boys from Long Island, had made its decision: "We won't go." And as I sat on my bed in the center of it all, I felt grateful. But, above all, I was filled with pride.

Dondre Green's story brought that childhood memory back to life. His golfing teammates, like my childhood friends, had an important decision to make: standing by their friend when it would cost them dearly. But when it came time to decide, no one hesitated. "Let's get out of here," one of them whispered.

"They just turned and walked toward the van," Dondre told us. "They didn't debate it. And the younger players joined us without looking back."

Dondre was astounded by the response of his friends—and the people of Louisiana. The whole state was outraged and tried to make it right. The Louisiana House of Representatives proclaimed a Dondre Green Day and passed legislation permitting lawsuits for damages, attorneys' fees and court costs against any private facility that invites a team, then bars any member because of race.

As Dondre concluded, his eyes glistened with tears. "I love my coach and my teammates for sticking by me," he said. "It goes to show that there are always good people who will not give in to bigotry. The kind of love they showed me that day will conquer hatred every time."

My friends, too, had shown that kind of love. As we sat in the hotel, a chaperone came in waving an envelope. "Boys!" he shouted. "I've just bought 13 tickets to the Senators-Tigers game. Anybody want to go?"

The room erupted in cheers. Not one of us had ever been to a professional baseball game in a real baseball park.

On the way to the stadium, we grew silent as our driver paused before the Lincoln Memorial. For one long moment, I stared through the marble pillars at Mr. Lincoln, bathed in that warm, yellow light. There was still no smile and no sign of hope in his sad and tired eyes.

". . . we here highly resolve . . . that this nation, under God, shall have a new birth of freedom . . . "

In his words and in his life, Lincoln had made it clear that freedom is not free. Every time the color of a person's skin keeps him out of an amusement park or off a country club fairway, the war for freedom begins again. Sometimes the battle is fought with fists and guns, but more often the most effective weapon is a simple act of love and courage.

Whenever I hear those words from Lincoln's speech at Gettysburg, I remember my 11 white friends, and I feel hope once again. I like to imagine that when we paused that night at the foot of his great monument, Mr. Lincoln smiled at last. As Dondre said, "The kind of love they showed me that day will conquer hatred every time."

Clifton Davis
actor, Amen

The Mirror

"Dr. Papaderos, what is the meaning of life?"

The usual laughter followed, and people stirred to go.

Papaderos held up his hand and stilled the room and looked at me for a long time, asking with his eyes if I was serious and seeing from my eyes that I was.

"I will answer your question."

Taking his wallet out of his hip pocket, he fished into a leather billfold and brought out a very small round mirror, about the size of a quarter.

And what he said went like this:

"When I was a small child, during the war, we were very poor and we lived in a remote village. One day, on the road, I found the broken pieces of a mirror. A German motorcycle had been wrecked in that place.

"I tried to find all the pieces and put them together, but it was not possible, so I kept only the largest piece. This one, and, by scratching it on a stone, I made it round. I began to play with it as a toy and became fascinated by the fact that I could reflect light into dark places where the sun would never shine—in deep holes and crevices and dark closets. It became a game for me to get light into the most inaccessible places I could find.

"I kept the little mirror, and, as I went about my growing up, I would take it out in idle moments and continue the challenge of the game. As I became a man, I grew to understand that this was not just a child's game but a metaphor for what I might do with my life. I came to understand that I am not the light or the source of light. But light—truth, understanding, knowledge—is there, and it will shine in many dark places only if I reflect it.

"I am a fragment of a mirror whose whole design and shape I do not know. Nevertheless, with what I have I can reflect light into the dark places of this world—into the black places in the hearts of men—and change some things in some people. Perhaps others may see and do likewise. This is what I am about. This is the meaning of my life."

Robert Fulghum

A Gift for Two

You never know what happiness a simple act of kindness will bring about.

Bree Abel

It was a beautiful day for sightseeing around downtown Portland. We were a bunch of counselors on our day off, away from the campers, just out for some fun. The weather was perfect for a picnic, so when lunch time came, we set our sights on a small park in town. Since we all had different cravings, we decided to split up, get what each of us wanted, and meet back on the grass in a few minutes.

When my friend Robby headed for a hot dog stand, I decided to keep her company. We watched the vendor put together the perfect hot dog, just the way Robby wanted it. But when she took out her money to pay him, the man surprised us.

"It looks a little on the cool side," he said, "so never mind paying me. This will be my freebie of the day."

We said our thanks, joined our friends in the park, and dug into our food. But as we talked and ate, I was distracted by a man sitting alone nearby, looking at us. I could tell that he hadn't showered for days. Another homeless person, I thought, like all the others you see in cities. I didn't pay much more attention than that.

We finished eating and decided to head off for more sightseeing. But when Robby and I went to the garbage can to throw away my lunch bag, I heard a strong voice ask, "There isn't any food in that bag, is there?"

It was the man who had been watching us. I didn't know what to say. "No, I ate it already."

"Oh," was his only answer, with no shame in his voice at all. He was obviously hungry, couldn't bear to see anything thrown away, and was used to asking this question.

I felt bad for the man, but I didn't know what I could do. That's when Robby said, "I'll be right back. Please wait for me a minute," and ran off. I watched curiously as she went across to the hot dog stand. Then I realized what she was doing. She bought a hot dog, crossed back to the trash can, and gave the hungry man the food.

When she came back to us, Robby said simply, "I was just passing on the kindness that someone gave to me."

That day I learned how generosity can go farther than the person you give to. By giving, you teach others how to give also.

Andrea Hensley

Life Just Isn't

What's important in life is how we treat each other.

Hana Ivanhoe, age 15

Throughout my junior year in high school I had been looking forward to the Junior Overnight, a retreat that was offered to the junior girls at my high school. The purpose was to talk about how our lives were going and to discuss our problems, concerns and worries about school, friends, guys, or whatever. We had some great discussions.

I went home from the retreat with a great feeling. I had learned a lot about people that I could put to good use. I decided to put the papers and notes I had received on the retreat in my journal, which is where I keep some of my most treasured items. Not thinking much about it, I set the journal on top of my dresser and finished unpacking.

I was feeling so great from the retreat that I went into the next week with high hopes. However, the week turned out to be an emotional disaster. A friend of mine really hurt my feelings, I had a fight with my mom, and I was worrying about my grades, particularly in English. To top it all off, I was worrying about the upcoming prom.

I literally cried myself to sleep almost every night. I had hoped that the Junior Retreat would have had a deeper impact on calming my nerves and helping me to be stress-free. Instead, I began to think that it had only been a temporary stress relief.

I woke up on Friday morning with a heavy heart and a bad attitude. I was also running late. I dressed quickly, grabbing a pair of socks out of my dresser drawer. As I slammed the drawer shut, my journal fell off the top of the dresser and its contents spilled all over the floor. As I knelt down to pick it up, one of the sheets of paper that had fallen out caught my eye. My retreat leader had given it me. I opened the folded sheet and read it.

Life isn't about keeping score. It's not about how many people call you and it's not about who you've dated, are dating or haven't dated at all. It isn't about who you've kissed, what sport you play, or which guy or girl likes you. It's not about your shoes or your hair or the color of your skin or where you live or go to school. In fact, it's not about grades, money, clothes, or colleges that accept you or not. Life isn't about if you have lots of friends, or if you are alone, and it's not about how accepted or unaccepted you are. Life just isn't about that.

But life is about who you love and who you hurt. It's about how you feel about yourself. It's about trust, happiness and compassion. It's about sticking up for your friends and replacing inner hate with love. Life is about avoiding jealousy, overcoming ignorance and building confidence. It's about what you say and what you mean. It's about seeing people for who they are and not what they have. Most of all, it is about choosing to use your life to touch someone else's in a way that could never have been achieved otherwise. These choices are what life's about.

I aced my next English test that day. I had a fun time with my friend that weekend and got the courage to talk to the boy that I liked. I spent more time with my family and made an effort to listen to my mom. I even found a great dress for the prom and had a wonderful time. And it wasn't luck or a miracle. It was a change in heart and a change in attitude on my part. I realized that sometimes I just need to sit back and remember the things in life that really matter—like the things I learned on my Junior Overnight.

I am a senior this year and preparing to go on my Senior Retreat. But that piece of paper is still in my journal, so that I can look at it whenever I need to remember what life is really about.

Katie Leicht, age 17

Tell the World for Me

I sought my soul
But my soul I could not see.
I sought my God
But my God eluded me.
I sought my brother
And I found all three.

Source Unknown

Some 14 years ago, I stood watching my university students file into the classroom for our opening session in the theology of faith. That was the day I first saw Tommy. He was combing his hair, which hung six inches below his shoulders. My quick judgment wrote him off as strange—very strange.

Tommy turned out to be my biggest challenge. He constantly objected to or smirked at the possibility of an unconditionally loving God. When he turned in his final exam at the end of the course, he asked in a slightly cynical tone, "Do you think I'll ever find God?"

"No," I said emphatically.

"Oh," he responded. "I thought that was the product you were pushing."

I let him get five steps from the door and then called out. "I don't think you'll ever find him, but I am certain he will find you." Tommy shrugged and left. I felt slightly disappointed that he had missed my clever line.

Later I heard that Tommy had graduated, and I was grateful for that. Then came a sad report: Tommy had terminal cancer. Before I could search him out, he came to me. When he walked into my office, his body was badly wasted, and his long hair had fallen out because of chemotherapy. But his eyes were bright and his voice, for the first time, was firm.

"Tommy! I've thought about you so often. I heard you were very sick," I blurted out.

"Oh, yes, very sick. I have cancer. It's a matter of weeks."

"Can you talk about it?"

"Sure. What would you like to know?"

"What's it like to be only 24 and know that you're dying?"

"It could be worse," he told me, "like being 50 and thinking that drinking booze, seducing women and making money are the real 'biggies' in life." Then he told me why he had come.

"It was something you said to me on the last day of class. I asked if you thought I would ever find God and you said no, which surprised me. Then you said, 'But he will find you.' I thought about that a lot, even though my search for God was hardly intense at that time.

"But when the doctors removed a lump from my groin and told me that it was malignant, I got serious about locating God. And when the malignancy spread into my vital organs, I really began banging against the bronze doors of heaven. But nothing happened. Well, one day I woke up, and instead of my desperate attempts to get some kind of message, I just quit. I decided I didn't really care about God, an afterlife, or anything like that.

"I decided to spend what time I had left doing something more important. I thought about you and something else you had said: 'The essential sadness is to go through life without loving. But it would be almost equally sad to leave this world without ever telling those you loved that you loved them.' So I began with the hardest one: my dad."

Tommy's father had been reading the newspaper when his son approached him.

"Dad, I would like to talk with you."

"Well, talk."

"I mean, it's really important."

The newspaper came down three slow inches. "What is it?"

"Dad, I love you. I just wanted you to know that."

Tommy smiled at me as he recounted the moment. "The newspaper fluttered to the floor. Then my father did two things I couldn't remember him doing before. He cried and he hugged me. And we talked all night, even though he had to go to work the next morning.

"It was easier with my mother and little brother," Tommy continued. "They cried with me, and we hugged one another, and shared the things we had been keeping secret for so many years. I was only sorry that I had waited so long. Here I was, in the shadow of death, and I was just beginning to open up to all the people I had actually been close to.

"Then one day I turned around and God was there. He didn't come to me when I pleaded with him. Apparently he does things in his own way and at his own hour. The important thing is that you were right. He found me even after I stopped looking for him."

"Tommy," I practically gasped, "I think you are saying something much more universal than you realize. You are saying that the surest way to find God is not by making him a private possession or an instant consolation in time of need, but rather by opening to love.

"Tommy," I added, "could I ask you a favor? Would you come to my theology-of-faith course and tell my students what you just told me?"

Though we scheduled a date, he never made it. Of course, his life was not really ended by his death, only changed. He made the great step from faith into vision. He found a life far more beautiful than the eye of humanity has ever seen or the mind ever imagined.

Before he died, we talked one last time. "I'm not going to make it to your class," he said.

"I know, Tommy."

"Will you tell them for me? Will you . . . tell the whole world for me?"

"I will, Tommy. I'll tell them."

John Powell, S.J.

Like People First

The more we know the better we forgive.
Whoever feels deeply, feels for all who live.

Madame de Staël

Craig, a close friend of mine in graduate school, brought energy and life into any room he entered. He focused his entire attention on you while you were talking, and you felt incredibly important. People loved him.

One sunny autumn day, Craig and I were sitting in our usual study area. I was staring out the window when I noticed one of my professors crossing the parking lot.

"I don't want to run into him," I said.

"Why not?" Craig asked.

I explained that the previous spring semester, the professor and I had parted on bad terms. I had taken offense at some suggestion he had made and had, in turn, given offense in my answer. "Besides," I added, "the guy just doesn't like me."

Craig looked down at the passing figure. "Maybe you've got it wrong," he said. "Maybe you're the one who's turning away—and you're just doing that because you're afraid. He probably thinks you don't like him, so he's not friendly. People like people who like them. If you show an interest in him, he'll be interested in you. Go talk to him."

Craig's words smarted. I walked tentatively down the stairs into the parking lot. I greeted my professor warmly and asked how his summer had been. He looked at me, genuinely surprised. We walked off together talking, and I could imagine Craig watching from the window, smiling broadly.

Craig had explained to me a simple concept, so simple I couldn't believe I'd never known it. Like most young people, I felt unsure of myself and came to all my encounters fearing that others would judge me—when, in fact, they were worrying about how I would judge *them.* From that day on, instead of seeing judgment in the eyes of others, I recognized the need people have to make a connection and to share something about themselves. I discovered a world of people I never would have known otherwise.

Once, for example, on a train going across Canada, I began talking to a man everyone was avoiding because he was weaving and slurring his speech as if drunk. It turned out that he was recovering from a stroke. He had been an engineer on the same line we were riding, and long into the night he revealed to me the history beneath every mile of track: Pile O'Bones Creek, named for the thousands of buffalo skeletons left there by Indian hunters; the legend of Big Jack, a Swedish track-layer who could lift 500-pound steel rails; a conductor named McDonald who kept a rabbit as his traveling companion.

As the morning sun began to tint the horizon, he grabbed my hand and looked into my eyes. "Thanks for listening. Most people wouldn't bother." He didn't have to thank me. The pleasure had been all mine.

On a noisy street corner in Oakland, California, a family

who stopped me for directions turned out to be visiting from Australia's isolated northwest coast. I asked them about their life back home. Soon, over coffee, they regaled me with stories of huge saltwater crocodiles "with backs as wide as car hoods."

Each encounter became an adventure, each person a lesson in life. The wealthy, the poor, the powerful and the lonely; all were as full of dreams and doubts as I. And each had a unique story to tell, if only I were willing to hear.

An old, stubble-bearded hobo told me how he'd fed his family during the Depression by firing his shotgun into a pond and gathering up the stunned fish that floated to the surface. A traffic patrolman confided how he'd learned his hand gestures by watching bullfighters and symphony conductors. And a young beautician shared the joy of watching residents in a nursing home smile after receiving a new hairstyle.

How often we allow such opportunities to pass us by. The girl who everyone thinks is homely, the boy with the odd clothes—those people have stories to tell, as surely as you do. And like you, they dream that someone is willing to hear.

This is what Craig knew. Like people first, ask questions later. See if the light you shine on others isn't reflected back on you a hundredfold.

Kent Nerburn

Reprinted by permission of Malcolm Hancock.

Lilacs Bloom Every Spring

When it comes down to it, we all just want to be loved.

Jamie Yellin, age 14

Today (here is my cue to sigh) is one of my bad days. Everything feels out of my reach, but I'm especially dreading my psychology class next hour. As a silly final project for the year, we are to bring a photo of ourselves that represents a truly happy time in our childhood.

The trouble was not in selecting a photo—I knew right away the one to bring. Framed on my desk is a picture of Grandma Sherrie, now dead, and myself, when I was eight years old. She had taken me on a lengthy bus ride to a lilac festival in the spring. We spent the afternoon sniffing, eyes closed, bent over lilac blossoms. The picture was taken by a really funny old man, who told us hilarious stories as he walked us to the bus stop late in the afternoon. We never saw him again, but looking back I wonder if he was smitten with Grandma Sherrie.

Looking at the picture, as I wait for my lunch period to end, I know my grandma's beauty isn't there in the photo—short, straight, silver hair, and large, slightly protuberant brown eyes. The nose is too big and the forehead is too high. She is short and a little squat. Beside her, clutching her hand, I am a smaller, younger replica. We even had the same narrow, skinny feet and unbelievably long toes. Had. Now it's just my ridiculous feet to laugh at, except that I haven't found anyone with whom it's quite as funny as it was with her. When she died two years ago, I lost some of my reality.

So this is the only picture I could bring. I can't miss an opportunity to bring her back a little bit, to celebrate her imprint on life. Even though I know that few, if any, will appreciate the gift I foolishly, eagerly share.

I sit down at my desk, feeling relief at arriving safely. Somehow the halls are where I feel the most isolated. Surrounded by people, I am more aware than ever of how far away I am from them. I have no one to walk with, or shriek gossip to. I see these same people every day, brush against them sometimes. But I don't know them any more than a stranger on the street. We don't even make eye contact.

As people trickle in, I sit with the picture in my lap, framed by my hands. *Why didn't I bring another? Why was I so sure my words could explain?*

The teacher steps to the front of the room. I don't like her any more than she likes me. She prefers students who stay after class to talk about boyfriends and complain about curfews. I stay after to show her articles about new treatments for autism. I'd like her to like me, even though I can't respect her.

She asks for volunteers to begin the presentations. She smiles expectantly at me in the front row. (Where else would I be?) I rise to my feet, the ultimate volunteer-to-go-firster. A voice from behind.

"I bet she brought a picture of her first set of encyclopedias." *Nope, sorry, that one's framed over the fireplace.*

Eyes, all these eyes looking at me with that blank stare reserved for observation without attention or thought.

"This is a photograph of my Grandma Sherrie and me when I was eight years old. She took me to a lilac festival. It was an annual event." *Event?* I should have said something else. "They had all sorts of lilacs, rare and common varieties, pinks and purples and whites. It was wonderful." *Boring.*

I looked down at the photo. The woman and the girl, holding hands framed by a tall hedge dotted with sprays of purple lilac blooms. The pair seems ready to march off and conquer the world, just the two of them in their sensible walking shoes.

"When I look at this picture, I can almost smell the lilacs. Especially now, in the spring. It was a perfect outing, and after we went home, my grandma made me spaghetti, and let me put chocolate sprinkles on my ice cream . . ." Getting a little off topic here. I'm losing the audience I never had.

"But it was a perfect day, um, like I said. It's hard to remember another day like that as I got older. My grandma got sick when I was nine . . ." suddenly, there are tears on my cheeks. ". . . and she never got better." Time to run, escape, at least sit down.

I thud into my chair, clutching the picture. No applause. The teacher abruptly, too cheerfully, calls on someone else. The class is soon over, after 10 or 12 years pass. I escape to the whirling chaos in the hallway.

Talk about a bad day.

But, like they say, there is always tomorrow. Which to me it seems to imply there's no use in getting through today, because you'll just have to do it again in less than 24 hours.

But here I am, tomorrow, at the door to my psych class, feeling like I just left. Only today, I'm late, having dropped a folder that spewed its contents with abandon. Everyone is looking at me. The day before I had broken two big rules. I not only displayed excessive emotion, but admitted that I really cared about something as inconsequential as a grandmother. Well, I'm invisible one day and the next the object of public scorn. Both unenviable life situations. I move to my desk. There is a paper shopping bag on the seat of the chair. Expecting a smelly gym uniform and tennis shoes, I look inside without thinking.

Oh. Oh. My God. I feel my outline melt.

The bag is full of lilac branches. I can smell them with my soul, can feel them with a part of me I thought had withered and died. *Am I still in my real life?* I look up (everyone is still staring blandly. But it must be one of them, some sentimental rebel in disguise). Which one?

I move the bag and sit down. The teacher is annoyed.

"Shall we begin, folks? Your presentations yesterday will be counted . . ."

There is a piece of paper tucked among the blossoms. I open it to find two lines:

We will find our right to be.
Until then, lilacs bloom every spring.

blue jean magazine

Paint Brush

I keep my paint brush with me
Wherever I may go,
In case I need to cover up
So the real me doesn't show.
I'm so afraid to show you me,
Afraid of what you'll do—that
You might laugh or say mean things.
I'm afraid I might lose you.

I'd like to remove all my paint coats
To show you the real, true me,
But I want you to try and understand,
I need you to accept what you see.
So if you'll be patient and close your eyes,
I'll strip off all my coats real slow.
Please understand how much it hurts
To let the real me show.

Now my coats are all stripped off.
I feel naked, bare and cold,
And if you still love me with all that you see,
You are my friend, pure as gold.

I need to save my paint brush, though,
And hold it in my hand,
I want to keep it handy
In case somebody doesn't understand.
So please protect me, my dear friend
And thanks for loving me true,
But please let me keep my paint brush with me
Until I love me, too.

Bettie B. Youngs

5

ON LEARNING

School has taught me not only how to learn in the classroom, but outside the classroom as well. Where do you think I learned how to climb, swing and skip? Where do you think I learned how to meet my best friend?

Jessie Braun, age 18

Egg Lessons

We should be careful to get out of an experience only the wisdom that is in it.

Mark Twain

Robby Rogers . . . my first love. What a great guy, too. He was kind, honest and smart. In fact, the more I think about him, the more reasons I find for loving him as much as I did. We had been going out for a whole year. As you know, in high school that's a very long time.

I don't remember why I was not at Nancy's party that Saturday night, but Robby and I had agreed we would see each other afterward. He would come over around 10:30. Robby always showed up when he said he would, so at 11:00 I started feeling sick. I knew something wasn't right.

On Sunday morning he woke me with a phone call. "We need to talk. Can I come over?"

I wanted to say, "No, you cannot come over here and tell me something is wrong." Instead, I said, "Sure," and hung up with a knot in my stomach.

I had been right. "I got together with Sue Roth last

night," Robby informed me, "and we're going out now." He followed with the usual, "I'm so confused. I would never do anything to hurt you, Kim. I'll always love you."

I must have turned white because I felt the blood leave my face. This wasn't what I expected; my reaction surprised me. I felt such anger that I was unable to complete a sentence. I was so hurt that everything but the pain in my heart seemed to be moving in slow motion.

"Come on, Kim, don't be like this. We can be friends, can't we?"

Those are the cruelest words to utter to someone you're dumping. I had loved him deeply, shared every little weakness and vulnerability with him—not to mention the four hours a day I had spent with him for the last year (not counting the phone time). I wanted to hit him really hard, over and over, until he felt as horrible as I did. Instead, I asked him to leave. I think I said something sarcastic like, "I hear Sue calling you."

As I sat on my bed and cried for hours, I hurt so bad that nothing could make it stop. I even tried eating an entire gallon of ice cream. I played all of our favorite songs again and again, torturing myself with memories of good times and kind words. After making myself ill with shameless self-indulgence, I made a decision.

I would turn to revenge.

My thinking went like this: Sue Roth is—was—one of my closest friends. Good friends do not throw themselves at your boyfriend when you're not around. Obviously, she should pay.

That weekend, I bought a few dozen eggs and headed for Sue's house with a couple of friends. I started out just venting a little anger, but it got worse. So when someone found an open basement window, we threw the remaining eggs inside. But that's not the worst part. The Roths were out of town for three days!

As I lay in my bed that night, I started to think about what we had done. *This is bad, Kim . . . this is really bad.*

Soon it was all over school. Robby and Sue were going out *and* someone had egged her house while she was out of town, *and* it was so bad that her parents had to hire a professional to get rid of the smell.

As soon as I got home from school, my mom was waiting to talk. "Kim, my phone has been ringing all day, and I don't know what to say. Please—you have to tell me. Did you do it?"

"No, Mom, I didn't." It felt really bad to lie to my mom.

My mother was furious when she got on the phone to call Mrs. Roth. "This is Ellen. I want you to stop accusing my daughter of throwing eggs at your house." She was yelling at Sue's mother now, her voice getting louder and louder. "Kim would *never* do such a thing, and I want you to stop telling people that she did!" She was really going now. "And what's more, *I want you to apologize to me and to my daughter!"*

I felt good about the way my mom was sticking up for me, but awful about the reality. The feelings were all sort of twisted inside of me, and I knew that I had to tell her the truth. I signaled for my mom to get off the phone.

She hung up, reached for the table and sat down. She knew. I cried and told her how sorry I was. Then she cried, too. I would have preferred anger, but she'd used all of that up on Mrs. Roth.

I called Mrs. Roth and told her I'd give her every penny of my baby-sitting savings to help pay for the damages. She accepted, but told me not to come over until she was ready to forgive me.

Mom and I stayed up late that night, talking and crying. She told me about the time her boyfriend left her for her sister. I asked her if she'd egged her own house, and she actually laughed. She told me that although I'd done a terrible thing, it made her furious to think about the things Mrs. Roth had said on the phone. "After all," Mom said, "what about the fact that her daughter steals boyfriends?"

Then she told me how hard it is sometimes being a parent because you want to yell at everyone who causes your child pain, but you can't. You have to stand back and watch while your children learn hard lessons on their own.

I told my mom how incredible it had felt to hear her defend me like that. And at the end of the night, I told her how special it was to spend this kind of time with her. She gave me a hug and said, "Good. We can spend next Saturday night together, and the one after that. I did tell you, didn't I, that you're grounded for two weeks?"

Kimberly Kirberger

A Long Walk Home

Experience: that most brutal of teachers.
But you learn, my God do you learn.

C. S. Lewis

I grew up in the south of Spain in a little community called Estepona. I was 16 when one morning, my father told me I could drive him into a remote village called Mijas, about 18 miles away, on the condition that I take the car in to be serviced at a nearby garage. Having just learned to drive, and hardly ever having the opportunity to use the car, I readily accepted. I drove Dad into Mijas and promised to pick him up at 4 P.M., then drove to a nearby garage and dropped off the car. Because I had a few hours to spare, I decided to catch a couple of movies at a theater near the garage. However, I became so immersed in the films that I completely lost track of time. When the last movie had finished, I looked down at my watch. It was six o'clock. I was two hours late!

I knew Dad would be angry if he found out I'd been watching movies. He'd never let me drive again. I decided to tell him that the car needed some repairs and that they had taken longer than had been expected. I drove up to the place where we had planned to meet and saw Dad waiting patiently on the corner. I apologized for being late and told him that I'd come as quickly as I could, but the car had needed some major repairs. I'll never forget the look he gave me.

"I'm disappointed that you feel you have to lie to me, Jason."

"What do you mean? I'm telling the truth."

Dad looked at me again. "When you did not show up, I called the garage to ask if there were any problems, and they told me that you had not yet picked up the car. So you see, I know there were no problems with the car." A rush of guilt ran through me as I feebly confessed to my trip to the movie theater and the real reason for my tardiness. Dad listened intently as a sadness passed through him.

"I'm angry, not with you but with myself. You see, I realize that I have failed as a father if after all these years you feel that you have to lie to me. I have failed because I have brought up a son who cannot even tell the truth to his own father. I'm going to walk home now and contemplate where I have gone wrong all these years."

"But Dad, it's 18 miles to home. It's dark. You can't walk home."

My protests, my apologies and the rest of my utterances were useless. I had let my father down, and I was about to learn one of the most painful lessons of my life. Dad began walking along the dusty roads. I quickly jumped in the car and followed behind, hoping he would relent. I pleaded all the way, telling him how sorry I was, but he simply ignored me, continuing on silently, thoughtfully and painfully. For 18 miles I drove behind him, averaging about 5 miles per hour.

Seeing my father in so much physical and emotional pain was the most distressing and painful experience that

I have ever faced. However, it was also the most successful lesson. I have never lied to him since.

Jason Bocarro

The Cost of Gratefulness

I was about 13. My father frequently took me on short outings on Saturdays. Sometimes we went to a park, or to a marina to look at boats. My favorites were trips to junk stores, where we could admire old electronic stuff. Once in a while we would buy something for 50 cents just to take it apart.

On the way home from these trips, Dad frequently stopped at the Dairy Queen for 10-cent ice cream cones. Not every single time; just often enough. I couldn't expect it, but I could hope and pray from the time we started heading home to that critical corner where we would either go straight for the ice cream or turn and go home empty-handed. That corner meant either mouth-watering excitement or disappointment.

A few times my father teased me by going home the long way. "I'm just going this way for variety," he would say, as we drove by the Dairy Queen without stopping. It was a game, and I was well fed, so we're not talking torture here.

On the best days he would ask, in a tone that made it sound novel and spontaneous, "Would you like an ice cream cone?" and I would say, "That sounds great, Dad!" I'd always have chocolate and he'd have vanilla. He would hand me 20 cents and I would run in to buy the usual. We'd eat them in the car. I loved my dad and I loved ice cream—so that was heaven.

On one fateful day, we were heading home, and I was hoping and praying for the beautiful sound of his offer. It came. "Would you like an ice cream cone today?"

"That sounds great, Dad!"

But then he said, "It sounds good to me too, Son. How would you like to treat today?"

Twenty cents! Twenty cents! My mind reeled. I could afford it. I got 25 cents a week allowance, plus some extra for odd jobs. But saving money was important. Dad told me that. And when it was my money, ice cream just wasn't a good use of it.

Why didn't it occur to me that this was a golden opportunity to give something back to my very generous father? Why didn't I think that he had bought me 50 ice cream cones, and I had never bought him one? But all I could think was "20 cents!"

In a fit of selfish, miserly ingratitude, I said the awful words that have rung in my ears ever since. "Well, in that case, I guess I'll pass."

My father just said, "Okay, Son."

But as we turned to head home, I realized how wrong I was and begged him to turn back. "I'll pay," I pleaded.

But he just said, "That's okay, we don't really need one," and wouldn't hear my pleading. We drove home.

I felt awful for my selfishness and ungratefulness. He didn't rub it in, or even act disappointed. But I don't think he could have done anything to make a deeper impression on me.

I learned that generosity goes two ways and gratefulness sometimes costs a little more than "thank you." On that day gratefulness would have cost 20 cents, and it would have been the best ice cream I'd ever had.

I'll tell you one more thing. We went on another trip the next week, and as we approached the crucial corner, I said, "Dad, would you like an ice cream cone today? My treat."

Randal Jones

I Try to Remember

1. Everybody Doesn't Have to Love Me

Not everybody has to love me or even like me. I don't necessarily like everybody I know, so why should everybody else like me? I enjoy being liked and being loved, but if somebody doesn't like me, I will still be okay and still feel like I am an okay person. I cannot make somebody like me, any more than someone can get me to like them. I don't need approval all the time. If someone does not approve of me, I will still be okay.

2. It Is Okay to Make Mistakes

Making mistakes is something we all do, and I am still a fine and worthwhile person when I make them. There is no reason for me to get upset when I make a mistake. I am trying, and if I make a mistake, I am going to continue trying. I can handle making a mistake. It is okay for others to make mistakes, too. I will accept mistakes in myself and also mistakes that others make.

3. Other People Are Okay and I Am Okay

People who do things I don't like are not necessarily bad people. They should not necessarily be punished just because I don't like what they do or did. There is no reason why other people should be the way I want them to be, and there is no reason why I should be the way somebody else wants me to be. People will be whatever they want to be, and I will be whatever I want to be. I cannot control other people or change them. They are who they are; we all deserve basic respect.

4. I Don't Have to Control Things

I will survive if things are different than what I want them to be. I can accept things the way they are, accept people the way they are, and accept myself the way I am. There is no reason to get upset if I can't change things to fit my idea of how they ought to be. There is no reason why I should have to like everything. Even if I don't like it, I can live with it.

5. I Am Responsible for My Day

I am responsible for how I feel and what I do. Nobody can make me feel anything. If I have a rotten day, I am the one who allowed it to be that way. If I have a great day, I am the one who deserves credit for being positive. It is not the responsibility of other people to change so that I can feel better. I am the one who is in charge of my life.

6. I Can Handle It When Things Go Wrong

I don't need to watch out for things to go wrong. Things usually go just fine, and when they don't, I can handle it.

I don't have to waste my energy worrying. The sky won't fall in; things will be okay.

7. It Is Important to Try

I can. Even though I may be faced with difficult tasks, it is better to try than to avoid them. Avoiding a task does not give me any opportunities for success or joy, but trying does. Things worth having are worth the effort. I might not be able to do everything, but I can do something.

8. I Am Capable

I don't need someone else to take care of my problems. I am capable. I can take care of myself. I can make decisions for myself. I can think for myself. I don't have to depend on somebody else to take care of me.

9. I Can Change

I don't have to be a certain way because of what has happened in the past. Every day is a new day. It's silly to think I can't help being the way I am. Of course I can. I can change.

10. Other People Are Capable

I can't solve other people's problems for them. I don't have to take on other people's problems as if they were my own. I don't need to change other people or fix up their lives. They are capable and can take care of themselves, and can solve their own problems. I can care and be of some help, but I can't do everything for them.

11. I Can Be Flexible

There is more than one way to do something. More than one person has had good ideas that will work. There is no one and only "best" way. Everybody has ideas that are worthwhile. Some may make more sense to me than others, but everyone's ideas are worthwhile, and everyone has something worthwhile to contribute.

Author Unknown
Submitted by Allison Stevenson

Mrs. Virginia DeView, Where Are You?

There are high spots in all of our lives, and most of them come about through encouragement from someone else.

George Adams

We were sitting in her classroom, giggling, jabbing each other and talking about the latest information of the day, like the peculiar purple-colored mascara Cindy was wearing. Mrs. Virginia DeView cleared her throat and asked us to hush.

"Now," she said smiling, "we are going to discover our professions." The class seemed to gasp in unison. Our professions? We stared at each other. We were only 13 and 14 years old. This teacher was nuts.

That was pretty much how the kids looked at Virginia DeView, her hair swirled back in a bun and her large, buck teeth gaping out of her mouth. Because of her physical appearance, she was always an easy target for snickers and cruel jokes among students.

She also made her students angry because she was demanding. Most of us just overlooked her brilliance.

"Yes; you will all be searching for your future professions," she said with a glow on her face—as though this was the best thing she did in her classroom every year. "You will have to do a research paper on your upcoming career. Each of you will have to interview someone in your field, plus give an oral report."

All of us went home confused. Who knows what they want to do at 13? I had narrowed it down, however. I liked art, singing and writing. But I was terrible in art, and when I sang my sisters screamed: "Oh, please shut up." The only thing left was writing.

Every day in her class, Virginia DeView monitored us. Where were we? Who had picked their careers? Finally, most of us had selected something; I picked print journalism. This meant I had to go interview a true-blue newspaper reporter in the flesh, and I was terrified.

I sat down in front of him barely able to speak. He looked at me and said: "Did you bring a pencil or pen?"

I shook my head.

"How about some paper?"

I shook my head again.

Finally, I think he realized I was terrified, and I got my first big tip as a journalist. "Never, never go anywhere without a pen and paper. You never know what you'll run into."

For the next 90 minutes, he filled me with stories of robberies, crime sprees and fires. He would never forget the tragic fire where four family members were killed in the blaze. He could still smell their burning flesh, he said, and he would never forget that horrid story.

A few days later, I gave my oral report totally from memory, I had been so mesmerized. I got an A on the entire project.

As we neared the end of the school year, some very resentful students decided to get Virginia DeView back for the hard work she put us through. As she rounded a corner, they shoved a pie into her face as hard as they could. She was slightly injured physically, but it was emotionally that she was really hurt. She didn't return to school for days. When I heard the story, I felt a deep, ugly pit fill my stomach. I felt shame for myself and my fellow students who had nothing better to do than pick on a woman because of how she looked, rather than appreciate her amazing teaching skills.

Years later, I forgot all about Virginia DeView and the careers we selected. I was in college scouting around for a new career. My father wanted me in business, which seemed to be sound advice at the time, except that I had no sense of business skills whatsoever. Then I remembered Virginia DeView and my desire at 13 to be a journalist. I called my parents.

"I'm changing my major," I announced.

There was a stunned silence on the end of the phone.

"What to?" my father finally asked.

"Journalism."

I could tell in their voices that my parents were very unhappy, but they didn't stop me. They just reminded me how competitive the field was and how all my life I had shied away from competition.

This was true. But journalism did something to me; it was in my blood. It gave me the freedom to go up to total strangers and ask what was going on. It trained me to ask questions and get answers in both my professional and personal life. It gave me confidence.

For the past 12 years, I've had the most incredible and satisfying reporting career, covering stories from murders to airplane crashes and finally settling in on my forté. I loved to write about the tender and tragic moments of people's lives because somehow I felt it helped them in some way.

When I went to pick up my phone one day, an incredible wave of memories hit me and I realized that had it not been for Virginia DeView, I would not be sitting at that desk.

She'll probably never know that without her help, I would not have become a journalist and a writer. I suspect I would have been floundering in the business world somewhere, with great unhappiness shadowing me each day. I wonder now how many other students in her class benefited from that career project.

I get asked all the time: "How did you pick journalism?"

"Well, you see, there was this teacher . . ." I always start out. I just wish I could thank her.

I believe that when people reflect back over their school days, there will be this faded image of a single teacher—their very own Virginia DeView. Perhaps you can thank her before it's too late.

Diana L. Chapman

"I imagine you'll be interested in one of the more highly visible occupations?"

What's Wrong?

A newly trained teacher named Mary went to teach at a Navajo Indian reservation. Every day, she would ask five of the young Navajo students to go to the chalkboard and complete a simple math problem from their homework. They would stand there, silently, unwilling to complete the task. Mary couldn't figure it out. Nothing she had studied in her educational curriculum helped, and she certainly hadn't seen anything like it in her student-teaching days back in Phoenix.

What am I doing wrong? Could I have chosen five students who can't do the problem? Mary would wonder. *No, it couldn't be that.* Finally she asked the students what was wrong. And in their answer, she learned a surprising lesson from her young Indian pupils about self-image and a sense of self-worth.

It seemed that the students respected each other's individuality and knew that not all of them were capable of doing the problems. Even at their early age, they understood the senselessness of the win-lose approach in the classroom. They believed no one would win if any students were shown up or embarrassed at the chalkboard.

So they refused to compete with each other in public.

Once she understood, Mary changed the system so that she could check each child's math problem individually, but not at any child's expense in front of his classmates. They all wanted to learn—but not at someone else's expense.

The Speaker's Sourcebook

The Eternal Gifts

In the darkest hour the soul is replenished and given strength to continue and endure.

Heart Warrior Chosa

"Is that true, or did you just put it on the bulletin board because it sounds catchy?"

"Is what true?" I asked without looking up from my desk.

"That sign you made that says, 'If you can conceive it and believe it you can achieve it'."

I looked up into the face of Paul, one of my favorite people, but most definitely not one of my best students. "Well, Paul," I said, "the man who wrote those words, Napoleon Hill, did so after years of research into the lives of great men and women. He discovered that concept, stated in many different ways, was the one thing they all had in common. Jules Verne put it another way when he said, 'Anything the mind of one man can imagine, the mind of another man can create'."

"You mean if I get an idea and really believe in it, I can do it?" He asked with an intensity that captured my total attention.

"From what I have seen and read, Paul, that's not a theory, but a law that has been proved throughout history."

Paul dug his hands into the hip pockets of his Levi's and walked in a slow circle around the room. Then he turned and faced me with a new energy. "Mr. Schlatter," he said, "I've been a below-average student my whole life, and I know it's going to cost me later in life. What if I conceived of myself as a good student and really believed it . . . that even *I* could achieve it?"

"Yes, Paul, but know this: If you really believe it, you'll act on it. I believe there is a power within you that will do great things to help you, once you make the commitment."

"What do you mean, commitment?" he asked.

"Well, there's a story about a preacher who drove out to the farm of a member of his congregation. Admiring the beauty of the place, he said, 'Clem, you and the Lord have certainly created a thing of beauty here'."

"'Thank you, preacher,' said Clem, 'but you should have seen it when the Lord had it all to himself.'

"In essence, Paul, God will give us the firewood, but we have to light the match."

A suspenseful silence followed. "All right," Paul said, "I'll do it. By the end of the semester, I'll be a B student."

It was already the fifth week of the term and in my class, Paul was averaging a D.

"It's a tall mountain, Paul, but I also believe you can achieve what you just conceived." We both laughed and he left my room to go to lunch.

For the next 12 weeks, Paul gave me one of the most inspirational experiences a teacher can have. He developed a keen curiosity as he asked intelligent questions. His new sense of discipline could be seen in a neater appearance and a fresh sense of direction in his walk. Very slowly, his average started to rise, he earned a commendation for improvement and you could see his self-esteem start to grow. For the first time in his life, other students started to ask him for his help. A charm and charismatic friendliness developed.

Finally came the victory. On a Friday evening, I sat down to grade a major test on the Constitution. I looked at Paul's paper for a long time before I picked up my red pen and started to grade it. I never had to use that pen. It was a perfect paper, his first A+. Immediately, I averaged his score into the rest of his grades and there it was, an A/B average. He had climbed his mountain with four weeks to spare. I called my colleagues to share the news.

That Saturday morning, I drove to school for a rehearsal of *Follow the Dream,* the play I was directing. I entered the parking lot with a light heart to be greeted by Kathy, the best actress in the play and one of Paul's best friends. Tears were streaming down her face. As soon as I got out of my car, she ran over to me and almost fell against me in a torment of sobs. Then she told me what had happened.

Paul was at a friend's house and they were looking at the collection of "unloaded" guns in the den. Being boys, they started to play cops and robbers. One boy had pointed an "unloaded" gun at Paul's head and pulled the trigger. Paul fell with a bullet lodged in his brain.

Monday, a student aide came in with a "check-out" notice for Paul. There was a box next to "book" to see if I had his test, and next to the box marked "grade" was written "unnecessary."

"That's what you say," I thought to myself, as I marked a big red B in the box. I turned my back to the class so they could not see the tears. Paul had earned that grade and it was here, but Paul was gone. Those new clothes he had bought with his paper route money were still in his closet, but Paul was gone. His friends, his commendation, his football award were still here, but Paul was gone. Why?

One good thing about total, complete grief is that it humbles a person to such an extent that there is no resistance to the voice of that loving, unleashed power that never leaves us.

"Build thee more stately mansions, oh, my soul." As the words of that old poem spoke to my heart, I realized that Paul did not leave everything behind. The tears started to dry and a smile came to my face as I pictured Paul still conceiving, still believing and still achieving, armed with his newly developed curiosity, discipline, sense of direction and self-esteem—those invisible mansions of the soul that we are here to cultivate.

He had left us with a great deal of wealth. Outside the church on the day of the funeral, I gathered my drama students around and announced that rehearsals would start the next day. In remembrance of Paul and all he had left us, it was time once again to follow the dream.

Jack Schlatter

Socrates

There once was an eager student who wanted to gain wisdom and insight. He went to the wisest of the town, Socrates, to seek his counsel. Socrates was an old soul and had great knowledge of many things. The boy asked the town sage how he too could acquire such mastery. Being a man of few words, Socrates chose not to speak, but to illustrate.

He took the child to the beach and, with all of his clothes still on, walked straight out into the water. He loved to do curious things like that, especially when he was trying to prove a point. The pupil gingerly followed his instruction and walked into the sea, joining Socrates where the water was just below their chins. Without saying a word, Socrates reached out and put his hands on the boy's shoulders. Looking deep into his student's eyes, Socrates pushed the student's head under the water with all his might.

A struggle ensued, and just before a life was taken away, Socrates released his captive. The boy raced to the surface and, gasping for air and choking from the salt water, looked around for Socrates in order to seek his retaliation on the sage. To the student's bewilderment, the old man was already patiently waiting on the beach. When the student arrived on the sand, he angrily shouted, "Why did you try to kill me?" The wise man calmly retorted with a question of his own: "Boy, when you were underneath the water, not sure if you would live to see another day, what did you want more than anything in the world?"

The student took a few moments to reflect, then went with his intuition. Softly he said, "I wanted to breathe." Socrates, now illuminated by his own huge smile, looked at the boy comfortingly and said, "Ah! When you want wisdom and insight as badly as you wanted to breathe, it is then you shall have it."

Retold by Eric Saperston

Challenge Days

Shared joy is double joy.
Shared sorrow is half sorrow.

Swedish Proverb

My name is Tony. I always looked out for myself because I thought no one else would, and I thought it would always be that way. That changed the day I got out of class for something called Challenge Day.

The people running it had big hopes of helping us join together and making us leaders. I just wanted to get out of class. I figured that after signing in I would sneak out.

In the school gym, I found myself sitting in a big circle, face to face with a hundred students that no one could have paid me to spend the day with. I was keeping up my front, my cool, but I was kind of nervous. I'm used to either sitting hidden in the back of a classroom waiting for a break, or skipping school and hanging with the guys. I wasn't used to not knowing what was going to happen.

I made fun of how a bunch of kids were dressed and of a girl who was fat. Some of the girls had worn pajamas and brought stuffed animals. Pretty stupid, I thought.

The day started with each of us standing up and saying our names into a microphone "loud and proud." A bunch of kids were really shy, but since I rap sometimes, I acted really cool when it was my turn. No one knew there was a lump in my throat. You see, I'm from a tough neighborhood, and showing your weakness only makes you a target. I was a target when I was real young, both for my brothers and for the people who called themselves my friends. We sure didn't know how to be friends, though. Fighting and putting each other down were a normal way of life.

Anyway, we started playing these games I thought were really childish. I hung back a little with my buddies, acting cool and not wanting to play like a little kid. After a couple of games, though, it didn't seem like anyone else was hanging back, and they were all having a good time. I thought, "Why not me?" I have to admit that I was playing a little rough, but it beat sitting on the edge.

What happened next was almost unbelievable. Carl, one of the only guys who is more feared and respected than me at school, was helping one of the leaders demonstrate how to give hugs. Everyone was laughing at first, but it was getting harder and harder to put anyone down that day. The leaders kept teaching us to open our hearts and minds, to share our true feelings and to give put-ups instead of put-downs. It wasn't what I was used to.

Then we did an exercise called "the power shuffle." Before the game started, the leaders talked about oppression. "Yeah," I thought, "like they really know what it's like to be oppressed. Here I am, a young Latino growing up in a white society. I get harassed and pushed around every day by store owners, teachers and all these adults who think I'm a gangster just because of the color of my skin. Yeah, I act hard, but what am I supposed to do when I have to watch my friends drop from drive-bys?"

The leaders said we had to be silent, to make it safe for everyone. They called out broad categories and asked us to cross over the line if we fit into the category. I was still snickering in my buddy's ear as the first few were called out.

But the leaders meant it about being quiet. One of the adults softly put his hand on me and said, "You'll want them to respect you; please respect them."

Category after category was called out. In silence, group after group, people crossed the line. Then a topic was called that I fit into, and I figured I would be the only one who experienced this kind of pain. "Cross the line if you've ever been hit, beaten or abused, in any way." I walked heavy in my shoes. Looking straight down as I walked, I turned around, having a hard time not laughing to cover what was going on inside me.

But as I looked up, half the group was walking with me. We stood together in silence, looked into each other's eyes, and for the first time in my life, I felt like I wasn't alone.

One by one we dropped our masks. I saw that these people, whom I had judged before, were in reality very much like me. Like me, they, too, knew how it felt to be hurt.

I walked back across the line. My friend tried to joke with me but it didn't seem right any more. Another topic was called, one where all the women and girls crossed. I had never seen before how much men and boys disrespect and hurt women. I became more uncomfortable as I noticed tears appearing in many of my friends' eyes.

We crossed the line next for having lost someone close to us in gang violence. So many of us crossed that line. It just wasn't right! I started feeling really angry inside, and tears were coming to my eyes. The leaders kept saying, "When the tears are on the outside, the inside is healing," and, "It takes a strong man to cry."

I had to make the choice of whether or not to have the courage to show my tears. I was still scared of being called names, but the tears came out. I cried, and with my tears I proved that I was a strong man.

Before we left that day, each of us stood up and shared our experiences. I stood up, again not sure if I should fight the tears or not. The leader encouraged me to look out at the group and ask if it was okay for a man to cry. So I did.

Then each person stood up in front of their chairs to show they respected me for showing my tears. Amazed, I started talking. I said I was sorry to a few of those people I had judged and pushed around in the halls because I thought they had it so much better than me. With tears in their eyes, they came up to me, one by one, and gave me a hug. Now I know what it is really like to share love with someone. I hope I can do this with my dad some day.

Here was a day I thought I was cutting from school, but instead I found myself telling the people I hurt that I was sorry, and people were saying the same thing to me. It was like we were all one family and we never knew it until that day. It wasn't magic—we just looked at each other in a different light.

Now it is up to us. Do we look through these eyes for just one day, or do we have the courage to remember that most people are just like us, and help others learn that it is safe to be themselves?

As told to Andrew Tertes

Please Hear What I'm Not Saying

Don't be fooled by me.
Don't be fooled by the face I wear.
For I wear a mask, a thousand masks,
masks that I'm afraid to take off,
and none of them is me.
Pretending is an art that's second nature to me,
but don't be fooled.
For God's sake don't be fooled.
I give you the impression that I'm secure,
that confidence is my name and coolness is my game,
that the water's calm and I'm in command,
and that I need no one.
But don't believe me.
My surface may seem smooth but my surface
is my mask, ever-varying and ever-concealing.
Beneath lies no complacence.
Beneath lies confusion and fear and aloneness.
But I hide this. I don't want anybody to know it.

I panic at the thought of my weakness and fear being
exposed.
That's why I frantically create a mask to hide behind,

a nonchalant sophisticated facade, to help me pretend,
to shield me from the glance that knows.
But such a glance is precisely my salvation.
My only hope, and I know it.
That is, if it's followed by acceptance,
if it's followed by love.
It's the only thing that can liberate me from myself,
from my own self-built prison walls,
from the barriers I so painstakingly erect.
It's the only thing that will assure me
of what I can't assure myself,
that I'm really worth something.
I don't like to hide.
I don't like to play superficial phony games.
I want to stop playing them.
I want to be genuine and spontaneous and me,
but you've got to help me.
You've got to hold out your hand
even when that's the last thing I seem to want.
Only you can wipe away from my eyes
the bland stare of the breathing dead.
Only you can call me into aliveness.

Each time you're kind and gentle and encouraging,
each time you try to understand because you really care,
my heart begins to grow wings, very small wings,
very feeble wings,
but wings!
With your power to touch me into feeling
you can breathe life into me.
I want you to know that.

Who am I, you may wonder.
I am someone you know very well.
For I am every man you meet,
and I am every woman you meet.

Author Unknown

I Am . . .

The words "I am . . ." are potent words; be careful what you hitch them to. The thing you're claiming has a way of reaching back and claiming you.

A. L. Kitselman

[EDITORS' NOTE: *Have you ever noticed how often people ask you what you are going to be, what you do, or what you are planning to do after college? For all of us who have suffered because what we do or who we're going to be doesn't cut it, here is the true answer. And let's remember this the next time someone says, "Oh, really? Well . . . there's nothing wrong with flipping burgers for a living. You should be proud."*]

I am an architect: I've built a solid foundation; and each year I go to that school I add another floor of wisdom and knowledge.

I am a sculptor: I've shaped my morals and philosophies according to the clay of right and wrong.

I am a painter: With each new idea I express, I paint a new hue in the world's multitude of colors.

I am a scientist: Each day that passes by, I gather new data, make important observations, and experiment with new concepts and ideas.

I am an astrologist: reading and analyzing the palms of life and each new person I encounter.

I am an astronaut: constantly exploring and broadening my horizons.

I am a doctor: I heal those who turn to me for consultation and advice, and I bring out the vitality in those who seem lifeless.

I am a lawyer: I'm not afraid to stand up for the inevitable and basic rights of myself and all others.

I am a police officer: I always watch out for others' welfare and I am always on the scene preventing fights and keeping the peace.

I am a teacher: By my example others learn the importance of determination, dedication and hard work.

I am a mathematician: making sure I conquer each one of my problems with correct solutions.

I am a detective: peering through my two lenses, searching for meaning and significance in the mysteries of life.

I am a jury member: judging others and their situations only after I've heard and understood the entire story.

I am a banker: Others share their trust and values with me and never lose interest.

I am a hockey player: watching out for and dodging those who try to block my goal.

I am a marathon runner: full of energy, always moving and ready for the next challenge.

I am a mountain climber: Slowly but surely I am making my way to the top.

I am a tight-rope walker: Carefully and stealthily I pace myself through every rough time, but I always make it safely to the end.

I am a millionaire: rich in love, sincerity and compassion, and I own a wealth of knowledge, wisdom, experience and insight that is priceless.

Most important, I am me.

Amy Yerkes

Sparky

For Sparky, school was all but impossible. He failed every subject in the eighth grade. He flunked physics in high school, getting a grade of zero. Sparky also flunked Latin, algebra and English. He didn't do much better in sports. Although he did manage to make the school's golf team, he promptly lost the only important match of the season. There was a consolation match; he lost that, too.

Throughout his youth Sparky was awkward socially. He was not actually disliked by the other students; no one cared that much. He was astonished if a classmate ever said hello to him outside of school hours. There's no way to tell how he might have done at dating. Sparky never once asked a girl to go out in high school. He was too afraid of being turned down.

Sparky was a loser. He, his classmates . . . everyone knew it. So he rolled with it. Sparky had made up his mind early in life that if things were meant to work out, they would. Otherwise he would content himself with what appeared to be his inevitable mediocrity.

However, one thing was important to Sparky—drawing. He was proud of his artwork. Of course, no one else appreciated it. In his senior year of high school, he submitted some cartoons to the editors of the yearbook. The cartoons were turned down. Despite this particular rejection, Sparky was so convinced of his ability that he decided to become a professional artist.

After completing high school, he wrote a letter to Walt Disney Studios. He was told to send some samples of his artwork, and the subject for a cartoon was suggested. Sparky drew the proposed cartoon. He spent a great deal of time on it and on all the other drawings he submitted. Finally, the reply came from Disney Studios. He had been rejected once again. Another loss for the loser.

So Sparky decided to write his own autobiography in cartoons. He described his childhood self—a little boy loser and chronic underachiever. The cartoon character would soon become famous worldwide. For Sparky, the boy who had such lack of success in school and whose work was rejected again and again, was Charles Schultz. He created the "Peanuts" comic strip and the little cartoon character whose kite would never fly and who never succeeded in kicking a football, Charlie Brown.

Bits & Pieces

Detention Can Be Fun

"Detention was really fun today," my son Ennis once told me, as if talking about a yacht club. "All the best people were there."

"I thought it was supposed to be for *punishment,*" I said.

"Oh, it can be for that too—if your friends aren't there or if Mrs. Piano is in a bad mood."

"She's the warden?"

"That's funny, Dad. They'd love you in detention because they love to have a good laugh."

"Yes, every prison needs some laughs. Tell me, why did you happen to get this particular honor today?"

"Dad, detention isn't anything bad."

"Sorry; I've been confused. So why were you invited to cocktails there?'

"Dad, you kill me."

"Don't rule it out."

"Well, *today's* detention . . ."

"You get detention every day?"

"I told you: it's nothing bad. Maybe it was in the Middle Ages, but believe me, it's changed."

"I believe you."

"Today I got it for throwing a book at James in history. Can you imagine that? Mr. Weinstock gave it to me just for throwing a book. I mean, a *grenade* I could understand."

"Just for throwing your history book?"

"Oh no, I don't have one of those."

"You're waiting for it to come as the Book-of-the-Month?"

"No, I lent it to Aaron."

"Aaron?"

"Well, he's trying hard to remember what he did with it. We've definitely ruled out his locker' cause there's no more room in there; and he doesn't think he left it at the mall."

"That's where I'd look for it."

"Anyway, Dad, I gotta tell ya the really great thing that happened there today. Jenny and George both got detention together. And they're going steady, y' see . . ."

"Like Bonnie and Clyde."

"Shakespeare, right?"

"Whatever."

"Anyhow, Jenny and George, they're two of the regulars, but mostly not together: one of 'em usually takes it free period and the other one after school. But today they were in sync."

"A penal *Madame Butterfly*."

"Shakespeare, right?"

"I'll look it up."

"Well, in the middle of the period, Jenny wrote George a note saying how much she loves him, and Mrs. Piano got her hands on it and she wanted to give him detention, but he already *had* it."

"A problem for the High Court. Does the Constitution protect you against getting detention in detention? Is it double jeopardy?"

"Dad, we're not talking about a quiz show here. Anyhow, George did something beautiful: he took the blame."

"How could he do that?"

"He said he wrote the note."

"But it was to him. He said he wrote the love letter to himself? You get more than detention for that."

"Well, it worked. It got Mrs. Piano mixed up so she didn't add any more detention."

"She probably wanted to be home by dinner."

"That's the kind of stuff that happens in detention, Dad. It's a great place to do schoolwork, if you ever have any, but you can also have some laughs."

"I can't imagine why a student would want to be anywhere else."

"You're probably kidding, but neither can I."

Bill Cosby

"So what if my grades are lousy? You always said it's not what you know, it's who you know."

If I Knew

You know how you always hear people say, "If I knew then what I know now . . ."?

Have you ever wanted to say . . . yeah . . . well . . . go on . . .

So here we go . . .

I would listen more carefully to what my heart says.

I would enjoy more . . . worry less.

I would know that school would end soon enough . . . and work would . . . well, never mind.

I wouldn't worry so much about what other people were thinking.

I would appreciate all my vitality and tight skin.

I would play more, fret less.

I would know that my beauty/handsomeness is in my love of life.

I would know how much my parents love me and I would believe that they are doing the best they can.

I would enjoy the feeling of "being in love" and not worry so much about how it works out.

I would know that it probably won't . . . but that something better will come along.

I wouldn't be afraid of acting like a kid.

I would be braver.

I would look for the good qualities in everyone and enjoy them for those.

I would not hang out with people just because they're "popular."

I would take dance lessons.

I would enjoy my body just the way it is.

I would trust my girlfriends.

I would be a trustworthy girlfriend.

I wouldn't trust my boyfriends. (Just kidding.)

I would enjoy kissing. Really enjoy it.

I would be more appreciative and grateful, for sure.

Kimberly Kirberger

Eleven

What they don't understand about birthdays and what they never tell you is that when you're eleven, you're also ten, and nine, and eight, and seven, and six, and five, and four, and three, and two, and one. And when you wake up on your eleventh birthday, you expect to feel eleven, but you don't. You open your eyes and everything's just like yesterday, only it's today. And you don't feel eleven at all. You feel you're still ten. And you are—underneath the year that makes you eleven.

Like some days you might say something stupid, and that's the part of you that's still ten. Or maybe some days you might need to sit on your mama's lap because you're scared, and that's the part of you that's five. And maybe one day when you're all grown up, maybe you will need to cry like if you're three, and that's okay. That's what I tell Mama when she's said and needs to cry. Maybe she's feeling three.

Because the way you grow old is kind of like an onion or like the rings inside a tree trunk or like my little wooden dolls that fit one inside the other, each year inside the next one. That's how being eleven years old is.

You don't feel eleven. Not right away. It takes a few days, weeks even, sometimes even months before you say Eleven when they ask you. And you don't feel smart eleven, not until you're almost twelve. That's the way it is.

Only today I wish I didn't have only eleven years rattling inside me like pennies in a tin Band-Aid box. Today I wish I was one hundred and two instead of eleven because if I was one hundred and two I'd have known what to say when Mrs. Price put the red sweater on my desk. I would've known how to tell her it wasn't mine instead of just sitting there with that look on my face and nothing coming out of my mouth.

"Whose is this?" Mrs. Price says, as she holds the red sweater up in the air for all the class to see. "Whose? It's been sitting in the coatroom for a month."

"Not mine," says everybody. "Not me."

"It has to belong to somebody," Mrs. Price keeps saying, but nobody can remember. It's an ugly sweater with red plastic buttons and a collar and sleeves all stretched out like you could use it for a jump rope. It's maybe a thousand years old and even if it belonged to me I wouldn't say so.

Maybe because I'm skinny, maybe because she doesn't like me, that stupid Sylvia Saldivar says, "I think it belongs to Rachel." An ugly sweater like that, all raggedy and old, but Mrs. Price believes her. Mrs. Price takes the sweater and puts it right on my desk, but when I open my mouth nothing comes out.

"That's not, I don't, you're not . . . not mine," I finally say in a little voice that was maybe when I was four.

"Of course it's yours," Mrs. Price says. "I remember you wearing it once." Because she's older and the teacher, she's right and I'm not.

Not mine, not mine, not mine, but Mrs. Price is already turning to page 32, and math problem four. I don't know why but all of a sudden I'm feeling sick inside, like the part of me that's three wants to come out of my eyes, only I squeeze them shut tight and bite down on my teeth real hard and try to remember today I am eleven, eleven. Mama is making a cake for me for me tonight, and when Papa comes home everybody will sing happy birthday, happy birthday to you.

But when the sick feeling goes away and I open my eyes, the red sweater's still sitting there like a big red mountain. I move the red sweater to the corner of my desk with my ruler. I move my pencil and books and eraser as far from it as possible. I even move my chair a little to the right. Not mine, not mine, not mine.

In my head I'm thinking how long till lunchtime, how long till I can take the red sweater and throw it over the schoolyard fence, or leave it hanging on a parking meter, or bunch it up into a little ball and toss it in the alley. Except when math period ends, Mrs. Price says loud and in front of everybody, "Now, Rachel, that's enough," because she sees I've shoved the red sweater to the tippy-tip corner of my desk and it's hanging all over the edge like a waterfall, but I don't care.

"Rachel," Mrs. Price says. She says it like she's getting mad. "You put that sweater on right now and no more nonsense."

"But it's not—"

"Now!" Mrs. Price says.

This is when I wish I wasn't eleven, because all the years inside of me—ten, nine, eight, seven, six, five, four, three, two and one—are pushing at the back of my eyes when I put one arm through one sleeve of the sweater, which smells like cottage cheese, and then the other arm through the other and stand there with my arms apart as if the sweater hurts me and it does, all itchy and full of germs that aren't even mine.

That's when everything I've been holding in since this morning, since when Mrs. Price put the sweater on my desk, finally lets go, and all of a sudden I'm crying in front of everybody. I wish I was invisible but I'm not. I'm eleven and it's my birthday today and I'm crying like I'm three in front of everybody. I put my head down on the desk and bury my face in my stupid clown-sweater arms. My face all hot and spit coming out of my mouth because I can't stop the little animal noises from coming out of me, until there aren't anymore tears left in my eyes, and it's just my body shaking like when you have the hiccups, and my whole head hurts like when you drink milk too fast.

But the worst part is right before the bell rings for lunch. That stupid Phyllis Lopez, who is even dumber than Sylvia Saldivar, says she remembers the red sweater is hers! I take if off right away and give it to her, only Mrs. Price pretends like everything's okay.

Today I'm eleven. There's a cake Mama's making for tonight, and when Papa comes home from work we'll eat it. There'll be candles and presents and everybody will sing happy birthday, happy birthday to you, Rachel, only it's too late.

I'm eleven today. I'm eleven, ten, nine, eight, seven, six, five, four, three, two and one, but I wish I was one hundred and two. I wish I was anything but eleven because I want today to be far away already, far away like a runaway balloon, like a tiny O in the sky, so tiny-tiny you have to close your eyes to see it.

Sandra Cisneros

6

TOUGH STUFF

You gain strength, courage and confidence by every experience by which you really stop to look fear in the face. You are able to say to yourself, "I lived through this horror. I can take the next thing that comes along."

Eleanor Roosevelt

I'll Always Be with You

On a quiet September night our 17-year-old son, Mike, got into his cherished yellow '68 Mustang, his heart broken after the sudden ending of his first romance. His girlfriend had told him she was going to get engaged to someone else. Sitting in the car he had so lovingly restored and treasured, Mike shot and killed himself. In the note he left, he wrote: "I wish I could have learned how to hate. . . . Don't blame yourselves, Mom and Dad. I love you." His note ended "Love, Mike, 11:45 P.M." At 11:52 P.M. that night, we and Mike's older brother, Vic, pulled into the driveway alongside Mike's car—seven minutes too late!

It wasn't long before stories about Mike started coming in from all sides. We heard many of them for the first time. His oldest friend, Danny, told us about the time he was frightened to have his picture taken in kindergarten. "It's easy. Just go like this," Mike assured him as he grinned from ear to ear, displaying the bright smile that became his trademark. Years later, when a classmate became a single parent, Mike helped her care for her baby. One of Mike's friends was shot in a drive-by shooting but recovered, with Mike's support. When his high school band went to Florida to march in the Orange Bowl parade, Mike assisted a fellow band member who was blind.

A young mother phoned to tell the story of how Mike had helped her when her car broke down. She and her children were stranded on the roadside when Mike came by. He stopped, showed her his driver's license to assure her he wouldn't hurt her and her children, and got her car started. He followed them home to make sure they arrived safely.

One of Mike's friends revealed the truth about why Mike never got the new transmission we thought he planned to install in his Mustang in preparation for the local drag race. Mike canceled his order for the transmission and instead bought two transmissions from a salvage yard—so his friend could get his car running, too. Mike had told us the reason he didn't buy the brand-new transmission was that it just wasn't right for the way he wanted his car to perform.

Mike's niece was born with cerebral palsy. He learned how to replace her tracheotomy tube and how to perform CPR, should the need arise. He learned sign language with her (the tracheotomy tube made it impossible for her to speak), and they would "sing" together in sign language.

In the days following Mike's death, many teenagers came to comfort us and asked if they could do anything to help. Our response to their question was: "Don't ever do this. Don't commit suicide. Reach out to someone and ask for help!" Before Mike's memorial service, Mike's close friends met with us to share their grief, tell their stories about their friendship with him and discuss the tragedy of teen suicide. We talked about ways to prevent teen suicide. This was how the Yellow Ribbon Project came to life.

We decided to establish a foundation dedicated to eliminating suicide, a leading cause of death among teens.

Within days after Mike's death, we began printing pocket-sized cards that read:

YELLOW RIBBON PROJECT
In loving memory of Michael Emme

THIS RIBBON CARD IS A LIFELINE! It carries the message that there are those who care and will help. If you are in need and don't know how to ask for help, take this card to a counselor, teacher, clergy, parent or friend and say:

"I NEED TO USE MY YELLOW RIBBON!"

Someone, remembering Mike's beloved yellow Mustang, had the idea of attaching yellow ribbons to the cards, which we did. At Mike's memorial service we set out a basket containing 500 of these yellow-ribbon cards. By the end of the service, the basket was empty (and Mike's Mustang was covered with 100 yellow miniature roses, put there by his friends).

Mike's tragic death made us decide to help others, just as Mike did during his life. In the time since Mike's death, the Yellow Ribbon Project has touched—and saved—the lives of teens around the world. We receive many letters from teenagers about the Yellow Ribbon Project with comments such as:

"Your Web site has helped me recover from my depression."

"I've tried to commit suicide several times. This time I found the Yellow Ribbon card in my pocket and held onto it until a friend came by and I was able to give them the card. They recognized that I was suicidal and got me help."

"Thank you for being there to let those without hope know that there is always someone who cares."

Mike's final letter to us contained another important message. In that letter he told us, "I'll always be with you." Every time we speak to a group of teenagers or receive a letter from a teen or child who needs help, we know Mike's words are true.

Dale and Dar Emme

[EDITORS' NOTE: *This story, which was first printed in* A 3rd Serving of Chicken Soup for the Soul *in April 1996, has resulted in an even greater distribution of The Yellow Ribbon Project. The following are excerpts from some of the letters the Emmes received.*]

> *My name is Jessica and I am a senior in high school. I was very deeply touched by your story. I am a survivor of depression and suicidal impulses. I've struggled with this for the past five years and if I hadn't had someone who reached out to help me, I would not be here.*
>
> *Last week a senior in high school shot himself. What if someone had stopped him and asked him how he was and really meant it? I think that would have made the difference between life and death.*
>
> *So if you could please send information, suggestions and ribbons, I would greatly appreciate it. I've wanted to get the message out about teen suicide but never knew how. Thank you for helping me.*
>
> *Jessica Magers*

> *I found out about The Yellow Ribbon Project in* A 3rd Serving of Chicken Soup for the Soul. *Your story really made me think about how much my friends and family mean to me, and if an occasion should arise when they do use their ribbon then I will be ever more grateful for your idea of creating The Yellow Ribbon Project. Thank you,*
>
> *Nicole Nero*

Two months ago I broke up with my boyfriend who I loved very much. I could not deal with the pain and emptiness so I attempted suicide. I spent the night in I.C.U., the pills I took caused me to stop breathing. Because I am only 16, a straight-A student with everything going for me, this event shocked me and I realized I have a lot to live for and also my parents could not bear it if I were dead. So I am writing to ask if I could get two of your yellow ribbons. One for me and for my best friend. Thank you very much,

Jen Vetter

[EDITORS' NOTE: *For information on The Yellow Ribbon Project, please see p. 336.*]

My Story

The journey in between what you once were and who you are now becoming is where the dance of life really takes place.

Barbara De Angelis

I never thought about killing myself; it just became a condition. Kind of like catching a cold. One minute you are fine, and the next minute you are sick. Whenever people would talk about suicide, I would think to myself, "I would never do that." Why would someone want to do something so final, so stupid?

For me, I just wanted the pain to stop. And it got to the point where I was willing to do whatever it took to make that happen. It started with the usual stuff . . .

I am 16. I spend the summer with my mom and during the school year I live with my dad. I feel like an inconvenience to both of them. At my mom's I have no room. My mom isn't there for me when I need her because she always has something more important to do. At least, that is how it feels.

I was having trouble with my friends. The ones I had

not lost already to "different lifestyles" were unable to help me. In their own words, my problems were "too much" for them. The intensity of my pain scared them, like it did me.

Oh, yeah . . . did I mention my boyfriend, John, had dumped me that day? My first boyfriend had left me, too. He said I had become impossible to love and now John was gone, too. And it wasn't that I would be without him that mattered . . . it was me. What was wrong with me? Why is it so hard to love me and why is it that when it gets hard, everyone bails?

I was alone. All I had were the voices in my head telling me I blew it, I was too needy, I was never going to be loved once someone really got to know me. I felt that I wasn't even good enough to be loved by my own parents.

You know how, when you are really hurting, you feel like you can just call the person (the boyfriend, the friend) and tell him or her how much it hurts and they'll say, "Oh, I am so sorry; I didn't mean to hurt you; hang on, I will be right there"? Well, I called and I was crying, and I said it hurts too much, please come talk to me. He said he couldn't help me . . . and he hung up.

I went into my mom's bathroom and took a bottle of Tylenol PM, some tranquilizers and a couple pain pills I had left from an injury. Soon the pain would be over.

I will spare you the gruesome details of what followed. It was a whole new kind of pain. Physically, I puked until I couldn't move. Emotionally, I was more scared than I have ever been. I did not want to die. (Statistics show that immediately after "attempting" suicide, the person desperately wants to live . . . not die, which makes it even sadder to think about those who do succeed.) Luckily for me, I did not die. But I hurt my body (my stomach still aches). And I scared and hurt a lot of people. I scared myself, but I didn't die and I can't even begin to tell you how happy I am about that.

I cringe every time someone else finds out. I did not want to write this story, but I did want to help anyone else who might be thinking about it or who is in a lot of pain.

It has been a month since that night. I have laughed at least 500 times, many of those real "pee your pants" kind of laughing. I have a therapist who really cares about me, and we are making real progress in building up my confidence. She is also helping my mom and dad be "better parents." I have realized that they really do care and that they are doing the best that they can. I have a new friend who has gone through some hard stuff herself. My intense feelings do not scare her, and we know what it means to "be there" for someone you care about. I have worked things out with some of my old friends and we are closer than ever. I have earned $500 and spent it all on myself . . . without guilt (well, maybe a little). And I am starting to forgive myself.

Oh, yeah . . . I met a guy. He is really sweet and he knows "my story." We have agreed to take things really slow.

These are only a few of the things I would have missed. Life gets really hard sometimes and really painful. For me, I couldn't feel everyone else's love because I had forgotten how to love myself. I'm learning now—learning how to accept, forgive and love myself. And I'm learning that things change. Pain *does* go away, and happiness is the other side. Although the pain comes back, so does the happiness. It is like waves in the ocean coming and going . . . coming and going . . . breathing in and breathing out.

Lia Gay, age 16

Somebody Should Have Taught Him

I went to a birthday party
but I remembered what you said.
You told me not to drink at all,
so I had a Sprite instead.
I felt proud of myself,
the way you said I would,
that I didn't choose to drink and drive,
though some friends said I should.
I knew I made a healthy choice and
your advice to me was right
as the party finally ended
and the kids drove out of sight.
I got into my own car,
sure to get home in one piece,
never knowing what was coming,
something I expected least.
Now I'm lying on the pavement.
I can hear the policeman say,
"The kid that caused this wreck was drunk."
His voice seems far away.
My own blood is all around me,

as I try hard not to cry.
I can hear the paramedic say,
"This girl is going to die."
I'm sure the guy had no idea,
while he was flying high,
because he chose to drink and drive
that I would have to die.
So why do people do it,
knowing that it ruins lives?
But now the pain is cutting me
like a hundred stabbing knives.
Tell my sister not to be afraid,
tell Daddy to be brave,
and when I go to heaven to
put "Daddy's Girl" on my grave.
Someone should have taught him
that it's wrong to drink and drive.
Maybe if his mom and dad had,
I'd still be alive.
My breath is getting shorter,
I'm getting really scared.
These are my final moments,
and I'm so unprepared.
I wish that you could hold me, Mom,
as I lie here and die.
I wish that I could say
I love you and good-bye.

Retold by Jane Watkins

Just One Drink

There's a small cross by the side of Highway 128, near the town of Boonville. If this cross could talk, it would tell you this sad story:

Seven years ago my brother, Michael, was at a friend's ranch. They decided to go out for dinner. Joe arrived and volunteered to drive—after just one drink.

Lightheartedly, the four friends traveled the winding road. They didn't know where it would end—nobody did. Suddenly, they swerved into the opposite lane, colliding with an oncoming car.

Back home we were watching *E.T.* on video in front of a warm fire. Then we went to bed. At 2:00 A.M. a police officer woke my mom with the devastating news. Michael had been killed.

In the morning, I found my mother and sister crying. I stood there bewildered. "What's wrong?" I asked, rubbing my sleepy eyes.

Mom took a deep breath. "Come here . . ."

Thus began a grueling journey through grief, where all roads lead to nowhere. It still hurts to remember that day.

The only thing that helps is telling my story, hoping

you will remember it if you are tempted to get into a car with someone who has had a drink—even just one drink.

Joe chose the road to nowhere. He was convicted of manslaughter and served time. However, the real punishment is living with the consequences of his actions. He left us with an ache in our hearts that will never go away, a nightmare that will haunt him—and us—for the rest of our lives. And a small cross by the side of Highway 128.

Chris Laddish, age 13
Dedicated with love to the memory of Michael Laddish

The Dance

Looking back on the memory of
The Dance we shared 'neath the stars above
For a moment all the world was right
How was I to know that you'd ever
say good-bye

[Chorus:]
And now I'm glad I didn't know
The way it all would end
The way it all would go
Our lives are better left to chance
I could have missed the pain
But I'd of had to miss the dance

Holding you I held everything
For a moment wasn't I a king
If I'd known how the king would fall
Well then who's to say I might have changed it all

[Repeat Chorus]

Our lives are better left to chance
I could have missed the pain
*But I'd of had to miss the dance**

Tony Arata

**The Dance was written by Tony Arata. ©1989 Morganactive Songs, Inc., and Pookie Bear Music (ASCAP). All rights reserved. Used by permission. Warner Bros. Publications U.S. Inc., Miami, FL 33014.*

The Premonition

Kyle, his mom Karen, and his sister Kari had been through their share of pain. When Kyle was twelve and Kari was nine, their father had walked out on the family in the middle of the night. They had little communication with him over the next few years, and received no financial help.

To make ends meet, Karen and her children moved in with her mother in Dallas, Texas, for a short period of time. Later, she was offered a job in Rock Hill, South Carolina, working for the gospel group The Happy Goodman Family. When the group moved their home base to Nashville, Karen, Kyle and Kari went along.

When Kyle entered his freshman year at Hillwood High School, Karen decided to settle down so that Kyle and Kari could both finish their remaining school years in one place. The family had finally arrived at a place where, for a moment, all the world was right.

Kyle grew into a handsome young man, as well as a talented athlete. He excelled in football, and it became a big part of his life. When he put his uniform on, you could see his eyes light up. His coach and teammates called him

'Hit Man' because he loved to hit people and wouldn't back down from anything. He was a good role model, and poured his whole heart and soul into each game.

His senior year, Kyle made the most tackles on his team and was named Defensive Player of the Year. He was determined to play for Austin Peay State University where he would attend college the following autumn.

Kyle and his family had overcome so much. Finally things were going well. Kyle was happy and filled with dreams. In fact, he co-wrote a poem about it with his friend.

Dreams

A lost young petal
Wondering souls
I see the dream you seek
Follow me please, if you dare.
The dream is coming
For you and me.
I return by your side
With a heart in my hand.
It is like a bright fire dancing
To the slow music turning.
My heart as smooth as ivory
Has turned to a lonely, sulfur.
I retire my heart now to you,
Love me because I love you.

Still, a sense that he may fall hung over Kyle. He was at a crossroads; and though he couldn't see what lay ahead, he had a premonition of what would befall him.

One night Kyle told his mother, "I've got the crazy feeling something is going to happen to me, and they are going to dedicate the annual to me." Karen told him to never think like that, and Kyle laughed in his usual laid-back way, saying, "Oh, Mom, it's just a crazy thought—nothing's gonna happen to me!"

Still the doubts troubled Kyle, as he wrote in this letter that was found tucked away in his room. It read:

> *This is to anyone. I'm writing because I need someone to talk to, someone to open myself to. I need to be held. Yes me. Even I am not made of brick. Although I'm strong, even strong things break down at times.*
>
> *Whoever reads, I don't want sympathy or talk, I just want someone to listen.*
>
> *I sit here laid back, tears are falling from my face. I'm so scared. I feel so alone, so lost, confused, sad . . . I realize I'm not going to have all the things I love forever.*
>
> *Starting off . . . my friends. God, I've never felt this way. I look at their faces in my mind. What's going to happen? Will I see my friend Kenneth's face forever? I doubt it, even though our love for each other may stay, eventually we'll separate. The same with Marv, Chris, Brew. Brew's dad said he might move to Pensacola. I dread the thought of losing somebody so close, God . . .*
>
> *And I'm going to college this year. God, I'm so scared, so afraid. I see Mom. God, I don't want to leave her. Sure I want to party, have a place of my own, but I'm so afraid of leaving because I love her and Kari so much.*
>
> *My grandparents are going to die soon. I can't see living without . . . God . . .*
>
> *Help . . .*

Football. I'm so scared, I love the game so much. What if I don't make college or get a scholarship? It will be the bloody last time to put on a pair of pads, and that hurts . . . BAD.

And Mandy. I love her so much, but, God, I'm not even going to have that forever . . . I mean, sure, you never know . . . but the only thing that makes me happy and I can talk to might not be here either. And also talking to her about problems of hers. God, this sucks so bad . . . I love you Mandy.

Wherever you may go in the future, I will love all of you . . . Mom, Kari, Marvin, Chris, Kenneth, Alec, Rodrik, Brian, Travis, Brian, Paul, Bobby. Trey, Brew. Mandy. Luke . . .

I mean, you know, all I've really, really, really, really got is myself, and then eventually I'm gone.

Well, I'm going. I love everybody. Thanks for listening, piece of paper, or whoever reads it.

Love, Peace.
Your buddy, Love, Son, Brother, 4 ever
I love U All—

That spring, Kyle went to a party. The friend that had driven Kyle had to leave early, so Kyle caught a ride with a young man later that evening when he was ready to go home. The young man, whom Kyle did not know well, had been drinking. Perhaps Kyle didn't realize this when he climbed into the back seat, but it was a mistake that would cost him and his family dearly.

The car carrying Kyle and three other young people was traveling more than 100 miles an hour when the driver lost control in a curve. Police reports estimate that the vehicle slid sideways approximately 130 feet, then went airborne for 46 feet. The 1992 Mustang finally came to a stop when its rear end slammed into a tree. Kyle was thrown from the car through the back window.

Karen answered a knock on the door at 1:00 A.M. and experienced what she now calls "a mother's worst nightmare." She was told that Kyle had been in an accident and was at St. Thomas Hospital in critical condition.

On the way to the hospital, Karen kept thinking of all the hard times she, Kyle, and Kari had shared, and how they had always pulled together to make it through. She just knew in her heart that they would be able to again.

Karen's hopes were soon dashed. "We did all we could," said the doctor. Kyle had died.

Though Kyle's pain was over, the pain his mother and his sister would endure had just begun. On Monday, March 30, 1992, (Karen's birthday) a memorial service for Kyle was held in the Hillwood High gymnasium. With all the students, friends, and teachers present, Kyle's football coach, Jerry Link, presented Karen with Kyle's jersey, number 82, which they had retired in his honor. He also handed her Kyle's cap and gown, which had just come in for graduation. Karen spoke to the crowd.

She told Kyle's fellow students—among them many of his closest friends—that they must continue on, and that they must realize how precious life really is. She asked them not to take chances, and to live each day the best way possible.

Karen looked out into the faces of the young audience. Tears rolled down their cheeks as they remembered Kyle. They reflected upon his bright smile, his crazy sense of humor, his athletic ability—but most of all, the way he seemed to really care about everyone around him. She knew that they all realized, as she did, that it really was worth the pain just to have known him.

As the school year came to a close, Hillwood High School's yearbook was dedicated to Kyle, and his premonition from months before sadly came true. Karen was presented with a yearbook signed by many of his friends and fellow students.

Bruce Burch

[EDITORS' NOTE: *Karen is now involved with Mothers Against Drunk Driving (MADD), and speaks to high school students, as well as to groups of DUI offenders.*]

Dead at 17

Agony claws my mind. I am a statistic. When I first got here, I felt very much alone. I was overwhelmed by grief, and I expected to find sympathy.

I found no sympathy. I saw only thousands of others whose bodies were as badly mangled as mine. I was given a number and placed in a category. The category was called "traffic fatalities."

The day I died was an ordinary school day. How I wish I had taken the bus! But I was too cool for the bus. I remember how I wheedled the car out of Mom. "Special favor," I pleaded. "All the kids drive." When the 2:50 P.M. bell rang, I threw my books in the locker. Free until tomorrow morning! I ran to the parking lot, excited at the thought of driving a car and being my own boss.

It doesn't matter how the accident happened, I was goofing off—going too fast, taking crazy chances. But I was enjoying my freedom and having fun. The last thing I remember was passing an old lady who seemed to be going awfully slow. I heard a crash and felt a terrific jolt. Glass and steel flew everywhere. My whole body seemed to be turning inside out. I heard myself scream.

Suddenly, I awakened. It was very quiet. A police officer was standing over me. I saw a doctor. My body was mangled. I was saturated with blood. Pieces of jagged glass were sticking out all over. Strange that I couldn't feel anything. Hey, don't pull that sheet over my head. I can't be dead. I'm only 17. I've got a date tonight. I'm supposed to have a wonderful life ahead of me. I haven't lived yet. I can't be dead!

Later I was placed in a drawer. My folks came to identify me. Why did they have to see me like this? Why did I have to look at Mom's eyes when she faced the most terrible ordeal of her life? Dad suddenly looked very old. He told the man in charge, "Yes—he is our son."

The funeral was weird. I saw all my relatives and friends walk toward the casket. They looked at me with the saddest eyes I've ever seen. Some of my buddies were crying. A few of the girls touched my hand and sobbed as they walked by.

Please—somebody—wake me up! Get me out of here. I can't bear to see Mom and Dad in such pain. My grandparents are so weak from grief they can barely walk. My brother and sister are like zombies. They move like robots. In a daze. Everybody. No one can believe this. I can't believe it, either.

Please don't bury me! I'm not dead! I have a lot of living to do! I want to laugh and run again. I want to sing and dance. Please don't put me in the ground! I promise if you give me just one more chance, God, I'll be the most careful driver in the whole world. All I want is one more chance. Please, God, I'm only 17.

John Berrio

I'll Be Looking for You, Ace

Dear Michael,

So, Ace, what's it like up in heaven? Everything it's cracked up to be? People say it's supposed to be beautiful; but really, how would anyone know? Maybe that's why I used to be so afraid of dying—because we do not know what is next. Oddly enough, my feelings have changed since you left.

I was at work that Saturday, December 6, with only an hour to go until I had to pick you up at Vinny's house. Then the phone rang. It was our sister, Lauren. I was expecting to hear the usual "Remember to bring home some shampoo." Instead, there were words that reverberated through my head: "Mike's been hit by a car."

I went numb, and I shook during the entire drive to St. John's Hospital. I remember praying that your face would not be disfigured and that you did not break too many bones. Death was not even a possibility. I figured you were too good a kid, too strong, too young (you were only 11) and too well-liked to be seriously hurt.

My worst nightmare could not compare with what I found facing me. I was ushered into the doctor's lounge, where our whole family and your friends were huddled. Phrases such as "Holding his own," "It could go either way" and "There's always hope with kids" floated past my ears. I sank onto a couch. While you were in surgery I prayed the hardest I ever prayed in my life. Then, a few hours later, the doctors let Lauren, Jeff and me up to see you in the intensive care unit.

There you were. Underneath the casts, bandages, bruises, stitches and tubes was the beautiful little brother I loved. The doctors said that even though you were in a coma, you might be able to hear, but I couldn't speak. Nothing I felt could be put into words. I wanted to give you the world, but I could only hold your hand. I kept thinking, *Come on, Mike. You can make it.*

At about 10:30 that night Lauren, Jeff and I went home while Mom and Dad stayed. We played some of your albums so loud the floor shook—you would have been so proud of us! After a while, I tried to fall asleep on the couch, but my mind raced. I kept thinking of how you and I danced the whole day together at cousin Becky's wedding, how you'd jump around in your room playing air guitar, and how you messed up your lines at the Christmas play tryouts so that Brian could get the part he wanted so badly. I thought how great life was with you; without you it would be unbearable. I was so scared.

We all did what we could for you. As an offering, Uncle Bob gave up smoking—and you know what a chain smoker he is! Your best friend, Matthew, went to church and lit 21 candles (your basketball number) for you. Lauren, Jeff and I were planning a party for you when you came home. Mom and Dad were going to get Ace Frehely to visit you.

All the hoping and planning and praying got us through that first night. In the morning, you were transferred to Columbia-Presbyterian Hospital, where it was thought that your chances for survival were greater. In Babies I.C.U. (don't get offended, Mike—Babies I.C.U. goes up to age 19!) a team of wonderful doctors and nurses stayed with you around the clock. I was there for you too, coaching you in my mind, as I used to cheer you on at your Little League games last spring. *Come on, Mike—give it your best shot. This is not a game. This is for real.*

Well, Ace, you made it through one more night. When we got to the hospital early Monday morning, you were having a CAT scan done. We were told we could see you afterward. You came back in cardiac arrest, with the doctors giving one last scramble for your life.

My mind was frantic. *You cannot die, Mike! You have too much to live for! What about the guitar lessons you were going to take—the band you were going to start with Matt and Vinny? What about the basketball team—you're the starting center. Wait, Mike, don't go. I love you too much to lose you. Keep fighting, please!*

Well, Ace, I know you did what you could. You could only fight so long with so much against you.

It was the worst moment in my life when I heard "He's gone." The room spun. I felt detached from my body, as if the pain of this startling reality was too much to bear. I wanted to die too, to be with you, to make sure you were okay.

After they took out all the tubes and monitors, the doctors let me in to see you once more. I felt that your soul was close. I wanted to shake your shoulders and have you open your eyes. Instead, I gave you a kiss and rested my face against yours, willing to do anything to bring you back. The only thing I could do was let you go.

Mike, I know you're still with me. I know you're helping me get on with my life. I learned so much from you. You taught me to live one day at a time, to appreciate everything that comes along, to laugh and have fun, to be honest, to accept people for what they are. And while 11 years is a short time, we filled them with so much happiness that can never be lost, even now.

The one thing you really did for me was take away my fear of death. I am no longer afraid. I know that God must have something wonderful waiting for a kid like you. My faith has also been strengthened, because if I did not believe in God and heaven, where would you be? Heaven has got to be beautiful with you there. I know that when my time comes, I will be looking for you. Could you be watching so we find each other? I really miss you, Ace, but I know that you are still with me, and I know we will see each other again.

I love you,
Jenn

Jennifer Lohrfink

"Gabby, You're Sooo Skinny"

I am a straight-A student. I am very involved in school activities and considered a "very together" teenager. Or at least, I was.

It all started innocently enough. I weighed about 125 pounds. I was not fat, but felt I could stand to lose a few pounds. A friend of mine had gone on a health kick and was getting great results from it—she was losing weight, she felt better and her friends were telling her how great she looked. I wanted to feel that way, too.

I began exercising and eating healthy snacks instead of the usual Coke-and-chips marathon watching the boob tube. Within a couple of weeks I had lost weight, I was feeling good, I cared more about what I wore and started feeling attractive in a way I had not experienced before. I would go to school and it seemed like everyone noticed. "Gabby, you look great," "Gabby, you look so beautiful," and "Gabby, you're so skinny." I don't think anything ever felt as good as those comments.

I was raised with the message that there is always room for improvement, so I figured if five pounds gets this much notice, just think what 10 will do! If cutting back to

1,000 calories works, imagine 500! I figure that was the moment I took off down the road to anorexia.

My previous successes didn't feel as good to me as the success of this weight thing. I think it had something to do with the control I felt I had. I lost weight at a fast rate, and every time I lost a pound I was elated. It was a euphoria that, now in looking back, I realize I became addicted to. I lived for that feeling.

I remember the first day I went the whole day without eating. When I got into bed that night I felt this emptiness in my stomach. But I also felt thinness: a feeling I had come to connect with achievement and success. I remember thinking, *If I can go a whole day without eating, then why not two?*

There were many days I did just that. In fact, I could go three days without eating.

I don't remember exactly when it happened, but it was sudden and total: No one said nice things to me and no one was complimenting me. Instead of seeing the logical conclusion, which was that I was taking this too far, I started feeling that I was failing and needed to try harder. I needed to lose more weight; I would have to get serious now!

I had days where all I ate was an apple, and then I went to bed at night feeling like a failure, feeling fat. It got to the point that any food in my stomach felt like too much. It felt dirty and disgusting. I belittled myself for being so weak. My life was becoming a hell. I felt that if I could just control myself a little more, it would get better. The truth is, all happiness had long ago slipped away, and my whole being was devoted to the moments of success that I felt when I lost another pound.

A part of me knew this was probably wrong, but that part of me was out of reach. It was there, just not able to talk louder than my illness. I needed help, and yet there was no way I could ask for it. I could not even admit it to the people who tried so desperately to give it to me.

Teachers, school nurses, friends—they all suspected I had a problem. My concern was only to put them off and convince them I was fine. I wonder if they really believed me, or if they just knew they couldn't help until I was ready.

I remember one night my dad brought home steak and announced to me that I was going to eat it and he was going to watch me. He would not take no for an answer. I cried and begged him not to make me do this. This thing sitting on my plate had become my worst enemy. It was pure fat; one bite would ruin everything. I had to make him understand I could not eat this, and that if he really loved me, be would not make me. I was crying, begging him to let go of this crazy idea, but he wouldn't. He said he would sit there all night. I had no choice, NO CHOICE! But this was supposed to be my choice. The one thing I had control over. Those words pushed a button in me and I no longer cared about him or his feelings. All I felt were anger and hate. I hated him for making me do this, for making me feel my pain and face how distorted my reality had become. I hated him for making me eat that disgusting, evil food.

All my life I had done things for everyone else. The grades, the manners, the awards—everything for them, nothing for me. This eating thing, this losing weight had become *mine.* It represented me and *my* choices, and now my dad was trying to take that away from me, too!

As I lay in bed that night crying and feeling fat, I knew I needed help. I knew I was hurting people I loved.

After staying up all night, I came to the conclusion that it wasn't my dad I hated. I hated ME! I realized that I wasn't in control. For the first time in my life, I understood that this was *my* problem. I needed to take control of my life—not let the disease control it.

Things didn't change overnight. In fact, it was one long road to recovery. But slowly, with the help of friends and family, I began to heal. Now that I'm at my ideal weight, I have stopped weighing myself altogether. I no longer peruse fashion magazines, either—I may not be "in style," but I feel just right!

Gabriella Tortes, age 17
As told to Kimberly Kirberger

Last Wish

Chris Hart was not your average 16-year-old. He was six-feet-eight-inches tall and weighed 260 pounds. In his freshman year of high school he played on the varsity football team; he could bench-press 250 pounds and squat 450. Then he was diagnosed with osteogenic sarcoma, a form of cancer. For a while it was in remission, then during his junior year it returned. A couple of months before Christmas in 1993, he was told by doctors that he probably did not have long to live.

That same year a local radio station sponsored a contest granting requests to people who wrote in with the best Christmas wishes. A member of our church wrote a letter to the radio station on Chris's behalf. Little did I know that when this letter was chosen, my world would change, too.

Chris's first wish was to have a stereo system for his truck. A local electronics firm obliged. His second wish was to see a Dallas Cowboys football game. That was his favorite team and he was their greatest fan. To his surprise, he not only got to see the Cowboys play, he actually met some of them in the locker room. Chris's third wish was more difficult to coordinate because of its sensitive nature. He wanted a date with a redhead.

At this point I should explain that I am a redhead.

My dad came home from church one night and told me about Chris and his three wishes, especially his third wish.

"Dad, I don't even know the guy," I said.

How could I go on a date with him? I didn't go to his school. I had never met him. My dad, who is a minister, had visited Chris several times and all he could say about him was that he was very nice, very tall and "big-boned." With some hesitation I said yes.

The date was scheduled for the week before Christmas. Before then Chris and I had only talked on the phone. He seemed sweet, but I was nervous about going out on a date, so I asked one of my best friends to join us. When Chris came to pick me up I was a little shocked by how he looked. He was huge, and bald from his chemotherapy treatments. He wore a hat, but took it off inside to be polite, exposing his hairless head. When we went to a local pizza restaurant, he had to duck to get through the door, and everybody stared at us.

After that he started to come to my house after school and we talked about our problems or watched movies. He told me how much he missed playing football, and sometimes we listened to music.

On Valentine's Day, a friend and I cooked a special dinner for Chris and her boyfriend, and we exchanged presents. Chris seemed pleased with the teddy bear and the new CD. He even asked me to go to his junior-senior prom.

Then I did something I'm still ashamed of. It started when the town newspaper did an article about Chris's three wishes. It was accompanied by a picture of the two of us in front of his truck. The caption said we dated. When kids from school saw the article and picture, they made comments. I tried to ignore them, but then one day, one of the popular seniors said to me, "Hey, I guess that guy couldn't find anybody better to date."

It really hurt. I was only a sophomore and still felt new to the town. I wanted people to like me. I didn't want them to think I was weird.

When Chris called, I said I was busy and couldn't talk. I made excuses, so he stopped coming over and we stopped going out. At night I cried myself to sleep because I knew I was being cruel, but I couldn't help it. Chris's prom was coming up and I knew I had to talk to him. Mom's friend had made a special dress for me and I had promised to go. So I called Chris and we made plans to go out to dinner with friends before the prom.

That night when he came to pick me up, we didn't talk much at first. He looked good in his tuxedo and sneakers (he couldn't find any black shoes big enough to fit). He had also lost a lot of weight. His class ring was so loose it kept falling off.

We joined our friends for dinner and started to laugh and joke like old times. On the way to the dance, Chris began to feel bad. We waited in the parking lot until he regained his strength.

The auditorium was beautifully decorated with an Egyptian theme. Everyone else was dancing and having a great time, but Chris still felt weak, so he could only sit and watch. While we were talking, the DJ interrupted the music and one of the football players took the microphone. He talked about Chris and how special he was. They dedicated the prom to Chris and gave him a plaque. It was one of his proudest moments.

After the prom I didn't care what people at my school thought. They could say whatever they wanted. Chris was my friend. I just hoped he could forgive me for the way I had treated him. That spring he became much worse and the doctors gave him two weeks to live. Every day for those two weeks I visited him. He had a huge bed set up in his bedroom with a lot of pillows, and together we watched TV and talked.

He wasn't afraid to talk about dying. I found it painful, but my dad said that just by listening to Chris, I was helping him.

Each day it got harder for Chris to concentrate. By the last few days he could barely recognize anybody. Saturday afternoon was the last time I got to visit Chris. As I was leaving, he called me back and asked for a hug. As I hugged him, he whispered, "I love you."

It was the first time he had said those words to me. He really had forgiven me.

Sunday morning I went straight home after church. My parents had suggested I join them at a restaurant for lunch, but I felt there was some reason I shouldn't. Only moments after I got home a phone call came from Chris's dad; Chris was dying. I called the restaurant where my parents were eating and they rushed home and took me to Chris's.

Family and friends were gathered around Chris's bed. He was breathing with great gasps, very slowly. I stood there but could say nothing. Words wouldn't come.

"Christi's here," my dad said softly. "We're all here and we love you." How could I say good-bye?

"Dear God," my dad prayed, "please be with Chris and all of those present and his family. Give us a sense of peace as you receive Chris into your loving arms."

I looked up to see Chris take his last breath. He was gone.

That was two years ago, and I still miss him.

Christi Galloway

Gold-Medal Winner

I spoke at a middle school in the spring of 1995. When the program was over, the principal asked me if I would pay a visit to a special student. An illness had kept the boy home, but he had expressed an interest in meeting me, and the principal knew it would mean a great deal to him. I agreed.

During the nine-mile drive to his home, I found out some things about Matthew. He had muscular dystrophy. When he was born, the doctors told his parents that he would not live to see 5, then they were told he would not make it to 10. He was 13 and from what I was told, a real fighter. He wanted to meet me because I was a gold-medal power lifter, and I knew about overcoming obstacles and going for your dreams.

I spent over an hour talking to Matthew. Never once did he complain or ask, "Why me?" He spoke about winning and succeeding and going for his dreams. Obviously, he knew what he was talking about. He didn't mention that his classmates had made fun of him because he was different; he just talked about his hopes for the future, and how one day he wanted to lift weights with me.

When we finished talking, I went into my briefcase and pulled out the first gold medal I won for power lifting and put it around his neck. I told him he was more of a winner and knew more about success and overcoming obstacles than I ever would. He looked at it for a moment, then took it off and handed it back to me. He said, "Rick, you are a champion. You earned that medal. Someday, when I get to the Olympics and win my gold medal, I will show it to you."

Last summer I received a letter from Matthew's parents telling me that Matthew had passed away. They wanted me to have a letter he had written to me a few days before.

Dear Rick,

My mom said I should send you a thank-you letter for the neat picture you sent me. I also wanted to let you know that the doctors tell me I don't have long to live anymore. It is getting very hard for me to breathe and I get tired very easy, but I still smile as much as I can. I know that I will never be as strong as you and I know we will never get to lift weights together.

I told you someday I was going to go to the Olympics and win a gold medal. I know now I will never get to do that. But I know I am a champion, and God knows that too. He knows I am not a quitter, and when I get to heaven, God will give me my gold medal, and when you get there, I will show it to you. Thanks for loving me.

Your Friend,
Matthew

Rick Metzger

Anne

Her real name was Annelies Marie, but people called her Anne. Except her mother. Sometimes when her mother was feeling especially impatient or sentimental, she called Anne by her real name.

Like most teenagers of any name or place, Anne was in love with life—one minute humming and giggling, then when somebody looked at her wrong or a dark thought came out from the corners of her mind, she fought tears and bit her lip. She wondered what it would be like to be in love, and took up almost a whole page in her diary when she got her first kiss. She wasn't precocious or brilliant. Her grades in school were average, at best. She was not beautiful—but she had spirit and spunk and could smile on the outside, and while those things did not save her life, they made her immortal.

Anne Frank.

It's odd, isn't it, that one of the bestsellers of all times was not written by a "writer" or a great "teacher" or a world leader. It was written by a teenage girl hiding in an attic.

Anne had two birthdays in that attic. She was barely 13 the summer afternoon in 1942 when her family gathered up a few things and walked in the pouring rain across Amsterdam to a warehouse above her father's grocery business. On August 1, 1944—two months after her 15th birthday—Nazi police burst through the door. Yanking open drawers, ripping mattresses, the police stuffed jewelry in their pockets and looked for hidden money. Then, shoving Anne and her family down the steps, into waiting cars, they drove off. No one immediately noticed the red-checkered diary left behind.

Anne was 16 when she came down with typhus in Bergen-Belsen. Her mother died of exhaustion, her sister of malnutrition. Only her father was found alive, liberated by Russians at Auschwitz. Anne never knew all this. She died three months before her 17th birthday.

Nor did she have any idea that years later, over 2,000 young people would march in the rain to Bergen-Belsen to place flowers on the mass grave into which she had been thrown like a piece of garbage.

"[No one] will be interested in the unbosoming of a 13-year-old schoolgirl," she writes in the first pages of her diary. She was wrong. That diary is translated into over 30 languages, her name a household word. The attic on the Prinsengracht Canal in Amsterdam is now a museum.

A week after the Franks' arrest, a family friend found the diary and, after the war, gave it to Anne's father. In 1947, though turned down by two Dutch publishing houses, it came out under the title *Diary of a Young Girl.* Ever since, people have turned to that attic prison where the only sunlight came from the unquenchable spirit of a teenage girl whom teachers had found average. Through this dreamy adolescent, we watch the world grow dark, fear moving through every aspect of life like a cancer on the loose.

We know from the outset how it will all end, but Anne sees things differently. Even as the news sputtering in over the radio grows worse and worse, Anne continues to write happy stories about elves, bears and an old dwarf. Even as she sits crammed up in the secret corner of a world gone mad, she talks about playing Ping-Pong and how good the sun feels on her face. Even after she loses one of her many private bouts with encroaching loneliness, she says she knows in her heart that people are basically kind, and that no matter what happens, good will win out.

Did it? Will it again?

A hundred years before Anne Frank wrote in her diary, an old British scholar, sitting in his soft leather chair and enjoying a good cigar, wrote these immortal words: "The pen is mightier than the sword." It was a teenage girl who not only proved it, but went one better:

In the long run, the sharpest weapon of all is a kind and gentle spirit.

Ina Hughs

Desiderata

Go placidly amid the noise and haste, and remember what peace there may be in silence. As far as possible without surrender be on good terms with all persons. Speak your truth quietly and clearly; and listen to others, even the dull and ignorant; they too have their story.

Avoid loud and aggressive persons, they are vexatious to the spirit. If you compare yourself with others, you may become bitter or vain, for always there will be greater and lesser persons than yourself. Enjoy your achievements as well as your plans.

Keep interested in your own career, however humble; it is a real possession in the changing fortunes of time. Exercise caution in your business affairs; for the world is full of trickery. But let this not blind you to what virtue there is; many persons strive for high ideals; and everywhere life is full of heroism.

Be yourself. Especially, do not feign affection. Neither be cynical about love; for in the face of all aridity and disenchantment it is perennial as the grass.

Take kindly the counsel of the years, gracefully surrendering the things of youth. Nurture strength of spirit to shield you in sudden misfortune. But do not distress yourself with imaginings. Many fears are born of fatigue and loneliness. Beyond a wholesome discipline, be gentle with yourself.

You are a child of the universe, no less than the trees and the stars; you have a right to be here. And whether or not it is clear to you, no doubt the universe is unfolding as it should.

Therefore be at peace with God, whatever you conceive Him to be, and whatever your labors and aspirations, in the noisy confusion of life keep peace with your soul.

With all its sham, drudgery and broken dreams, it is still a beautiful world. Be cheerful. Strive to be happy.

Max Ehrmann

7

MAKING A DIFFERENCE

Great opportunities to help others seldom come, but small ones surround us every day.

Sally Koch

What Is Success?

What is success?
To laugh often and much;
To win the respect of intelligent people
and the affection of children;
To earn the appreciation of honest critics
and endure the betrayal of false friends;
To appreciate beauty;
To find the best in others;
To leave the world a bit better, whether by
a healthy child, a garden patch
or a redeemed social condition;
To know even one life has breathed
easier because you have lived;
This is to have succeeded.

Ralph Waldo Emerson

Be Cool . . . Stay in School!

In the eighth grade, I was student-body president of Erwin Middle School in Asheville, North Carolina. I considered this quite an honor since there were over 1,000 students in the school. At the end of the year, I was asked to make a speech at the ceremony where my class was promoted to high school. I knew this had to be more than just the brief comments a student might normally give. We're the class of 2000, so I wanted my speech to be as special as we were.

I spent several nights lying in bed, thinking about what to say. Many things crossed my mind, but none of them involved all my classmates. Then one night, it hit me. Erwin High School has the highest dropout rate of any high school in our county. What better goal could we have than for every single one of us to graduate? What if I could get my class to become the first class in the history of our public school system to enter high school as freshmen and all graduate? Wouldn't that be awesome?

The speech I gave on graduation day was only 12 minutes long, but what it started is unbelievable. When I issued the challenge to my classmates to become the first class in history to enter high school as freshmen and all graduate, the entire audience, including the parents, grandparents and teachers, erupted in applause. As I showed the personalized certificates and signs each student would get, I could tell they were really enthused. At the end of my speech the whole audience jumped to its feet with a standing ovation. It was all I could do to keep my composure and not break down and cry. I'd had no idea my challenge would bring this kind of response.

Throughout the summer, I worked on developing a program to carry our commitment into high school. I gave speeches to civic clubs and groups, and talked with several of my classmates. I told our high school principal that I wanted to start a "Dropout Patrol," made up of students who would be willing to help and support other students during bad times. I told him I wanted to design a special shirt to identify members of our class and would like to sell these to make money to publish a class directory. Then I told him I thought it would be good if we could have some type of party to celebrate if we made it through a whole semester without losing anyone.

"I'll go you one better than that," he told me. "I'll throw your class a party at the end of each grading period if you don't lose anyone." That was really exciting because a grading period was only six weeks: just 30 school days. The plan was beginning to come together.

Throughout the summer, word began to spread about our challenge. I appeared on local television and radio, the newspaper asked me to write a guest column and calls started coming in from everywhere. One day I received a call from CBS News in New York. One of their researchers had found my newspaper article and they were interested in featuring our class on their *48 Hours* program. Ken Hamblin, the Black Avenger on national talk radio, featured us in his August 1996 publication, *Ken Hamblin Talks with America.* He invited me to appear on his show and tell the country about our commitment. All this was amazing, because I had told our class we could become the most famous class in America if we all made it to graduation. We were just beginning, and we were already drawing national attention.

As I write this story, our journey is just beginning. We have the first 12 weeks of school behind us. Our pledges are hanging in the school lobby across from the principal's office. Across from them is a large glass case where we mounted a piece of sheet metal with a huge hourglass painted on it. In the top of the hourglass there is a round magnetic dot for each day we have remaining in high school. We have appointed a committee of "Dropout Patrol" members to monitor the hourglass. Each day they move a dot from the top to the bottom. This lets us track our progress in a way the entire class can watch. We began with 720 dots in the top, but now 60 of them have been moved to the bottom and we have earned our second party. It's fun to watch the dots move.

We are just starting a difficult four-year journey, but we have already made a significant impact. Last year, by the end of the second grading period, 13 kids had dropped out of the freshman class. So far this year, not a single person who signed the pledge has quit, and the "Dropout Patrol" has become the largest organized group in the school.

Businesses are seeing what a program run completely by kids can do, and they are throwing their support behind us. We have banks, car dealers, furniture stores, restaurants and more where we can get discounts for our entire family when we show our "Dropout Patrol" ID cards. Others are donating U.S. Savings Bonds and merchandise that we use to reward kids for supporting our program.

The Erwin High "Committed Class of 2000" would like to encourage your class to start a program like ours. Wouldn't it be awesome if the entire class of 2000, nationwide, had a 100 percent graduation rate? Who knows? Maybe it can!

Jason Summey, age 15

[EDITORS' NOTE: *You can contact Jason by writing to P.O. Box 16844, Asheville, NC 28816, or by calling (704) 252-3573.*]

The Leader

If only they knew how hard it is for me.
I'm turning 16, the world I begin to see.
My friends began to change, right before my eyes,
and now they seem to laugh, and tell all sorts of lies.
They hang around together in groups of three or four;
the language they use . . . it isn't gentle anymore.
The kids that seem most lonely wind up in their pack,
and those that stand alone, they talk behind their back.
Somehow I feel rejected because I don't conform.
Those that step to their own beat don't seem to be the norm.
I've watched a few just fade away, with drugs and alcohol;
and many more have given up, too many to recall.
Alcohol is an option for everyone in my school.
I've lost a friend to booze again; I will not be a fool.
And sex, it seems so open, for everyone to explore.
Three girls I know that came to school don't come here anymore.
If only I could make a difference, what could I do or say?
I would go to school and try my best each and every day.
There is one thing I'd like to do before I graduate.
I'd like to touch them one by one before it is too late.

Tony Overman

Courage in Action

A couple of years ago, I witnessed courage that ran chills up and down my spine.

At a high school assembly, I had spoken about picking on people and how each of us has the ability to stand up for people instead of putting them down. Afterwards, we had a time when anyone could come out of the bleachers and speak into the microphone. Students could say thank-you to someone who had helped them, and some people came up and did just that. A girl thanked some friends who had helped her through family troubles. A boy spoke of some people who had supported him during an emotionally difficult time.

Then a senior girl stood up. She stepped over to the microphone, pointed to the sophomore section and challenged her whole school. "Let's stop picking on that boy. Sure, he's different from us, but we are in this thing together. On the inside he's no different from us and needs our acceptance, love, compassion and approval. He needs a friend. Why do we continually brutalize him and put him down? I'm challenging this entire school to lighten up on him and give him a chance!"

All the time she shared, I had my back to the section where that boy sat, and I had no idea who he was. But obviously the school knew. I felt almost afraid to look at his section, thinking the boy must be red in the face, wanting to crawl under his seat and hide from the world. But as I glanced back, I saw a boy smiling from ear to ear. His whole body bounced up and down, and he raised one fist in the air. His body language said, "Thank you, thank you. Keep telling them. You saved my life today!"

Bill Sanders

Turning Up Your Light

Those who bring sunshine to the lives of others cannot keep it from themselves.

James M. Barrie

More than three decades ago, I was a sophomore at a large high school in Southern California. The student body of 3,200 was a melting pot of ethnic differences. The environment was tough. Knives, pipes, chains, brass knuckles and an occasional zip gun were commonplace. Fights and gang activity were weekly events.

After a football game in the fall of 1959, I left the bleachers with my girlfriend. As we walked down the crowded sidewalk, someone kicked me from behind. Turning around, I discovered the local gang, armed with brass knuckles. The first blow of the unprovoked attack immediately broke my nose, one of several bones to be broken in the pounding. Fists came from every direction as the 15 gang members surrounded me. More injuries. A brain concussion. Internal bleeding. Eventually, I had to have surgery. My doctor told me that if I had been hit in the head one more time, I probably would have died.

Fortunately, they did not harm my girlfriend.

After I recovered medically, some friends approached me and said, "Let's go get those guys!" That was the way problems were "resolved." After being attacked, evening the score became a priority. A part of me said, "Yes!" The sweet taste of revenge was clearly an option.

But another part of me paused and said no. Revenge did not work. Clearly, history had demonstrated time and again that reprisal only accelerates and intensifies conflict. We needed to do something differently to break the counterproductive chain of events.

Working with various ethnic groups, we put together what we called a "Brotherhood Committee" to work on enhancing racial relationships. I was amazed to learn how much interest fellow students had in building a brighter future. Not all bought in to doing things differently. While small numbers of students, faculty and parents actively resisted these cross-cultural exchanges, more and more individuals joined in on the effort to make a positive difference.

Two years later, I ran for student body president. Even though I ran against two friends, one a football hero and the other a popular "big man on campus," a significant majority of the 3,200 students joined me in the process of doing things differently. I will not claim that the racial problems were fully resolved. We did, however, make significant progress in building bridges between cultures, learning how to talk with and relate to different ethnic groups, resolving differences without resorting to violence and learning how to build trust in the most difficult of circumstances. It's amazing what happens when people are on speaking terms with one another!

Being attacked by the gang those many years ago was clearly one of my toughest life moments. What I learned, however, about responding with love rather than returning hate has been a powerful force in my life. Turning up our light in the presence of those whose light is dim becomes the difference that makes the difference.

Eric Allenbaugh

The Oyster

There once was an oyster
Whose story I tell,
Who found that some sand
Had got into his shell.
It was only a grain,
But it gave him great pain.
For oysters have feelings
Although they're so plain.

Now, did he berate
The harsh workings of fate
That had brought him
To such a deplorable state?
Did he curse at the government,
Cry for election,
And claim that the sea should
Have given him protection?

No—he said to himself
As he lay on a shell,
Since I cannot remove it,

I shall try to improve it.
Now the years have rolled around,
As the years always do,
And he came to his ultimate
Destiny—stew.

And the small grain of sand
That had bothered him so
Was a beautiful pearl
All richly aglow.
Now the tale has a moral;
For isn't it grand
What an oyster can do
With a morsel of sand?

What couldn't we do
If we'd only begin
With some of the things
That get under our skin.

Author Unknown

Courage in a Fire

Melinda Clark pulled the blanket up under Courtney's chin and whispered, "Good night, Corky." It was 10:00 P.M. and time for bed. Melinda grinned and patted the huge lump under the covers created by Courtney's three-foot panda. The two sisters shared the same room, but 13-year-old Melinda didn't mind at all. Courtney, who was only four, seemed like her baby, too.

Melinda jumped under her own covers, but she didn't pull them up. Even though it was February and there was snow frozen on the ground outside, it seemed unusually warm that night, especially for Everett, Pennsylvania.

Something wet slopped along her cheek. "Oh, Beau. You're a good dog." The miniature collie licked her again. His tail thumped alongside her bed as she rubbed his sable fur.

Melinda's nose twitched at the smoky odor in the air. It was probably just the wood stove downstairs. Fumes traveled up the staircase easily. Melinda shut her eyes.

Two-year-old Justin startled her as he burst through the doorway. He ran over to Melinda's bed and banged his fists on her. "Mom hurt!" His face flushed red.

"What?" Melinda jumped up. The carpet felt very warm as she dropped her bare feet onto the floor. The smoky smell was stronger as she stood up.

What was going on? She rubbed her tingling cheeks and ran into the hall between the two second-story bedrooms. She paused. As she opened the door at the top of the stairs, smoke sucked up the steps in swirls. Orange flames crackled and leaped toward her like snatching fingers. She covered her hot face and screamed.

"Wayne!" She turned and yelled for her 12-year-old brother. Although his bedroom light was on, she couldn't even see his bed through the ballooning smoke. But Wayne fought through the gray haze and stumbled into her. He was in his underwear.

"My window!" Melinda yelled.

Together they ran into Melinda's room to the double windows, where Wayne began struggling with the stubborn latch on the chest-high ledge.

"Pull! Shove it."

"I'm yanking!"

The fiberglass curtains melted down the sides of the window. Flecks of hot plastic burned into Wayne's bare back.

Melinda smashed her fist against the latch. *If they couldn't get it open, they were going to die . . .*

Wayne banged at the latch, too.

Suddenly it budged, then slipped open. But as they shoved on the window, it held tightly shut, swollen from the waves of heat.

Courtney yanked on Melinda's pink nightgown, screaming and crying. She coughed and choked in the acrid fumes.

Melinda's eyes stung. She gritted her teeth. They weren't going to die from these flames! "Shove, Wayne! Together! Now!" They banged on the window. "Again!

Harder!" She coughed. She threw all her 100 pounds behind the thrust.

Wayne shoved, too, and together they finally forced the stubborn window open.

Melinda told Wayne to climb out on the plastic porch roof. She handed Courtney over the window. Then Melinda pulled herself over the window ledge.

The three children walked to the edge of the roof, looking for a way down. Wayne jumped to the ground to catch the younger kids.

Suddenly Melinda looked at Wayne, her eyes round circles. "Justin. Where's Justin? *Justin!*" She screamed. He had been right with them!

Without pausing for a breath, she turned around and climbed back over the hot window ledge.

"Justin!" she called.

She dropped onto her hands and knees and crawled low on the hot carpet. She found the closet and felt her hands around. No Justin. She tried to call, but she choked. Her throat felt like hot coals. Yanking on the tangled nightie under her burning knees, she bumped into Courtney's five-foot-tall toy dog and duck, knocking them both over.

Could Justin have gone back into his bedroom? If he had, she'd never make it through the smoke and flames, which now sucked up the open staircase and window as if a vacuum were outside the window.

Stretching out flat, she felt under Courtney's bed. No Justin.

She coughed in spasms and grabbed at her throat. She couldn't breathe. She wasn't going to make it.

As she crawled toward the window she heard a noise coming from under her bed. She scrambled across the floor and reached underneath the bed, her hand bumping into fur. Beau. He whimpered again and licked her hand. She searched her fingers past Beau and touched hair.

Justin. He was there hiding, too. *Thanks for whimpering, Beau,* she thought.

She grabbed Justin by his hair and pulled him out. He clung to her like a baby koala as she crawled back toward the window.

She lifted him over the window ledge and climbed out behind, gasping for mouthfuls of air. But as she stepped onto the plastic roof, her foot crashed through melting plastic up to her knee. She ripped her leg out of the hole and moved to the edge of the roof.

A second later, the picture window below them exploded. Shattering glass flew out 30 feet.

Courtney and Justin screamed and pulled at Melinda's arms.

"Beau!" Melinda yelled. She looked behind at the flames licking out the bedroom window. "Oh, Beau!" She tried to swallow, and without another pause, she pushed both younger children off the roof and into the snow 18 feet below. She leaped behind them, practically smashing Justin as she hit the ground.

A trooper who had seen the fire from the road scooped up the children and carried them across the glass and snow to his car.

"Mommy!" Justin cried.

"Where's Mom?" Melinda asked. She ran up to the neighbor's porch just as her mom ran across the snow to wrap Melinda in her arms. "I was calling 911," she choked, as she grabbed Wayne in a hug. "I was down in the basement changing the wash. I saw you at the top of the stairs. I yelled at you to get out."

The trooper carried the little ones into the neighbor's house. They called their dad, who was working the night shift at Everite Door Manufacturing.

Melinda dropped onto a beanbag chair. The voices and faces swirled around her. She passed out for a few moments. When she came to, she was in an ambulance. The red light flashed. The siren screamed. She drifted in and out of consciousness several more times before reaching the hospital.

Melinda was treated for smoke inhalation, as were her brothers and sister. Melinda's nightgown was melted in spots and although it stuck to her skin, her body beneath it wasn't burned.

Both she and Wayne suffered minor burns, however. Melinda's leg was scratched and burned from where it had broken through the roof, while Wayne's back was burned in small spots from the fiberglass curtains. Courtney and Justin received scratches in their tumble from the overhang. Their pajamas were scorched. But all four children were alive.

Justin kept repeating, "An angel picked me up and threw me out the window. It was a real angel. I know it."

Melinda smiled. She hugged Justin and closed her eyes.

No one could determine the cause of the fire.

"It wasn't until the next day when we went back that I got really scared," Melinda remembers. "When we walked into the downstairs, it was really strange. Some things were burned, and other things weren't. Like the fish was still alive, swimming in his bowl in the dining room. But our bedrooms were ruined."

Her brown eyes suddenly filled with tears. "Beau didn't make it." She looked down. "I had to leave him under my bed."

But Justin did make it because Melinda crawled back into the flames to save her brother. Her fast action and courage wouldn't let her give up. She was an angel, indeed.

Barbara A. Lewis

The Most Mature Thing I've Ever Seen

Every student at Monroe High School knew about it. Nobody did it. Nobody.

Lunchtime at Monroe High School was consistent. As soon as the bell that ended the last morning class started ringing, the students swarmed toward their lockers. Then those who didn't eat in the cafeteria headed with their sack lunches toward the quad. The quad was a large, treeless square of concrete in the center of campus. It was the meeting-and-eating place.

Around the quad the various school cliques assembled. The druggies lined up on the south side. The punkers were next to them. On the east side were the brothers. Next to them were the nerds and brains. The jocks stood on the north side next to the surfers. The rednecks were on the west side. The socialites were in the cafeteria. Everybody knew their place.

This arrangement did create some tension. But for all the tension generated on the perimeter of the quad at lunchtime, it was nothing compared with the inside of the quad.

The inside was no-man's land.

Nobody at Monroe walked across the middle of the quad. To get from one side to the other, students walked around the quad. Around the people. Around the stares.

Everybody knew about it, so nobody did it.

Then one day at the beginning of spring, a new student arrived at Monroe. Her name was Lisa. She was unfamiliar to the area; in fact, she was new to the state.

And although Lisa was pleasant enough, she did not quickly attract friends. She was overweight and shy, and the style of her clothes was not . . . right.

She had enrolled at Monroe that morning. All morning she had struggled to find her classes, sometimes arriving late, which was especially embarrassing. The teachers had generally been tolerant, if not cordial. Some were irritated; their classes were already too large, and now this added paperwork before class.

But she had made it through the morning to the lunch bell. Hearing the bell, she sighed and entered the crush of students in the hall. She weaved her way to her locker and tried her combination three, four, five times before it banged open. Standing in front of her locker, she decided to carry along with her lunch all of her books for afternoon classes. She thought she could save herself another trip to her locker by eating lunch on the steps in front of her next class.

So Lisa began the longest walk of her life—the walk across campus toward her next class. Through the hall. Down the steps. Across the lawn. Across the sidewalk. Across the quad.

As Lisa walked she shifted the heavy books, alternately resting the arm that held her light lunch. She had grabbed too many books; the top book kept slipping off, and she was forced to keep her eye on it in a balancing act as she moved past the people, shifting the books from arm to arm, focusing on the balanced book, shuffling forward, oblivious to her surroundings.

All at once she sensed something: The air was eerily quiet. A nameless dread clutched her. She stopped. She lifted her head.

Hundreds of eyes were staring. Cruel, hateful stares. Pitiless stares. Angry stares. Unfeeling, cold stares. They bore into her.

She froze, dazed, pinned down. Her mind screamed, No! This can't be happening!

What happened next people couldn't say for sure. Some later said she dropped her book, reached down to pick it up, and lost her balance. Some claimed she tripped. It didn't matter how it happened.

She slipped to the pavement and lay there, legs splayed, in the center of the quad.

Then the laughter started, like an electric current jolting the perimeter, charged with a nightmarish quality, wrapping itself around and around its victim.

And she lay there.

From every side fingers pointed, and then the taunt began, building in raucous merriment, building in heartless insanity: "You! You! You! YOU!"

And she lay there.

From the edge of the perimeter a figure emerged slowly. He was a tall boy, and he walked rigidly, as though he were measuring each step. He headed straight toward the place where the fingers pointed. As more and more students noticed someone else in the middle, the calls softened, and then they ceased. A hush flickered over the crowd.

The boy walked into the silence. He walked steadily, his eyes fixed on the form lying on the concrete.

By the time he reached the girl, the silence was deafening. The boy simply knelt and picked up the lunch sack and the scattered books, and then he placed his hand under the girl's arm and looked into her face. And she got up.

The boy steadied her once as they walked across the quad and through the quiet perimeter that parted before them.

The next day at Monroe High School at lunchtime a curious thing happened. As soon as the bell that ended the last morning class started ringing, the students swarmed toward their lockers. Then those who didn't eat in the cafeteria headed with their sack lunches across the quad.

From all parts of the campus, different groups of students walked freely across the quad. No one could really explain why it was okay now. Everybody just knew. And if you ever visit Monroe High School, that's how it is today.

It happened some time ago. I never even knew his name. But what he did, nobody who was there will ever forget.

Nobody.

Susan Doenim
Submitted by Leon Bunker

Broken Wing

You were born with wings. Why prefer to crawl through life?

Rumi

Some people are just doomed to be failures. That's the way some adults look at troubled kids. Maybe you've heard the saying, "A bird with a broken wing will never fly as high." I'm sure that T. J. Ware was made to feel this way almost every day in school.

By high school, T. J. was the most celebrated troublemaker in his town. Teachers literally cringed when they saw his name posted on their classroom lists for the next semester. He wasn't very talkative, didn't answer questions and got into lots of fights. He had flunked almost every class by the time he entered his senior year, yet was being passed on each year to a higher grade level. Teachers didn't want to have him again the following year. T. J. was moving on, but definitely not moving up.

I met T. J. for the first time at a weekend leadership retreat. All the students at school had been invited to sign up for ACE training, a program designed to have students become more involved in their communities. T. J. was one of 405 students who signed up. When I showed up to lead their first retreat, the community leaders gave me this overview of the attending students: "We have a total spectrum represented today, from the student body president to T. J. Ware, the boy with the longest arrest record in the history of town." Somehow, I knew that I wasn't the first to hear about T. J.'s darker side as the first words of introduction.

At the start of the retreat, T. J. was literally standing outside the circle of students, against the back wall, with that "go ahead, impress me" look on his face. He didn't readily join the discussion groups, didn't seem to have much to say. But slowly, the interactive games drew him in. The ice really melted when the groups started building a list of positive and negative things that had occurred at school that year. T. J. had some definite thoughts on those situations. The other students in T. J.'s group welcomed his comments. All of a sudden T. J. felt like a part of the group, and before long he was being treated like a leader. He was saying things that made a lot of sense, and everyone was listening. T. J. was a smart guy and he had some great ideas.

The next day, T. J. was very active in all the sessions. By the end of the retreat, he had joined the Homeless Project team. He knew something about poverty, hunger and hopelessness. The other students on the team were impressed with his passionate concern and ideas. They elected T. J. co-chairman of the team. The student council president would be taking his instruction from T. J. Ware.

When T. J. showed up at school on Monday morning, he arrived to a firestorm. A group of teachers were protesting to the school principal about his being elected co-chairman. The very first communitywide service project was to be a giant food drive, organized by the

Homeless Project team. These teachers couldn't believe that the principal would allow this crucial beginning to a prestigious, three-year action plan to stay in the incapable hands of T. J. Ware. They reminded the principal, "He has an arrest record as long as your arm. He'll probably steal half the food." Mr. Coggshall reminded them that the purpose of the ACE program was to uncover any positive passion that a student had and reinforce its practice until true change can take place. The teachers left the meeting shaking their heads in disgust, firmly convinced that failure was imminent.

Two weeks later, T. J. and his friends led a group of 70 students in a drive to collect food. They collected a school record: 2,854 cans of food in just two hours. It was enough to fill the empty shelves in two neighborhood centers, and the food took care of needy families in the area for 75 days. The local newspaper covered the event with a full-page article the next day. That newspaper story was posted on the main bulletin board at school, where everyone could see it. T. J.'s picture was up there for doing something great, for leading a record-setting food drive. Every day he was reminded about what he did. He was being acknowledged as leadership material.

T. J. started showing up at school every day and answered questions from teachers for the first time. He led a second project, collecting 300 blankets and 1,000 pairs of shoes for the homeless shelter. The event he started now yields 9,000 cans of food in one day, taking care of 70 percent of the need for food for one year.

T. J. reminds us that a bird with a broken wing only needs mending. But once it has healed, it can fly higher than the rest. T. J. got a job. He became productive. He is flying quite nicely these days.

Jim Hullihan

Passing the Dream

She sat on the bench, feeding the birds.
Just throwing crumbs, not saying a word.
I sat down with my beads and braids,
Proclaiming what a mess her generation had made.
I spoke of poverty, and the war in 'Nam.
What is the use of going on?

She replied softly:

"All my life, I have worked for change.
Today, I give you my dream.
You can make a difference, with the small things you do.
The future is entirely left to you.
If things go wrong and you feel down,
Open your eyes and look around.
Don't look for someone to blame.
Search for an inspiration, to rise again.
The changes you make may not always be seen.
But perhaps you can give a child the chance to dream.
So get to work, and maybe find
A small solution to help humankind.

All my life, I have worked for change.
Today I give you my dream."

Today I decided to take a walk.
I passed a teen loudly playing his boom box.
He turned his music down low
And we chatted for a minute or so.
He spoke of the homeless, and the streets filled with crime.
Couldn't my generation have found the time
To ease some of this discord
By feeding the hungry, and housing the poor?

I replied softly:

"All my life, I have worked for change.
Today, I give you my dream.
I hope you make our world a better place.
But you must work diligently; just keep pace
With the changes and dreams of the generation to come.
But with a little luck, a small battle may be won.
Someday, we will merge. And in time you will be
The older generation looking back to see
How you have answered all these questions you ask.
Fixing tomorrow is now your task.
All my life, I have worked for change.
Today, I give you my dream."

Penny Caldwell

8

GOING FOR IT!

Having a dream isn't stupid, Norm.
It's not having a dream that's stupid.

Cliff Clavin, Cheers

The Girl Next Door

Do you remember
Many years ago
When we were young,
How we used to play together
Every day?

It seems like yesterday—
The childhood world
Of clowns and cotton candy
And summer days
That never seemed to end
When we played hide 'n' seek
From four o'clock till dusk
Then sat outside on someone's stoop
And listened to the crickets
And slapped away mosquitoes
And talked about our dreams
And what we'd do when we grew up
Until our mothers called us in.

And do you remember
That one winter when it snowed
For days and days on end
And we tried to build an igloo
Like the Eskimos?
Or when we made a game
Of raking leaves
All up and down the street
Until we'd made the biggest pile
The world had ever seen
And then we jumped in it?
Or how about the time
We gathered honeysuckle
From your yard
And sold it to the neighbors?
And the grand day when finally
The training wheels came off our bikes
And we were free
To explore the whole world
In an afternoon
So long as we stayed
On our own street.

But those days passed by furtively
And we grew up, as children do
Until we reached a day when we
Assumed that we were too grown-up
To play amid the trees on summer nights . . .
and when I see you now
You've changed in ways I can't explain
You're like a rose that blooms before its time
And falls a victim to
The February frost.

Because the waist on your jeans is getting tight
Symbolic of a youth that's not your own
And your face is pale and green—
You don't look well.
I see you scowling at the street
From the window in your room,
It's so rare to see you smiling anymore.
And when a car pulls up outside
You run downstairs and out the door
With a suitcase in each hand
And the car speeds away
And the girl next door is gone.

And I long once more
For the summer days
When I stood on your porch
And banged on your door
And bade you come outside to greet
the afternoon's adventures.

Won't you come out to play, once more?
For we are still so young . . .

Amanda Dykstra, age 14

I'll Be Back

Although the world is full of suffering, it is also full of the overcoming of it.

Helen Keller

Linda and Bob Samele braced themselves as they approached the door to the hospital room. *Keep calm,* Linda told herself as she reached for the knob. *You don't want to upset him any more than he already is.*

That sleety afternoon of December 23, 1988, their 15-year-old son, Chris, had been riding with five friends from the Sameles' hometown of Torrington, Connecticut, to nearby Waterbury. Suddenly, the teenagers' laughter turned to screams as their car skidded on an icy patch and slammed into a guardrail. Three of the kids, including Chris, were catapulted out the rear window. One died instantly, another was seriously injured.

Chris had been found sitting on the median, staring with dazed eyes at a torrent of blood gushing from his left thigh. Twenty feet away was his left leg, severed through the knee by a guardrail cable. He was rushed to

Waterbury Hospital for surgery. His parents had to wait almost seven hours to see him.

Now Linda's eyes filled with tears at the sight of her son in the hospital bed. Bob, a Torrington letter carrier, took Chris's hand. "Dad, I lost my leg," the young man said softly to his father. Bob nodded and squeezed his hand tighter. After a brief silence, Chris added, "What's going to happen to my basketball career?"

Bob Samele struggled to control his emotions. The game had been Chris's passion since early childhood, and already he was becoming a local legend. The previous season, as an eighth-grader at St. Peter's, he had compiled a remarkable 41-point average. Now a freshman at Torrington High, Chris had scored a total of 62 points in two junior-varsity games. "Someday I'm going to play at Notre Dame in front of thousands," Chris would say to his parents with a grin. "And you'll be there to watch me."

Looking down at his crippled son, Bob Samele searched for words. "You know, Chris," he managed at last, "there's a big group of people in the waiting room, including Coach Martin."

Chris's face brightened. Then, with a determined voice, he said, "Dad, tell Coach I'll be back next season. I'm going to play basketball again."

Chris underwent three more operations on his leg in seven days. From the start, his surgeons saw that the jumble of torn nerves, arteries and muscles made it impossible to reattach the severed limb. Chris would need a prosthesis.

During his three-and-a-half-week hospital stay he had a steady stream of visitors. "Don't feel bad for me," Chris would say whenever he sensed pity. "I'll be just fine." Behind his strong spirits lay an indomitable will forged by religious faith. Many of his doctors and nurses were uncomprehending.

"How are you dealing with all this, Chris?" a psychiatrist asked one day. "Do you ever feel sorry for yourself?"

"No," the boy replied, "I don't see where that is going to help."

"Don't you feel bitter or angry?"

"No," Chris said. "I try to be positive about it all."

When the persistent psychiatrist finally left his room, Chris told his parents, "*He's* the one that needs help."

Chris worked hard in the hospital to recover his strength and coordination. When he was strong enough he would flip a Nerf ball through a hoop that a friend had attached to the wall alongside his bed. His demanding therapy included upper-body exercises for crutches and workouts to improve his balance.

Two weeks into his hospital stay, the Sameles gambled on an additional therapy: They took Chris in a wheelchair to a Torrington High basketball game. "Keep a close watch on him," the nurses warned, concerned about his reaction.

The boy remained unusually quiet when he was wheeled into the noisy gym. As he passed before the bleachers, however, friends and teammates began calling out his name and waving. Then Frank McGowan, Torrington High's assistant principal, announced over the public-address system, "We have a very special friend here tonight. Everyone, please welcome back Chris Samele!"

Startled, Chris looked around and saw that all 900 people in the gym had risen to their feet, cheering and applauding. Tears welled up in the boy's eyes. It was a night he would never forget.

On January 18, 1989, not quite a full month after the accident, Chris was able to return home. To keep up with schoolwork, he was visited each afternoon by a tutor. When he wasn't studying, he was being driven back to Waterbury Hospital for more therapy. Physical pain—sometimes searing—was part of his daily life. At times, watching television with his parents, he rocked back and forth in silent reaction to the ache radiating from his stump.

Then one frigid afternoon, Chris struggled onto his crutches and hobbled around the corner to the old garage where he had learned to shoot. Putting the crutches down, he picked up a basketball and glanced around to make sure no one was watching. Finally, hopping about on his right leg, he began tossing the ball at the hoop. Several times he lost his balance and slammed down on the asphalt. Each time he picked himself up, hopped over to retrieve the ball and continued shooting. After 15 minutes he was exhausted. *This is going to take longer than I thought,* he said to himself, as he began the slow walk back into the house.

Chris got his first prosthetic device on March 25, Good Friday. Excited by the new limb, he asked Ed Skewes, director of the hospital's prosthetic and orthotic department, whether this meant he could begin playing basketball right away. Surprised to see Chris serious, Skewes replied, "Let's take this a day at a time." The doctor knew that it's usually about a year before a person can walk comfortably with a prosthesis, let alone play sports.

In the basement at home, Chris spent long hours learning to walk with his artificial leg. Hard as it was to shoot baskets on one leg, he found it even more difficult with the prosthesis. Most of his shots were way off the mark, and he often crashed to the pavement.

In his darkest moments, Chris remembered a conversation with his mother. After a particularly discouraging day, he had asked if she really thought he'd ever play again. "You'll have to work even harder at basketball now," she replied. "But, yes—I think you can do it." She was right, he knew. It all came down to hard work—and refusing to give in.

Chris returned to Torrington High in early April and was immediately one of the gang again—except on the basketball court. After school, Chris's friends would play on an outdoor court. For several weeks, he watched from the sidelines as they flew past. Then one afternoon in early May, he went out suited to play. His surprised buddies made way as he came unhesitatingly onto the court.

From the first, Chris began shooting from the outside, and he felt a thrill whenever the ball swished through the net. But when he tried to drive, hop-skipping toward the basket, or leap for a rebound, he fell to the ground. "Come on, Chris, you can do it!" his friends shouted. But Chris knew the truth: he couldn't do it—not as he used to.

In a game during a summer tournament, he went up hard for a rebound and broke the foot of his prosthesis. As he hopped off the court, he thought, *Maybe I'm just kidding myself. Maybe I'm not up to this.*

Ultimately, however, he told himself there was only one thing to do: push himself even harder. So he began a daily regimen of shooting, dribbling and weight-lifting. After each workout, he carefully removed the artificial leg and four sweat socks he wore over his stump to cushion the prosthesis. Then he showered, groaning slightly as he rubbed soap over the blisters. Before long, the pain was eased by the sense that he was seeing flashes of the old self. *I'm going to do it. And not next year. This year!*

The Monday after Thanksgiving, jayvee head coach Bob Anzellotti called together the crowd of boys, all nervous and expectant, who were vying for a spot on the Torrington High junior varsity basketball team. His eyes stopped on Chris Samele.

During the two days of tryouts, no one had pushed himself harder than Chris. He dribbled through defenders, dived after loose balls—whatever it took to show everyone he could still play. He even took 10 laps around the gym each day with the others—moving far slower than everyone else, but never failing to finish.

The morning after the last practice, Chris joined the rush to check the roster. *You've done all you could,* he told himself as he peered over the shoulders of others at the list. And there it was—*Samele.* He was back on the squad!

Later that week, Coach Anzellotti called his players together for a team meeting. "Each year's squad has a captain, who is selected for the example he sets. This year's captain will be . . . Chris Samele." The players erupted with cheers.

On the night of December 15, just eight days shy of a year since the accident, 250 people settled into their seats to watch the game that would bring Chris back to the basketball court.

In the locker room, Chris's hand trembled slightly as he pulled on his maroon jersey. "You're going to be all right, Chris," Coach Anzellotti said. "Just don't expect too much the very first night." Chris nodded. "I know," he said softly. "Thanks."

Soon he was running with his teammates onto the court for pre-game practice. Nearly everyone in the stands stood to cheer. Moved by the sight of their son in a Torrington High uniform once again, Linda and Bob fought back tears. *God,* Linda prayed silently, *please don't let him be embarrassed.*

Despite his efforts to calm down, Chris carried his nervousness onto the court. During warmups, most of his shots clanged off the rim. "Take it easy; relax," Coach Anzellotti whispered. "Don't rush it."

When the players finally came out to the center of the court for the tip-off, Chris was starting at guard. With the opening jump ball, he began playing a tight and awkward game. He managed to keep up, but his movements were jerky, his rhythm off. Several times when he shot the ball, it failed even to touch the rim of the basket. Usually when that happens, kids in the stands taunt, "Air ball! Air ball!" This time, they were silent.

After playing eight minutes, Chris was given a long breather. With two minutes left in the half he was put back in. *Come on, Chris,* he told himself, *this is what you've worked for. Show them you can do it.* Seconds later, he worked himself free 20 feet from the basket, and a teammate whipped him a pass. It was a tough range for anyone—a long three-pointer. Without hesitation, Chris planted himself and launched a high, arching shot. The ball sailed toward the rim—and swished cleanly through the net.

The gym erupted in shouts and cheers. "Thatta way, Chris!" Bob Samele yelled, his voice cracking with emotion.

A minute later, Chris grabbed a rebound amid a tangle of arms. Muscling up, he flipped the ball against the backboard. Once again, it sliced through the basket. And again cheers exploded. By now, tears were streaming down Linda Samele's face as she watched her son hop-skip down the court, his fist raised in triumph. *You did it, Chris,* she kept saying to herself. *You did it.*

Chris continued to go all out, to the delight of the crowd. Only once did he lose his footing and tumble to the floor. When the final buzzer sounded, he had scored 11 points, and Torrington had won.

At home later that night, Chris broke into a wide grin. "I did okay, Dad, didn't I?"

"You did just great," Bob answered, giving his son a big hug.

After chatting briefly about the game, Chris, still wearing a look of joy, made his way up the stairs to his bedroom. In his mind, his parents knew, this night was only the beginning.

As Linda turned out the lights, she recalled an afternoon shortly following the accident when she was driving her son home from therapy. Chris was quiet, staring out the car window; then suddenly he broke the silence. "Mom, I think I know why this happened to me." Startled, Linda replied, "Why, Chris?"

Still looking out the window, Chris said simply, "God knew I could handle it. He saved my life because he knew I could handle it."

Jack Cavanaugh

[EDITORS' NOTE: *Samele went on to star with the varsity basketball team at Torrington High School during his junior and senior years. Chris also played both singles and doubles on the school tennis team. He has played on the varsity tennis team at Western New England College in Springfield, Massachusetts, and has played intramural basketball at Western New England and in summer leagues in the Torrington area. Samele hopes to become a basketball coach.*]

Just Me

From the time I was little, I knew I was great
'cause the people would tell me, "You'll make it—just wait."
But they never did tell me how great I would be
if I ever played someone who was greater than me.

When I'm in the back yard, I'm king with the ball.
To swish all those baskets is no sweat at all.
But all of a sudden there's a man in my face
who doesn't seem to realize that I'm king of this place.

So the pressure gets to me; I rush with the ball.
My passes to teammates could go through the wall.
My jumpers not falling, my dribbles not sure.
My hand is not steady, my eye is not pure.

The fault is my teammates—they don't understand.
The fault is my coaches—what a terrible plan.
The fault is the call by that blind referee.
But the fault is not mine; I'm the greatest, you see.

Then finally it hit me when I started to see
that the face in the mirror looked exactly like me.

It wasn't my teammates who were dropping the ball,
and it wasn't my coach shooting bricks at the wall.

That face in the mirror that was always so great
had some room for improvement instead of just hate.
So I stopped blaming others and I started to grow.
My play got much better and it started to show.

And all of my teammates didn't seem quite so bad.
I learned to depend on the good friends I had.
Now I like myself better since I started to see
that I was lousy being great—I'm much better being me.

Tom Krause

True Height

If you don't daydream and kind of plan things out in your imagination, you never get there. So you have to start someplace.

Robert Duvall

His palms were sweating. He needed a towel to dry his grip. A glass of ice water quenched his thirst, but hardly cooled his intensity. The Astroturf he was sitting on was as hot as the competition he faced today at the National Junior Olympics. The pole was set at 17 feet. That was three inches higher than his personal best. Michael Stone confronted the most challenging day of his pole-vaulting career.

The stands were still filled with about 20,000 people, even though the final race had ended an hour earlier. The pole vault is truly the glamour event of any track-and-field competition. It combines the grace of a gymnast with the strength of a body builder. It also has the element of flying, and the thought of flying as high as a two-story building is a mere fantasy to anyone watching such an event. Today and now, it is not only Michael Stone's reality and dream—it is his quest.

As long as Michael could remember, he had always dreamed of flying. Michael's mother read him numerous stories about flying when he was growing up. Her stories were always ones that described the land from a bird's eye view. Her excitement and passion for details made Michael's dreams full of color and beauty. Michael had this one recurring dream. He would be running down a country road. He could feel the rocks and chunks of dirt at his feet. As he raced down the golden-lined wheat fields, he always out-ran the locomotives passing by. It was at the exact moment he took a deep breath that he lifted off the ground. He would soar like an eagle.

Where he flew always coincided with his mother's stories. Wherever he flew was with a keen eye for detail and the free spirit of his mother's love. His dad, on the other hand, was not a dreamer. Bert Stone was a hard-core realist. He believed in hard work and sweat. His motto: *If you want something, work for it!*

From the age of 14, Michael did just that. He began a very careful and regimented weight-lifting program. He worked out every other day with weights, with some kind of running work on alternate days. The program was carefully monitored by Michael's coach, trainer and father. Michael's dedication, determination and discipline were a coach's dream. Besides being an honor student and only child, Michael Stone continued to help his parents with their farm chores. Michael's persistence in striving for perfection was not only his obsession but his passion.

Mildred Stone, Michael's mother, wished he could relax a bit more and be that "free dreaming" little boy. On one occasion she attempted to talk to him and his father about this, but his dad quickly interrupted, smiled and said, "You want something: work for it!"

All of Michael's vaults today seemed to be the reward for his hard work. If Michael Stone was surprised, thrilled or arrogant about clearing the bar at 17 feet, you couldn't tell. As soon as he landed on the inflated landing mat, and with the crowd on their feet, Michael immediately began preparing for his next attempt at flight. He seemed oblivious of the fact he had just surpassed his personal best by one foot and that he was one of the final two competitors in the pole-vaulting event at the National Junior Olympics.

When Michael cleared the bar at 17 feet, 2 inches and 17 feet, 4 inches, again he showed no emotion. Constant preparation and determination were his vision. As he lay on his back and heard the crowd moan, he knew the other vaulter had missed his final jump. He knew it was time for his final jump. Since the other vaulter had fewer misses, Michael needed to clear this vault to win. A miss would get him second place. Nothing to be ashamed of, but Michael would not allow himself the thought of not winning first place.

He rolled over and did his ritual of three finger-tipped push-ups along with three Marine-style push-ups. He found his pole, stood and stepped on the runway that led to the most challenging event of his 17-year-old life.

The runway felt different this time. It startled him for a brief moment. Then it all hit him like a wet bale of hay. The bar was set at nine inches higher than his personal best. *That's only one inch off the national record,* he thought. The intensity of the moment filled his mind with anxiety. He began shaking the tension from his body. It wasn't working. He became more tense. *Why was this happening to him now,* he thought. He began to get nervous. Fear would be a more accurate description. What was he going to do? He had never experienced these feelings. Then out of nowhere, and from the deepest depths of his soul, he envisioned his mother. Why now? What was his mother doing in his thoughts at a time like this? It was simple. His mother always used to tell him that when you felt tense, anxious, or even scared, to take deep breaths.

So he did. Along with shaking the tension from his legs, he gently laid his pole at his feet. He began to stretch out his arms and upper body. The light breeze that was once there was now gone. He could feel a trickle of cold sweat running down his back. He carefully picked up his pole. He felt his heart pounding. He was sure the crowd did, too. The silence was deafening. When he heard the singing of some distant robins in flight, he knew it was his time to fly.

As he began sprinting down the runway, something felt wonderfully different, yet familiar. The surface below him felt like the country road he used to dream about. The rocks and chunks of dirt, the visions of the golden wheat fields seemed to fill his thoughts. When he took a deep breath, it happened. He began to fly. His take-off was effortless. Michael Stone was now flying, just like in his childhood dreams. Only this time he knew he wasn't dreaming. This was real. Everything seemed to be moving in slow motion. The air around him was the purest and freshest he had ever sensed. Michael was soaring with the majesty of an eagle.

It was either the eruption of the people in the stands or the thump of his landing that brought Michael back to earth. On his back with that wonderful hot sun on his face, he could only envision the smile on his mother's face. He knew his dad was probably smiling too, even laughing. Bert would always do that when he got excited: smile and then sort of giggle. What he didn't know was that his dad was hugging his wife and crying. That's right: Bert "if-you-want-it-work-for-it" Stone was crying like a baby in his wife's arms. He was crying harder than Mildred had ever seen before. She also knew he was crying the greatest tears of all: tears of pride. Michael was immediately swarmed with people hugging and congratulating him on the greatest accomplishment thus far in his life. He later went on that day to clear 17 feet $6\frac{1}{2}$ inches: National and International Junior Olympics record.

With all the media attention, endorsement possibilities and swarming herds of heartfelt congratulations, Michael's life would never be the same. It wasn't just because he won the National Junior Olympics and set a new world record. And it wasn't because he had just increased his personal best by $9\frac{1}{2}$ inches. It was simply because Michael Stone is blind.

David Naster

Helen Keller and Anne Sullivan

Knowledge is love and light and vision.

Helen Keller

[EDITORS' NOTE: *Helen Keller became ill at age two and was left blind and deaf. For the next five years she grew up in a world of darkness and emptiness. She was afraid, alone and without any anchor. This is the story of her meeting the teacher who would change her life.*]

The most important day I remember in all my life is the one on which my teacher, Anne Mansfield Sullivan, came to me. I am filled with wonder when I consider the immeasurable contrasts between the two lives which it connects. It was the third of March, 1887, three months before I was seven years old.

On the afternoon of that eventful day, I stood on the porch, dumb and expectant. I guessed vaguely from my mother's signs and from the hurrying to and fro in the house that something unusual was about to happen, so I went to the door and waited on the steps. The afternoon sun penetrated the mass of honeysuckle that covered the porch, and fell on my upturned face. My fingers lingered almost unconsciously on the familiar leaves and blossoms which had just come forth to greet the sweet Southern spring. I did not know what the future held of marvel or surprise for me. Anger and bitterness had preyed upon me continually for weeks and a deep languor had succeeded this passionate struggle.

Have you ever been at sea in a dense fog, when it seemed as if a tangible white darkness shut you in, and the great ship, tense and anxious, groped her way toward the shore with plummet and sounding-line, and you waited with beating heart for something to happen? I was like that ship before my education began, only I was without compass or sounding-line, and had no way of knowing how near the harbor was. "Light! Give me light!" was the wordless cry of my soul, and the light of love shone on me in that very hour.

I felt approaching footsteps. I stretched out my hand as I supposed it was my mother. Someone took it, and I was caught up and held close in the arms of her who had come to reveal all things to me, and, more than all things else, to love me.

The morning after my teacher came she led me into her room and gave me a doll. The little blind children at Perkins Institution had sent it and Laura Bridgman had dressed it; but I did not know this until afterward. When I played with it a little while, Miss Sullivan slowly spelled into my hand the word "d-o-l-l." I was at once interested in this finger play and tried to imitate it. When I finally succeeded in making the letters correctly I was flushed with childish pleasure and pride. Running downstairs to my mother I held up my hand and made the letters for doll. I did not know that I was spelling a word or even that words existed; I was simply making my fingers go in monkey-like imitation. In the days that followed I learned to spell in this uncomprehending way a great many words, among them pin, hat, cup, and a few verbs like sit, stand, and walk. But my teacher had been with me several weeks before I understood that everything has a name.

One day, while I was playing with my new doll, Miss Sullivan put my big rag doll into my lap also, spelled "d-o-l-l" and tried to make me understand that "d-o-l-l" applied to both. Earlier in the day we had had a tussle over the words "m-u-g" and "w-a-t-e-r." Miss Sullivan had tried to impress it upon me that "m-u-g" is mug and that "w-a-t-e-r" is water, but I persisted in confounding the two. In despair she had dropped the subject for the time, only to renew it at the first opportunity. I became impatient at her repeated attempts and, seizing the new doll, I dashed it upon the floor. I was keenly delighted when I felt the fragments of the broken doll at my feet. Neither sorrow nor regret followed my passionate outburst. I had not loved the doll. In the still, dark world in which I lived there was no strong sentiment or tenderness. I felt my teacher sweep the fragments to one side of the hearth, and I had a sense of satisfaction that the cause of my discomfort was removed. She brought me my hat, and I knew I was going out into the warm sunshine. This thought, if a wordless sensation may be called a thought, made me hop and skip with pleasure.

We walked down the path to the well-house, attracted by the fragrance of the honeysuckle with which it was covered. Someone was drawing water and my teacher placed my hand under the spout. As the cool stream gushed over one hand she spelled into the other the word water, first slowly, then rapidly. I stood still, my whole attention fixed upon the motions of her fingers. Suddenly I felt a misty consciousness as of something forgotten—a thrill of returning thought; and somehow the mystery of language was revealed to me. I knew then that "w-a-t-e-r" meant the wonderful cool something that was flowing over my hand. That living word awakened my soul, gave it light, hope, joy, set it free! There were barriers still, it is true, but barriers that could in time be swept away.

I left the well-house eager to learn. Everything had a name, and each name gave birth to a new thought. As we returned to the house, every object that I touched seemed to quiver with life. That was because I saw everything with the strange, new sight that had come to me. On entering the door I remembered the doll I had broken. I felt my way to the hearth and picked up the pieces. I tried vainly to put them together. Then my eyes filled with tears; for I realized what I had done, and for the first time I felt repentance and sorrow.

I learned a great many new words that day. I do not remember what they all were; but I do know that mother, father, sister, teacher were among them—words that were to make the world blossom for me, "like Aaron's rod, with flowers." It would have been difficult to find a happier child than I was as I lay in my crib at the close of that eventful day and lived over the joys it had brought me, and for the first time longed for a new day to come.

Helen Keller

[EDITORS' NOTE: *Helen went on to graduate cum laude from Radcliffe. She then devoted the rest of her life to teaching and giving hope to the blind and deaf, as her teacher had done. She and Anne remained friends until Anne's death.*]

The Gravediggers of Parkview Junior High

People are always blaming their circumstances for what they are. I don't believe in circumstances. The people who get on in this world are the people who get up and look for the circumstances they want, and, if they can't find them, they make them.

George Bernard Shaw

The most important lessons we are taught in school go beyond answering the questions on a test correctly. It is when the lessons change us by showing us what we are really capable of accomplishing. We can, with the use of band instruments, make beautiful music. We can, with the use of a paint brush and canvas, show people how we see the world. We can, with the hard work of a team, beat the odds and win the game. However, no multiple choice or true/false test will ever teach us the greatest lesson of all: We are the stuff of which winners are made.

Not long after the release of the film *Jeremiah Johnson,*

starring Robert Redford, our seventh-grade class was discussing the story. We talked about the fact that this rough and tough mountain man was also kind and gentle. We discussed his deep love of nature and his wishes to be part of it. Our teacher, Mr. Robinson, then asked us a most unusual question. Where did we think Jeremiah Johnson was buried? We were shocked when he told us the final resting place of the great mountain man was about 100 yards away from the San Diego Freeway in Southern California.

Mr. Robinson asked us, "So, do you believe this was wrong?"

"Yes!" we all chimed in.

"Do you feel something should be done to change it?" he asked with a sly grin.

"Yes!" we replied with an enthusiasm born of youthful innocence.

Mr. Robinson stared at us, and after a few moments of suspenseful silence, he asked a question that would change the way some of us viewed life forever. "Well, do you think you could do it?"

"Huh?"

What was he talking about? We were just a bunch of kids. What could we do?

"There is a way," he said. "It's a way filled with challenge and probably some disappointment . . . but there is a way." Then he said he would help us but only if we promised to work hard and pledge to never give up.

As we agreed, little did we know that we were signing on to the most adventurous voyage of our lives thus far.

We began by writing letters to everyone we could think of who could help us: local, state and federal representatives, the cemetery owners, even Robert Redford. Before long, we started getting answers that thanked our class for the interest, but "there was absolutely nothing that could be done." Many would have given up at that point. Had it not been for our promise to Mr. Robinson not to quit, we would have. Instead, we kept writing.

We decided that we needed more people to hear about our dream so we contacted the newspapers. Finally a reporter from the *Los Angeles Times* came to our class and interviewed us. We shared what we had been trying to do and how discouraging it was that no one seemed to care. We hoped that our story would raise public interest.

"Did Robert Redford ever contact you?" the reporter asked.

"No," we replied.

Two days later our story made the front page of the paper, telling how our class was trying to right an injustice to an American legend, and that no one was helping us, not even Robert Redford. Next to the article was a picture of Robert Redford. That same day, as we were sitting in the classroom, Mr. Robinson was called to the office to take a phone call. He came back with a glow on his face like we had never seen before. "Guess who that was on the phone!"

Robert Redford had called and said he received hundreds of letters every day and that ours somehow had never reached him, but he was very interested in helping us achieve our goal. Suddenly our team was not only getting bigger, it was getting more influential and powerful.

Within a few months, after all the proper documents were filed, our teacher and a few of the students went to the cemetery and observed the removal of the remains. Jeremiah Johnson had been buried in an old wooden casket that had been reduced to a few rotted boards, and nothing but a few bones were left of the mountain man. All were carefully gathered up by the cemetery workers and placed in a new casket.

Then a few days later, at a ranch in Wyoming, a ceremony was held in honor of Jeremiah Johnson, and his final remains were placed to rest in the wilderness he had loved so much. Robert Redford was one of the pallbearers.

From then on, throughout the school, our class was referred to as the "Gravediggers," but we preferred to think of ourselves as the "Dream Lifters." What we learned that year was not just about how to write effective letters, how our government works, or even what you have to go through to accomplish such a simple thing as moving a grave site. The lesson was that nothing can beat persistence. A bunch of kids at the beginning of our teenage years had made a change.

We learned that we were the stuff of which winners are made.

Kif Anderson

Adulthood

After the dishes are washed and the sink rinsed out, there remains in the strainer at the bottom of the sink what I will call, momentarily, some "stuff." A rational, intelligent, objective person would say that this is simply a mixture of food particles too big to go down the drain, composed of bits of protein, carbohydrates, fat and fiber. Dinner dandruff.

Furthermore, the person might add that not only was the material first sterilized by the high heat of cooking, but further sanitized by going through the detergent and hot water of the dishpan, and rinsed. No problem.

But any teenager who has been dragooned into washing dishes knows this explanation is a lie. That stuff in the bottom of the strainer is toxic waste—deadly poison—a danger to health. In other words, about as icky as icky gets.

One of the very few reasons I had any respect for my mother when I was 13 was because she would reach into the sink with her bare hands—BARE HANDS—and pick up that lethal gunk and drop it into the garbage. To top that, I saw her reach into the wet garbage bag and fish around in there looking for a lost teaspoon BARE-HANDED—a kind of mad courage. She found the spoon in a clump of coffee grounds mixed with scrambled egg remains and the end of the vegetable soup. I almost passed out when she handed it to me to rinse off. No teenager who wanted to live would have touched that without being armed with gloves, a face mask and stainless-steel tongs.

Once, in school, I came across the French word *ordure,* and when the teacher told me it meant "unspeakable filth" I knew exactly to what it referred. We had it every night. In the bottom of the sink.

When I reported my new word to my mother at dish-washing time, she gave me her my-son-the-idiot look and explained that the dinner I had just eaten was in just about the same condition in my stomach at the moment, rotting, and it hadn't even been washed and rinsed before it went down my drain. If she had given me a choice between that news and being hit across the head with a two-by-four, I would have gone for the board.

I lobbied long and hard for a disposal and an automatic dishwasher, knowing full well that they had been invented so that *nobody* would *ever* have to touch the gunk again.

Never mind what any parent or objective adult might tell me, I knew that the stuff in the sink drainer was lethal and septic. It would give you leprosy, or something worse. If you should ever accidentally touch it, you must never touch any other part of your body with your finger until you had scalded and soaped and rinsed your hands. Even worse, I knew that the stuff could congeal and mush up and mutate into some living thing that would crawl out of the sink during the night and get loose in the house.

Why not just use rubber gloves, you ask? Oh, come on. Rubber gloves are for sissies. Besides, my mother used her bare hands, remember. My father never came closer than three feet to the sink in his life. My mother said he was lazy. But I knew that he knew what I knew about the gunk.

Once, after dinner, I said to him that I bet Jesus never had to wash dishes and clean the gunk out of the sink. He agreed. It was the only theological discussion we ever had.

My father, however, would take a plunger to the toilet when it was stopped up with even worse stuff. I wouldn't even go in the room when he did it. I didn't want to know.

But now. Now, I am a grown-up. And have been for some time. And I imagine making a speech to a high school graduating class. First, I would ask them, "How many of you would like to be an adult, an independent, on-your-own citizen?" All would raise their hands with some enthusiasm. And then I would give them this list of things that grown-ups do:

—clean the sink strainer
—plunge out the toilet
—clean up babies when they poop and pee
—wipe runny noses
—clean up the floor when the baby throws strained spinach
—clean ovens and grease traps and roasting pans
—empty the kitty box and scrape up the dog doo
—carry out the garbage
—pump out the bilges
—bury dead pets when they get run over in the street

I'd tell the graduates that when they can do these things, they will be adults. Some of the students might not want to go on at this point. But they may as well face the truth.

It can get even worse than the list suggests. My wife is a doctor, and I won't tell you what she tells me she has to do sometimes. I wish I didn't know. I feel ill at ease sometimes being around someone who does those things. And also proud.

A willingness to do your share of cleaning up the mess is a test. And taking out the garbage of this life is a condition of membership in a community.

When you are a kid, you feel that if they really loved you, they wouldn't ever ask you to take out the garbage. When you join the ranks of the grown-ups, you take out the garbage because you love them. And by "them" I mean not only your own family, but the family of mankind.

The old cliché holds firm and true.
Being an adult *is* dirty work
But someone has to do it.

Robert Fulghum

Teenagers' Bill of Rights

Our Rights with Friends:

We all have the right and the privilege to have friends. We can choose our friends based on our own likes and dislikes. We don't have to like the same people everyone else likes or not like someone because they aren't in our "group." Friendship is a personal thing.

We can ask from our friends that they be trustworthy. If we share something with them and ask them not to tell everyone, we can expect that they will keep it just between us. We will give them the same right. If they don't, they have betrayed our trust and our friendship.

It is okay to be honest with our friends. If they do something that hurts us or concerns us, we can talk to them about it. We will be open to their being honest also. This does not mean it is okay to be mean to each other, just that we can talk honestly about our feelings.

We have the right to be respected for the decisions we make. Some of our friends may not understand the choices we make, but they are our choices. In return, we take responsibility for them.

With Parents and Other Adults:

We have the right to have our feelings respected and not compared to the feelings of puppies . . . or any other such put downs. Our feelings are strong and sometimes confusing. It helps if you take our feelings seriously and listen to us before disregarding them.

We feel we have the right to make decisions (some, not all) for ourselves. If we make mistakes we will learn from them, but it is time for us to be more responsible.

Whenever possible, exclude us from your fights. We understand that fighting is part of every relationship, but it is painful for us to be involved. Don't put us in the middle of *any* problem you have with each other.

We agree to treat you with respect and ask that you respect us in return. This includes respecting our privacy.

With Everyone:

We have the right to be loved unconditionally, and our goal is to love you the same.

We have the right to speak our minds, love ourselves, feel our feelings, and strive for our dreams. Please support us by believing in us rather than fearing for us.

Lia Gay, 16; Jamie Yellin, 14;
Lisa Gumenick, 14; Hana Ivanhoe, 15;
Bree Able, 15; Lisa Rothbard, 14

The Boy Who Talked with Dolphins

From what we get we can make a living, what we give, however, makes a life.

Arthur Ashe

It began as a deep rumble, shattering the predawn silence. Within minutes on that January morning in 1994, the Los Angeles area was in the grip of one of the most destructive earthquakes in its history.

At Six Flags Magic Mountain theme park, 20 miles north of the city, three dolphins were alone with their terror. They swam frantically in circles as heavy concrete pillars collapsed around their pool and roof tiles crashed into the water.

Forty miles to the south, 26-year-old Jeff Siegel was thrown from his bed with a jarring thump. Crawling to the window, Jeff looked out at the convulsing city and thought of the creatures who mattered more to him than anything else in the world. *I've got to get to the dolphins,* he told himself. *They rescued me, and now they need me to rescue them.*

To those who had known Jeff from childhood, a more unlikely hero could not have been imagined.

Jeff Siegel was born hyperactive, partially deaf and lacking normal coordination. Since he couldn't hear words clearly, he developed a severe speech impediment that made it almost impossible for others to understand him. As a preschooler, the small, sandy-haired child was taunted as a "retard" by other kids.

Even home was no refuge. Jeff's mother was unprepared to deal with his problems. Raised in a rigid, authoritarian household, she was overly strict and often angry at his differences. She simply wanted him to fit in. His father, a police officer in their middle-class Los Angeles community of Torrance, worked extra jobs to make ends meet and was often gone 16 hours a day.

Anxious and frightened on the first day of kindergarten, five-year-old Jeff climbed over the schoolyard fence and ran home. Furious, his mother hauled him back to school and forced him to apologize to the teacher. The entire class overheard. As the mispronounced and barely intelligible words were dragged out of him, he became instant prey for his classmates. To fend off the hostile world, Jeff kept to isolated corners of the playground and hid in his room at home, dreaming of a place where he could be accepted.

Then one day when Jeff was nine, he went with his fourth-grade class to Los Angeles' Marineland. At the dolphin show, he was electrified by the energy and exuberant friendliness of the beautiful animals. They seemed to smile directly at him, something that happened rarely in his life. The boy sat transfixed, overwhelmed with emotion and a longing to stay.

By the end of that school year, Jeff's teachers had labeled him emotionally disturbed and learning-disabled. But testing at the nearby Switzer Center for children with disabilities showed Jeff to be average-to-bright, though so anxiety-ridden that his math test score came out borderline retarded. He transferred from public school to the

Center. Over the next two years he became less anxious, and his academic achievement improved dramatically.

At the start of seventh grade he returned, unwillingly, to public school. Tests now showed his I.Q. in the 130s, the gifted range. And years of therapy had improved his speech. But to his classmates, Jeff was still the same victim.

Seventh grade was unfolding as the worst year of Jeff's life—until the day his father took him to Sea World in San Diego. The minute the boy saw the dolphins, the same rush of joy welled up in him. He stayed rooted to the spot as the sleek mammals glided past.

Jeff worked to earn money for an annual pass to Marineland, closer to his home. On his first solo visit, he sat on the low wall surrounding the dolphin pool. The dolphins, accustomed to being fed by visitors, soon approached the astonished boy. The first to swim over was Grid Eye, the dominant female in the pool. The 650-pound dolphin glided to where Jeff sat and remained motionless below him. *Will she let me touch her?* he wondered, putting his hand in the water. As he stroked the dolphin's smooth skin, Grid Eye inched closer. It was a moment of sheer ecstasy for the young boy.

The outgoing animals quickly became the friends Jeff never had, and since the dolphin area was isolated at the far end of Marineland, Jeff often found himself alone with the playful creatures.

One day Sharky, a young female, glided just below the surface until her tail was in Jeff's hand. She stopped. *Now what?* he wondered. Suddenly Sharky dived a foot or so below the surface, pulling Jeff's hand and arm underwater. He laughed and pulled back without letting go. The dolphin dived again, deeper. Jeff pulled back harder. It was like a game of tug-of-war.

When Sharky surfaced to breathe, boy and dolphin faced each other for a minute, Jeff laughing and the dolphin open-mouthed and grinning. Then Sharky circled and put her tail back in Jeff's hand to start the game again.

The boy and the 300-to-800 pound animals often played tag, with Jeff and the dolphins racing around the pool to slap a predetermined point or give each other hand-to-flipper high-fives. To Jeff, the games were a magical connection that he alone shared with the animals.

Even when there were summer crowds of 500 around the pool, the gregarious creatures recognized their friend and swam to him whenever he wiggled his hand in the water. Jeff's acceptance by the dolphins boosted his confidence, and he gradually emerged from his dark shell. He enrolled in a course at a nearby aquarium and devoured books on marine biology. He became a walking encyclopedia on dolphins and, to his family's amazement, braved his speech impediment to become a volunteer tour guide.

In 1983 Jeff wrote an article for the American Cetacean Society's newsletter, describing his experiences with Marineland dolphins. He was unprepared for what followed. Embarrassed by the extent to which he'd been playing with the dolphins without the park's knowledge, Marineland management revoked his pass. Jeff returned home numb with disbelief.

For their part, Jeff's parents were relieved. They could see no benefit to the time their strange, misfit son was spending with dolphins until a day in June 1984 when Bonnie Siegel took an unexpected long-distance phone call. That evening she asked her son, "Did you enter some kind of contest?"

Sheepishly, Jeff confessed that he'd written an essay for a highly coveted Earthwatch scholarship worth more than $2,000. The winner would spend a month in Hawaii with dolphin experts. Now, telling his mother about it, he expected a tirade. Instead, she said quietly, "Well, you won."

Jeff was ecstatic. Best of all, it was the first time that his parents realized he might achieve his dream of someday sharing his love of dolphins.

Jeff spent the month in Hawaii, teaching dolphins strings of commands to test their memories. In the fall, he fulfilled another condition of the scholarship by giving a talk on marine mammals to fellow students at Torrance High School. Jeff's report was so enthusiastic that it earned him, at last, grudging respect from his peers.

After graduation, Jeff struggled to find work in marine research, supplementing the low pay with minimum-wage moonlighting. He also earned an associate's degree in biology.

In February 1992 he showed up in the office of Suzanne Fortier, director of marine-animal training at Six Flags Magic Mountain. Though holding down two jobs, he wanted to do volunteer work with Magic Mountain's dolphins on his days off. Fortier gave him the chance—and was immediately amazed. Of the 200 volunteers she'd trained in 10 years, she'd never seen anyone with Jeff's intuitive ability with dolphins.

In one instance, her crew needed to move a sick 600-pound dolphin named Thunder to another park. The animal had to be transported in a nine-by-three-foot tank. During the journey, Jeff insisted on riding in the truck bed with Thunder's tank to try to calm the anxious animal. When Fortier later called from the cab of the truck to ask how Thunder was doing, Jeff replied, "He's fine now. I'm cradling him." *Jeff's actually in the tank with Thunder!* Fortier realized. For four hours, Jeff floated inside the cool tank, holding Thunder in his arms.

Jeff continued to amaze co-workers with his rapport with the animals. His favorite at Magic Mountain was Katie, a 350-pound, eight-year-old dolphin who greeted him exuberantly and swam with him for hours.

Once again, as at Marineland, Jeff could interact with the dolphins and find affection in return. Little did he dream how severely his love would be tested.

As Jeff struggled to reach Magic Mountain on the morning of the earthquake, freeways were collapsing, and caved-in roads often forced him to backtrack. *Nothing is going to stop me,* he vowed.

When Jeff finally reached Magic Mountain, the water in the 12-foot-deep dolphin pool was halfway down, and more was draining from the crack in the side. The three dolphins there when the quake hit—Wally, Teri and Katie—were in a frenzy. Jeff lowered himself to a ledge five feet down and tried to calm them.

To ease the dolphins through the continuing tremors, Jeff attempted to distract them by playing games, but it didn't work. Worse, he had to reduce their food: The pool's filtration system had shut down, creating the additional risk that an accumulation of their body waste would further contaminate the water.

Jeff remained with the dolphins that night as temperatures fell into the 30s. He was still there through the next day, and the next, and the next.

On the fourth day a road opened, and staffers secured a truck to transfer Wally, Teri and Katie to the dolphin pool at Knott's Berry Farm. But first, someone had to get them into their transport tanks. Transporting a dolphin is normally a routine procedure, after it has been safely guided through a tunnel and hoisted on a canvas sling. But the water level in the connecting tunnel was too low for the animals to swim through. The three dolphins would have to be caught in open water and then maneuvered into canvas slings.

Staffer Etienne Francois and Jeff volunteered for the jobs. As much as he trusted the dolphins, Jeff knew the likelihood of getting hurt or bitten by them in an open-water capture was almost 100 percent.

Wally was easily removed from the pool, but Teri and Katie became erratic. Each time Jeff and Etienne closed in on Katie, the powerful dolphin fended them off with her hard, pointed beak.

For almost 40 minutes the men struggled as Katie butted and whacked them with her thrashing tail. Finally, just before they maneuvered her into a sling, she sank her needle-sharp teeth into Jeff's hand. Ignoring the bleeding, Jeff helped capture Teri and hoist her into the transport tank.

When the dolphins reached Knott's Berry Farm, Katie was exhausted but calm. Later, Fortier told friends that Jeff's courage and leadership had been essential in safely transporting the dolphins.

Today, Jeff is a full-time dolphin trainer at Marine Animal Productions in Gulfport, Mississippi, where he organizes programs for schools.

One day, before he left for Mississippi, Jeff gave a demonstration to 60 children from the Switzer Center at one of the aquariums where he had taught. He saw that a boy named Larry slipped off to play alone. Realizing Larry was an outcast, as he himself had been, Jeff called him forward and asked the boy to stand next to him. Then Jeff plunged his arms into a nearby tank and hauled up a harmless but impressive three-foot horn shark. As the children gasped, he allowed Larry to carry the dripping creature proudly around the room.

After the session, Jeff received a letter reading: "Thank you for the magnificent job you did with our children. They came back glowing from the experience. Several told me about Larry getting to carry the shark. This was probably the happiest and proudest moment of his life! The fact that you were once a student here added to it. You are a model of hope that they, too, can 'make it' in life." The letter was from Janet Switzer, the Center's founder.

For Jeff, that afternoon held an even more gratifying moment. As he spoke, he saw his mother and father in the audience, watching intently. From the look on their faces, Jeff could tell they were proud of their son at last.

Jeff has never earned more than $14,800 a year in his life, yet he considers himself a rich man and an exceptionally lucky one. "I'm completely fulfilled," he says. "The dolphins did so much for me when I was a child. They gave me unconditional love. When I think about what I owe the dolphins . . ." His voice trails off momentarily, and he smiles. "They gave me life. I owe them everything."

Paula McDonald

Wild Thing

Face the thing you fear, and you do away with that fear.

Source Unknown

With the wind biting my face and the rain soaking though my clothes, it didn't seem like July. I watched a puddle form at the foot of my sleeping bag as the 10-foot plastic sheet jerry-rigged above me gave way to the wind. I hadn't eaten for almost a day, and a rumble in my stomach demanded why I was in the Northern Cascades of Oregon—alone, soaked—in the first place. With two more days alone in the wilds ahead of me, I had plenty of time to think about that question.

I'd always been impressed by people who had been in Outward Bound, basically because I'd always lumped myself in the I-could-never-do-that category. For one thing, I just assumed I was too small and urban; I'm no granola. I also wasn't a big risk-taker. I'd always relied a lot on my family, friends and boyfriend, and I evaluated myself on how well I met their expectations of me.

Signing up for an Outward Bound course the summer

after my junior year in high school was a chance to break away from that. After all, the courses are described as "adventure-based education programs that promote self-discovery through tough, outdoor activities." Exactly what I needed; I'd be facing challenges away from my usual supporters. As the starting date approached, though, I became increasingly terrified. I'd never attempted mountain climbing, white-water rafting, back-packing, rappelling or rock climbing, and I was plagued by fears that I'd fail at one or all of them. I begged my mother to cancel for me. No such luck.

I shouldn't have worried so much. For most of the people on the course, it was their first time with Outward Bound, too. Then again, the course was pretty hard because I had to adjust to a different way of day-to-day living.

For starters, I've always been a big fan of showers. I usually take one a day, and it was tough to forgo this ritual for three weeks. I also never realized how handy toilets were until they disappeared from my life, toilet paper and all. (We used leaves and snow.) On the whole, though, these inconveniences seemed less important as the course progressed. Besides, I was far too busy to sit around and watch my leg hair grow.

The first week, my group rafted 100 miles down the Deschutes River. I was soaked, shocked and exhilarated. Then we climbed Mount Jefferson, the second highest peak in Oregon. Every time I gazed at that snowy, 10,000-foot peak, I felt a combination of panic and delight. The delight faded, however, the first time I strapped on my backpack. It was so heavy that I needed someone to help me put it on. And then I could barely walk in a straight line. Eventually, I got the hang of it and could actually feel myself getting stronger. Somehow we made it up Mount Jefferson in five days. At the peak, I decided I could do anything I set my mind to, which was good since the solo component of my course—that three-day bonding session with myself—was next.

For solo, my instructors dropped me off in a clearing in the woods with very little equipment and minimal food. I was alone with a pencil, some paper and my thoughts. Sure, I was bored at first and a little scared, but honestly, it was one of the coolest things I've ever done. I realized how little time I actually spent alone, and I kind of enjoyed my own company.

Overall, during the three weeks of my course, I became a new woman. I discovered parts of myself that I had no idea existed. I can't even count the times that I thought I couldn't give any more, and somehow I'd find the strength to carry out the task at hand, and carry it out well. I loved that feeling, and I didn't lose it. Back home, my grades soared with this realization that personal limits didn't have to exist unless I let them.

My experiences with Outward Bound are invaluable, but that doesn't mean I'm going to give up my dreams of a career (and modern plumbing) and live in the woods. I will, however, forever be grateful for what I got out of the course: Before I went I always thought, *I can't do this.* Now I think, *I'm not afraid to try.*

Jennifer Philbin

To Track Down My Dream

It was the district track meet—the one we had been training for all season. My foot still hadn't healed from an earlier injury. As a matter of fact, I had debated whether or not I should attend the meet. But there I was, preparing for the 3,200-meter run.

"Ready . . . set . . ." The gun popped and we were off. The other girls darted ahead of me. I realized I was limping and felt humiliated as I fell farther and farther behind.

The first-place runner was two laps ahead of me when she crossed the finish line. "Hooray!" shouted the crowd. It was the loudest cheer I had ever heard at a meet.

"Maybe I should quit," I thought as I limped on. "Those people don't want to wait for me to finish this race." Somehow, though, I decided to keep going. During the last two laps, I ran in pain and decided not to compete in track next year. It wouldn't be worth it, even if my foot *did* heal. I could never beat the girl who lapped me twice.

When I finished, I heard a cheer—just as enthusiastic as the one I'd heard when the first girl passed the finish line. "What was that all about?" I asked myself. I turned around and sure enough, the boys were preparing for their race. "That must be it; they're cheering for the boys."

I went straight to the bathroom where a girl bumped into me. "Wow, you've got courage!" she told me.

I thought, "Courage? She must be mistaking me for someone else. I just lost a race!"

"I would have never been able to finish those two miles if I were you. I would have quit on the first lap. What happened to your foot? We were cheering for you. Did you hear us?"

I couldn't believe it. A complete stranger had been cheering for me—not because she wanted me to win, but because she wanted me to keep going and not give up. Suddenly I regained hope. I decided to stick with track next year. One girl saved my dream.

That day I learned two things:

First, a little kindness and confidence in people can make a great difference to them.

And second, strength and courage aren't always measured in medals and victories. They are measured in the struggles we overcome. The strongest people are not always the people who win, but the people who don't give up when they lose.

I only dream that someday—perhaps as a senior—I will be able to win the race with a cheer as big as the one I got when I lost the race as a freshman.

Ashley Hodgeson

From Crutches to a World-Class Runner

A number of years ago in Elkhart, Kansas, two brothers had a job at the local school. Early each morning their job was to start a fire in the potbellied stove in the classroom.

One cold morning, the brothers cleaned out the stove and loaded it with firewood. Grabbing a can of kerosene, one of them doused the wood and lit the fire. The explosion rocked the old building. The fire killed the older brother and badly burned the legs of the other boy. It was later discovered that the kerosene can had accidentally been filled with gasoline.

The doctor attending the injured boy recommended amputating the young boy's legs. The parents were devastated. They had already lost one son, and now their other son was to lose his legs. But they did not lose their faith. They asked the doctor for a postponement of the amputation. The doctor consented. Each day they asked the doctor for a delay, praying that their son's legs would somehow heal and he would become well again. For two months, the parents and the doctor debated on whether to amputate. They used this time to instill in the boy the belief that he would someday walk again.

They never amputated the boy's legs, but when the bandages were finally removed, it was discovered that his right leg was almost three inches shorter than the other. The toes on his left foot were almost completely burned off. Yet the boy was fiercely determined. Though in excruciating pain, he forced himself to exercise daily and finally took a few painful steps. Slowly recovering, this young man finally threw away his crutches and began to walk almost normally. Soon he was running.

This determined young man kept running and running and running—and those legs that came so close to being amputated carried him to a world record in the mile run. His name? Glenn Cunningham, who was known as the "World's Fastest Human Being," and was named athlete of the century at Madison Square Garden.

The Speaker's Sourcebook

If

If you can keep your head when all about you
Are losing theirs and blaming it on you;
If you can trust yourself when all men doubt you,
But make allowance for their doubting too;
If you can wait and not be tired by waiting,
Or being lied about, don't deal in lies,
Or being hated don't give way to hating,
And yet don't look too good, nor talk too wise;

If you can dream—and not make dreams your master;
If you can think—and not make thought your aim,
If you can meet with Triumph and Disaster
And treat those two impostors just the same;
If you can bear to hear the truth you've spoken
Twisted by knaves to make a trap for fools,
Or watch the things you gave your life to; broken,
And stoop and build 'em up with worn-out tools;

If you can make one heap of all your winnings
And risk it on one turn of pitch-and-toss,
And lose, and start again at your beginnings,

And never breathe a word about your loss;
If you can force your heart and nerve and sinew
To serve your turn long after they are gone,
And so hold on when there is nothing in you
Except the Will which says to them: "Hold on!"

If you can talk with crowds and keep your virtue,
Or walk with Kings—nor lose the common touch,
If neither foes nor loving friends can hurt you,
If all men count with you, but none too much;
If you can fill the unforgiving minute
With sixty seconds worth of distance run,
Yours is the Earth and everything that's in it,
And—which is more—you'll be a Man, my son!

Rudyard Kipling

No-Hair Day

Whatever you are doing, love yourself for doing it. Whatever you are feeling, love yourself for feeling it.

Thadeus Golas

If you are turning 16, you stand in front of the mirror scrutinizing every inch of your face. You agonize that your nose is too big and you're getting another pimple—on top of which you are feeling dumb, your hair isn't blonde, and that boy in your English class has not noticed you yet.

Alison never had those problems. Two years ago, she was a beautiful, popular and smart eleventh-grader, not to mention a varsity lacrosse goalie and an ocean lifeguard. With her tall, slender body, pool-blue eyes and thick blonde hair, she looked more like a swimsuit model than a high school student. But during that summer, something changed.

After a day of life-guarding, Alison couldn't wait to get home, rinse the saltwater out of her hair and comb through the tangles. She flipped her sun-bleached mane forward. "Ali!" her mother cried, "what did you do?" She discovered a bare patch of skin on the top of her daughter's scalp. "Did you shave it? Could someone else have done it while you were sleeping?" Quickly, they solved the mystery—Alison must have wrapped the elastic band too tightly around her pony tail. The incident was soon forgotten.

Three months later, another bald spot was found, then another. Soon, Alison's scalp was dotted with peculiar quarter-sized bare patches. After diagnoses of "it's just stress" with remedies of topical ointments, a specialist began to administer injections of cortisone, 50 to each spot, every two weeks. To mask her scalp, bloody from the shots, Alison was granted permission to wear a baseball hat to school, normally a violation of the strict uniform code. Little strands of hair would push through the scabs, only to fall out two weeks later. She was suffering from a condition of hair loss known as alopecia, and nothing would stop it.

Alison's sunny spirit and supportive friends kept her going, but there were some low points. Like the time when her little sister came into her bedroom with a towel wrapped around her head to have her hair combed. When her mother untwisted the towel, Alison watched the tousled thick hair bounce around her sister's shoulders. Gripping all of her limp hair between two fingers, she burst into tears. It was the first time she had cried since the whole experience began.

As time went on a bandanna replaced the hat, which could no longer conceal her balding scalp. With only a handful of wispy strands left, the time had come to buy a wig. Instead of trying to resurrect her once-long blonde hair, pretending as though nothing had been lost, Alison opted for a shoulder-length auburn one. Why not? People cut and dyed their hair all the time. With her new look, Alison's confidence strengthened. Even when the wig blew off from an open window of her friend's car, they all shared in the humor.

But as the summer approached, Alison worried. If she couldn't wear a wig in the water, how could she lifeguard again? "Why—did you forget how to swim?" her father asked. She got the message.

After wearing an uncomfortable bathing cap for only one day, she mustered up the courage to go completely bald. Despite the stares and occasional comments from less-than-polite beachcombers—"Why do you crazy punk kids shave your heads?"—Alison adjusted to her new look.

She arrived back at school that fall with no hair, no eyebrows, no eyelashes, and with her wig tucked away somewhere in the back of her closet. As she had always planned, she would run for school president, changing her campaign speech only slightly. Presenting a slide show on famous bald leaders from Gandhi to Mr. Clean, Alison had the students and faculty rolling in the aisles.

In her first speech as the elected president, Alison addressed her condition, quite comfortable answering questions. Dressed in a T-shirt with the words "Bad Hair Day" printed across the front, she pointed to her shirt and said, "When most of you wake up in the morning and don't like how you look, you may put on this T-shirt." Putting on another T-shirt over the other, she continued. "When I wake up in the morning, I put on this one." It read, "No-Hair Day." Everybody cheered and applauded. And Alison, beautiful, popular and smart—not to mention varsity goalie, ocean lifeguard and now, school president with the pool-blue eyes—smiled back from the podium.

Jennifer Rosenfeld and Alison Lambert

I Did It!

The task ahead of us is never as great as the power behind us.

Alcoholics Anonymous

MAY 1989

My high school graduation was only one month away, and I was more determined than ever to roll across the graduation stage in my manual wheelchair. You see, I was born with a disease called cerebral palsy and because of it, am not able to walk. In order to practice for graduation, I began using my manual wheelchair daily at school.

It was very difficult pushing myself around campus all day while lugging four or five school books, but I did it. During the first couple of days of using my manual wheelchair at school, everyone offered to give me a push from class to class, but after a few times of my teasingly remarking, "I don't need your help or want your pity," everyone got the hint and let me huff and puff myself around school.

I had always received tremendous satisfaction from using my manual wheelchair, but when I began to push myself around school, the personal rewards were far greater than I ever imagined. I not only saw myself differently, but my classmates, too, seemed to view me on a different level. My classmates knew of my perseverance and determination and respected me because of them. I couldn't have been more pleased about the emotional and physical liberation that my insistence on using my manual wheelchair was bringing to my life.

My electric wheelchair was a tremendous source of freedom for me while I was growing up. It gave me the independence to move about in ways that I was not able to do under my own power. However, as I became older, I realized that the electric wheelchair that had once given me so much freedom was quickly becoming an obstacle of confinement. I felt that I was an independent person except for the fact that I was limited by my dependency on my electric wheelchair. The very thought of being dependent on anything for the rest of my life frustrated me.

To me, graduating from high school in my manual wheelchair was a symbolic point in my life. I wanted to enter my future as an independent young man—I was not going to allow myself to be carried across the graduation stage by an electric wheelchair. I didn't care if it took me 20 minutes to push across the stage, I was going to do it.

JUNE 14, 1989

Graduation. That evening all of the graduates marched around the pavilion in caps and gowns and to our seats on the stage. I sat proudly in my manual wheelchair among the first row of my graduating class.

When the announcer called my name, I realized that everything I had striven for as a child was now a reality. The independent life that I had worked so hard for was now within my grasp.

I pushed myself ever so slowly toward the front of the stage. I looked up from my concentration on pushing my wheelchair and realized that everyone on the pavilion was giving me a standing ovation. I proudly accepted my diploma, turned to my fellow classmates, held my diploma above my head, and yelled as loud as I could, "I did it . . . I did it!"

Mark E. Smith

Growing

I'm leaving now to slay the foe—
Fight the battles, high and low.
I'm leaving, Mother, hear me go!
Please wish me luck today.

I've grown my wings, I want to fly,
Seize my victories where they lie.
I'm going, Mom, but please don't cry—
Just let me find my way.

I want to see and touch and hear,
Though there are dangers, there are fears.
I'll smile my smiles and dry my tears—
Please let me speak my say.

I'm off to find my world, my dreams,
Carve my niche, sew my seams,
Remember, as I sail my streams—
I'll love you, all the way.

Brooke Mueller

New Beginnings

June, 1996

Dear Graduate,

Well, this is it! Graduation is over and you're ready to begin life's journey! I know you have lots of mixed feelings. That's the weird thing about most of life's big moments—very rarely do they consist of one emotion. But that's okay. It helps to make the good times more precious and the not-so-good times bearable.

I've spent a lot of time trying to figure out what sage advice I could pass along. That's one of the hard parts about being a parent—determining what should be said and what should be left for you to discover. I finally decided just to offer a little insight to life's basic questions. Some people go through their whole lives without ever giving them any thought. Too bad—as you search for the answers, you can make some wonderful discoveries. They can also be frustrating; just when you think you've found the answer, you'll find the need to ask another question. (Which explains why even at my incredibly advanced age, I still don't have any answers!) At any rate, I hope that sharing this little piece of myself and my soul will somehow help to carry you through when the questions come along.

Who? It took me a while to realize that this is probably the most important question of all. Take time to discover who you are and be your own person. Strive to be honest, respectful and happy. When you are at peace with yourself, everything else will fall into place. Just be careful not to wrap your identity in possessions. Allow yourself to grow and change. And remember always that you are not alone—you have your family, your friends, your guardian angel and God (not necessarily in that order!).

What? This is a tricky one, and at first this question had me fooled. I thought the question was, "What will I do today?" However, I found that things really got interesting when I instead asked, *"What is my passion?"* Discover what it is that burns inside and keeps you going, then nurture it. Take it apart and build it back together. Do whatever you want with it, but never let it from your sight. Do it because that's what you love to do. The joy it brings you will keep you going through some of the doldrums of life.

When? This is the sneaky one. Do not ignore it. It will keep you balanced. Some things are best done now. Procrastination usually just creates more work. But keep in mind that there is a season for everything, and some things are better left for another day. As hard as it may be, remember to take time to rest and enjoy the miracle of each new day. With practice, you will learn the pleasure of doing some things now and the unique delight of waiting and planning for others.

Where? Surprisingly, this is the easiest one. You will always have the answer with you if you keep your home in your heart and put your heart into wherever you call home. Be an active part of your community and you will discover the special charm that will endear it to you.

Remember always that the simplest act of kindness can make an enormous difference, and that you *can* change the world.

Why? Never stop asking this one. It's the one that will keep you growing. Let it. Let it challenge you when you've become too complacent. Let it shout at you when you are making decisions. Let it whisper to you when you lose sight of who you are or where you want to be. But you also need to be careful with this one. Sometimes the answer does not come for years, and sometimes it doesn't come at all. Recognizing that basic fact can keep you sane and allow you to move on.

How? Ah, this is the one on which I can't advise you! This is the one you will answer in your own special way. But you've come so far in the past few years, I know that you'll do fine. Just remember to believe in yourself and in miracles. Remember that the greatest discoveries come after stumbling over questions. And please remember—always—that I love you.

Congratulations on your new beginning.

Love,

Mom

Paula (Bachleda) Koskey

More Chicken Soup?

Many of the stories and poems that you have read in this book were submitted by readers like you who have read other *Chicken Soup for the Soul* books. In the near future, we are planning to publish *A 2nd Helping of Chicken Soup for the Teenage Soul, Chicken Soup for a Friend's Soul, Chicken Soup for the Parent's Soul, Chicken Soup for the Pet Lover's Soul* and *Chicken Soup for the Teacher's Soul.* We would love to have you contribute a story, poem, quote or cartoon to one of these future books.

This may be a story you write yourself or one you clip out of the school newspaper, the local newspaper, a church bulletin or a magazine. It might be something you read in a book or find on the Internet. It could also be a favorite poem, quotation or cartoon you have saved. Please send us as much information as possible about where it came from.

Send a copy of your stories or other pieces to us in an envelope marked with the name of the particular book to which you are submitting at this address:

Chicken Soup for the Soul
P.O. Box 30880 • Santa Barbara, CA 93130
phone: 800-237-8336 • fax: 805-563-2945
e-mail: soup4soul@aol.com

We are also compiling a book entitled *The Chicken Soup for the Soul Letters,* in which we will publish letters, stories and poems about how the stories in all the *Chicken Soup for the Soul* books have impacted people's lives. Please write to us and tell us how these stories have made a difference in your life at home, at school, at work and with your friends. We would love to hear from you.

You can also contact us at the above address for speaking engagements and for a brochure describing our other books, tapes and workshops, or visit our Web site at http://www.chickensoup.com.

Supporting Teenagers

In the spirit of supporting teenagers everywhere, we have selected the following organizations to receive a portion of the profits that are generated from the sale of this book:

Challenge Days is a program committed to making our schools and the world a better place for children. To end teasing, violence and oppression on campus, adults and youth are brought together. Hearts and minds are opened, unleashing the power to create positive change. To book workshops or receive information, contact:

Challenge Associates
P.O. Box 23824 • Pleasant Hill, CA 94523
phone: 510-930-6206 • fax: 510-935-3120

The Yellow Ribbon Project is a nonprofit organization that helps to prevent teen suicides. You can learn more about this organization by reading "I'll Always Be With You" on p. 206.

You may contact this organization for help in setting up a yellow ribbon program in your school or community, or to receive a yellow ribbon for yourself or your friends:

The Yellow Ribbon Project
P.O. Box 644 • Westminster, CO 80030
phone: 303-429-3530 • fax: 303-426-4496
e-mail: light4life@yellowribbon.org
Web site: www.yellowribbon.org

Motivational Media Assemblies (MMA) is a non-profit educational company serving schools in the United States, Canada, Australia and Taiwan. Over the last 11 years, MMA has brought its powerful multimedia programs to 38 million students in 40,000 schools nationwide.

These programs, along with a custom follow-up curriculum have proved to be one of the most powerful tools to facilitate students' positive attitudinal and behavioral changes. Special emphasis is placed on the areas of substance abuse education and conflict resolution.

To receive information about the organization contact:

Motivational Media Assemblies
148 S. Victory • Burbank, CA 91502
phone: 818-848-1980

Who Is Jack Canfield?

Jack Canfield is a bestselling author and one of America's leading experts in the development of human potential. He is both a dynamic and entertaining speaker and a highly sought-after trainer with a wonderful ability to inform and inspire audiences to open their hearts, love more openly and boldly pursue their dreams.

Jack spent his teenage years in Martins Ferry, Ohio, and Wheeling, West Virginia, with his sister Kimberly (Kirberger), and his two brothers, Rick and Taylor. They have all spent most of their professional careers educating, counseling and empowering teens. Rick is a psychotherapist in Phoenix, Arizona, who specialized in working with teens for many years, and Taylor is currently a special-education teacher in Tampa, Florida. Jack admits to being shy and lacking in self-confidence in high school, but through a lot of hard work he managed to earn letters in three sports and graduate third in his class.

After graduating from college, Jack taught high school in the inner city of Chicago and in Iowa. Much of his professional career after that has been spent teaching teachers how to empower teenagers to believe in themselves and to go for their dreams. In recent years Jack has expanded this to include adults in both educational and corporate settings.

He is the author and narrator of several bestselling audio- and videocassette programs, including *Self-Esteem and Peak Performance, How to Build High Self-Esteem* and *The GOALS Program.* He is a regularly consulted expert for radio and television broadcasts and has published 14 books—all bestsellers within their categories—including 10 *Chicken Soup for the Soul* books, *The Aladdin Factor, Heart at Work, 100 Ways to Build Self-Concept in the Classroom* and *Dare to Win.*

Jack addresses over 100 groups each year. His clients include professional associations, school districts, government agencies, churches and corporations. His clients have included schools and school districts in all 50 states; over 100 education associations including the American School Counselors Association, the California Peer Counselors Association and Californians for a Drug Free Youth; and corporate clients such as AT&T, Campbell Soup, Clairol, Domino's Pizza, GE, New England Telephone, Re/Max, Sunkist, Supercuts and Virgin Records.

Jack conducts an annual eight-day Training of Trainers program in the areas of building self-esteem and achieving peak performance. It attracts educators, counselors, parenting trainers, corporate trainers, professional speakers, ministers and others interested in developing their speaking and seminar leading skills in these areas.

For further information about Jack's books, tapes and training programs, or to schedule him for a presentation, please contact:

The Canfield Training Group
P.O. Box 30880 • Santa Barbara, CA 93130
phone: 800-237-8336 • fax: 805-563-2945
e-mail: soup4soul@aol.com

Who Is Mark Victor Hansen?

Mark Victor Hansen is a professional speaker who, in the last 20 years, has made over 4,000 presentations to more than 2 million people in 32 countries. His presentations cover sales excellence and strategies; personal empowerment and development; and how to triple your income and double your time off.

Mark has spent a lifetime dedicated to his mission of making a profound and positive difference in people's lives. Throughout his career, he has inspired hundreds of thousands of people to create a more powerful and purposeful future for themselves while stimulating the sale of billions of dollars worth of goods and services.

Mark is a prolific writer and has authored *Future Diary, How to Achieve Total Prosperity* and *The Miracle of Tithing.* He is coauthor of the *Chicken Soup for the Soul* series, *Dare to Win* and *The Aladdin Factor* (all with Jack Canfield) and *The Master Motivator* (with Joe Batten).

Mark has also produced a complete library of personal empowerment audio- and videocassette programs that have enabled his listeners to recognize and use their innate abilities in their business and personal lives. His message has made him a popular television and radio personality, with appearances on ABC, NBC, CBS, HBO, PBS and CNN. He has also appeared on the cover of numerous magazines, including *Success, Entrepreneur* and *Changes.*

Mark is a big man with a heart and spirit to match—an inspiration to all who seek to better themselves.

You can contact Mark at:

P.O. Box 7665
Newport Beach, CA 92658
phone: 714-759-9304 or 800-433-2314
fax: 714-722-6912

Who Is Kimberly Kirberger?

Kimberly Kirberger has enjoyed many successes in her life, but the one of which she is most proud is being called friend by many teenagers. When she began compiling *Chicken Soup for the Teenage Soul* with Jack and Mark, she decided that all the final decisions should be made by teenagers themselves. To accomplish this, she convened and worked with a group of teens who first identified the issues they wanted to see covered and then helped her select the stories that best covered them. The most important thing to Kimberly was that this book be for teenagers and teenagers only.

Kimberly is the managing editor of the *Chicken Soup for the Soul* series of books. She works closely with the authors, coauthors, editors and contributors, making sure the books all contain that special *Chicken Soup* magic. Since there are currently over 30 *Chicken Soup* books being written, compiled and edited, she has her hands full.

Kimberly is also an internationally respected jewelry designer and creator of the Kimberly Kirberger Collection. It is sold in 150 of the finest boutiques and department stores in the nation, including Nordstrom. Most recently she has become known for her "Charms for the Soul," which contain inspirational quotes inspired by the *Chicken Soup for the Soul* series. She has designed jewelry for numerous television shows and movies, including *Melrose Place, Friends* and *Mrs. Doubtfire.*

Kimberly is also proud to call Jack Canfield her brother and confirms that from the time they were both young, she knew he would do something great and kind. She recalls how he used to come home from college and engage her in stories that both entertained and taught lessons.

Kimberly is the coauthor of the forthcoming *Chicken Soup for the Parent's Soul* and *A 2nd Helping of Chicken Soup for the Teenage Soul.* For further information about Kimberly's jewelry or future *Chicken Soup* books, please contact:

Kimberly Kirberger
P.O. Box 936 • Pacific Palisades, CA 90272
phone: 310-573-3656 • fax: 310-573-3657
e-mail: jewels24@aol.com

Contributors

Several of the stories in this book were taken from books or magazines we have read. These sources are acknowledged in the Permissions section. Many of the stories and poems were contributed by authors and professional speakers who specialize in working with teens. If you would like to contact them for information on their books, tapes and seminars, you can reach them at the addresses and phone numbers provided below.

Most of the stories were contributed by readers like yourself who had read our previous *Chicken Soup for the Soul* books and who responded to our request for stories.

Over half of these stories were written by teens. We have included information about them as well.

Dr. Eric Allenbaugh is a management consultant, a national keynote speaker and bestselling author of *Wake-Up Calls: You Don't Have to Sleepwalk Through Your Life, Love or Career.* Eric has been a guest on nearly 300 television and radio talk shows regarding leadership and life issues. His seminars are frequently described as "life changing." He can be reached at Allenbaugh Associates, Inc., in Lake Oswego, Oregon, at 503-635-3963 or via e-mail at eric@allenbaugh.com.

Kif Anderson is establishing a reputation as a unique speaker who blends magic, motivation and merriment to lift his audiences to new heights of inspiration. He writes a monthly column for the on-line magazine *Lighten Up! America* and is an author of many works on magic. Kif is presently working on his first major book, titled *Reaching Beyond Perceived Realities.* In 1991 he was honored with the distinguished Comedy Magician of the Year Award. Kif can be reached at P.O. Box 577, Cypress, CA 90630, by e-mail at magicalmotivator @the mall.net, or by calling 562-272-7363.

Rebecca Barry is a freelance writer living in Manhattan. She is a former columnist for *Seventeen* and has contributed to a wide variety of magazines, including *Vogue, Mademoiselle, Swing, Maxim, Cosmopolitan* and *Time Out New York.* She is currently working on a collection of essays and can be reached through Writer's House Literary Agency.

blue jean magazine is an alternative to the beauty- and glamour-focused magazines targeted at young women. *blue jean* is advertising-free and includes no beauty tips, fashion spreads or supermodels. The editorial board, which is the driving force of *blue jean magazine,* is comprised of a diverse group of young women who stay true to what really matters: publishing what young women are thinking, saying and doing. *blue jean* profiles real young women on the verge of changing the world. For more information, call 716-654-5070.

Jason Bocarro is currently pursuing his doctorate at Texas A&M University. Originally from London, England, Jason has spent the last five years working with troubled youths in Nova Scotia, New Hampshire and Texas. He is the coauthor of the monograph *Alternatives to Incarceration: Prevention or Treatment* and is currently working on a new book, *Humorous Stories Within Education.* He can be reached at 306 First St., College Station, TX 77840 or by calling 409-846-8207.

Eva Burke is a student at Central Florida Community College and plans to transfer to the University of Central Florida to finish her degree in social work. Eva has been writing since she was a child, and her first love in writing has always been poetry. She can be reached at P.O. Box 14787, Gainseville, FL 32604.

Dave Carpenter has been a full-time freelance cartoonist and humorous illustrator since 1981. His cartoons have appeared in *Barron's*, the *Wall Street Journal, Forbes, Better Homes & Gardens, Good Housekeeping, Woman's World, First,* the *Saturday Evening Post* and numerous other publications. Dave can be reached at P.O. Box 520, Emmetsburg, IA 50536, phone: 712-852-3725.

Jack Cavanaugh covers sports for the *New York Times.* He also has written extensively for *Sports Illustrated* and a number of other national publications, including *Reader's Digest*, the *Sporting News, Golf Digest, Tennis* magazine and *American Way*, the in-flight publication of American Airlines. As a sportswriter, he has covered hundreds of major sports events, including the Olympics, the World Series, the Super Bowl, scores of title fights, the U.S. Open tennis and golf tournaments, the Masters golf tournament, and the Davis Cup. During a breakaway period from print journalism, he was a news reporter for ABC News for six years and, later, for CBS News for two years. Cavanaugh has taught writing courses at the University of Connecticut and at Norwalk Community and Technical College in Norwalk, Connecticut. His book *Damn the Disabilities: Full Speed Ahead* was published in 1995. He lives in Wilton, Connecticut.

Diana L. Chapman has been a journalist for more than 11 years, working for such newspapers as the *San Diego Union, Los Angeles Copley Newspapers* and the *Los Angeles Times.* She specializes in human interest stories. Diana was diagnosed with multiple sclerosis in 1992 and is currently working on a book involving health issues. She has been married for eight years and has one son, Herbert "Ryan" Hart. She can be reached by calling 310-548-1192 or writing to P.O. Box 414, San Pedro, CA 90733.

Nick Curry III was born in Korea and then adopted by an American family when he was four years old. This all-American boy was president of his class, played soccer and baseball, and "will golf for food"! He attends The Golf Academy of the South in Orlando, Florida, and can be reached on the golf course or at home (4207 Tacon St., Tampa, FL 33629), or by calling 813-831-9444.

Amanda Dykstra is in the ninth grade at Oakland Mills High School in Columbia, Maryland. She has always wanted to be a writer. This is her first published poem. She can be reached at Minerva382@aol.com.

Melissa Esposito wrote this essay while in high school in 1992. She was 16 at the time. Today Melissa is a sophomore in college. She misses her two little sisters, Emma and Kathryn. Kathryn was born after Melissa wrote the essay, and Melissa welcomed her into the family without the anxiety Emma originally created.

Christi Galloway is a freshman nursing student at Tarleton State University in Stephenville, Texas. She graduated from Early High School, Early, TX, in 1996. She is an active member of the First United Methodist Church of Early. She can be reached at P.O. Box 3281, Early, TX 76803.

Jennie Garth has been playing the role of "Kelly" in Fox Television's *Beverly Hills, 90210* for seven years. Among its ensemble cast, Jennie has since become one of the break-out stars of one of the most successful series ever for the Fox network. She began starring in telefilms in 1993, such as Danielle Steel's "Star" and also starred in and was executive producer of "Without Consent" for ABC. She went on to produce her most recent project, "A Loss of Innocence." Jennie was born in Champaign, Illinois, moved to Phoenix when she was 13, and at 15 moved to L.A. with her mother to pursue Jennie's dream of acting.

Lia Gay is a 16-year-old high school student who lives in Santa Monica, California. She loves to write stories and poems, and plans to pursue writing as a career. She played a large part in developing the concept and compiling the stories in this book, and plans to join the author for portions of the book tour. You can reach her through Kimberly Kirberger at 310-573-3655.

Randy Glasbergen has more than 20,000 cartoons and illustrations that have been published by magazines and newspapers around the world. He is also the author of many books. When you're online, be sure to visit "Today's Cartoon by Randy Glasbergen" http://www.norwich.net/~randyg/toon.thml, or e-mail him at randyg@norwich.net.

E. J. Green graduated from college magna cum laude in 1992. After graduation she created her own company. E. J. is continuing her educational process along non-traditional lines. She has achieved Levels I and II certification in pranic energy healing. She conducts breath balancing workshops and is a Tai Chi instructor. E. J. may be reached at 801 Stone St., Clermont, IA 52135, or by calling 319-423-5112.

Lisa Gumenick is a 15-year-old freshman at Palisades High School in Pacific Palisades, California. She lives with her mom, dad and sister. Her older brother attends Brown University. Lisa loves friends, talking, dancing and drawing.

Malcolm Hancock was a freelance cartoonist who was published internationally in publications as diverse as *Playboy, Boy's Life* and *National Review.* A paraplegic following a tragic accident at the age of 17, Mal spent his life communicating the humor in human existence. Mal died in 1993 after a valiant fight against cancer.

Barbara Hauck is currently a sophomore in high school and enjoys her cat, athletics, music, math, computers, writing and drawing. A polo enthusiast, Barbara hopes to attend a college where she can play polo competitively. She can be reached at 13923 Boquita Drive, Del Mar, CA 92014.

Andrea Hensley has worked for the Salvation Army Camps, a program that reaches out to children, for five summers. Currently, Andrea works as a substitute teacher in the Renton School District. Andrea can be reached at 12037 64th Ave. South, Seattle, WA 98178.

Jennifer Love Hewitt stars as Sarah Reeves on the Golden Globe-winning FOX drama series, *Party of Five.* She can be seen on the big screen in three new films this year: *I Know What You Did Last Summer, Trojan War* and *Telling You.* A gifted vocalist, her latest album on Atlantic Records, *Jennifer Love Hewitt,* was released in 1996.

Ashley Hodgson, age 15, began her writing career with a winning personal hero essay in fifth grade. Her writing achievements sparked ambition in other areas: academics (4.0 GPA), speech, track (she has run since sixth grade) and science projects. She can be reached at 810 College, Kennett, MO 63857, phone: 573-888-1581.

Jim Hullihan is an internationally recognized film producer and leadership retreat designer whose motivational media assemblies programs annually appear before 4 million people. As the creator of America's first CD-ROM magazine for teens entitled *Sweet! Digizine,* Jim is the leading motivation expert in U.S. secondary education. He can be reached at 148 S. Victory, Burbank, CA 91502, or by calling 818-848-1980.

Randal Jones is a professional speaker and resident of Re: Think. He teaches seminars on thinking skills and personal management, helping people live and work deliberately for maximum effectiveness and satisfaction. He can be reached at 4307 Lealand Lane, Nashville, TN 37204, or by calling 615-292-8585.

Mary Ellen Klee is an acupuncturist working in Santa Monica, Calif. Since 1971, she has been a student and teacher of the Arica method and practice developed by Oscar Ichazo. She has had a home in Big Sur, Calif., for over 30 years and is a trustee of the Esalen Institute. Starting with a teenage diary, writing has been a hobby and refuge for most of her life.

Paula (Bachleda) Koskey is the happy mother of two wonderful hormone hostages (a.k.a. teenagers), HopeAnne and Luke, and one post teen (whew!), Jesse. She would like to thank her children for all their inspiration and encouragement—and Clairol for covering the gray. She maintains her balance by writing, walking, eating chocolate and believing in miracles. Paula is the author of a children's book entitled *Secrets of Christmas.* She can be reached by writing 1173 Cambridge, Berkley, MI 48072, or by calling 810-542-0376.

Tom Krause has been an educator/coach in Missouri for the past 18 years. His many experiences with students of all ages have led to a collection of short stories and poems. You can contact Tom at P.O. Box 274, Aurora, MO 65605, or call 417-678-4904.

Chris Laddish is a freshman at Terra Linda High School in San Rafael, Calif. He has always enjoyed writing and has won first place in the Philips Literary Writing contest two years in a row. He hopes to become a screenwriter or journalist. Chris enjoys mountain biking, in-line skating and exploring the Internet. He is the youngest of six children and has lived in San Rafael his entire life.

Alison Lambert is a member of the class of 2000 at the University of Pennsylvania in Philadelphia. She is a certified emergency medical technician with the Newtown Square volunteer fire company #1 in Newtown, Pennsylvania. Ali is also an ocean lifeguard in Long Beach Township, New Jersey. She can be reached at 8 Denford Dr., Newtown Square, PA 19073, phone: 610-356-0909, e-mail: alambert@sas.upenn.edu.

A. J. Langer is best known for her role as Rayanne Graff on the groundbreaking ABC drama series *My So-Called Life*. Her story is dedicated with all her love and appreciation to her friends, her kindergarten group.

Katie Leicht is from Indianapolis, Indiana. She attends Cathedral High School and is involved in cheerleading and enjoys volunteering, especially in anti-peer pressure programs for kids. She can be reached at 431 Round Hill Rd., Indianapolis, IN 46260.

Barbara Lewis has won more than 30 awards for excellence in teaching and writing and for her students' projects. She is the author of several books, including *The Kid's Guide to Social Action* and *The Kid's Guide to Service Projects*. She can be contacted through Free Spirit Publishing, 400 First Ave. N., Suite 616, Minneapolis, MN 55401, or by calling 1-800-735-7323.

Jennifer Lohrfink was born and raised in Yonkers, New York. She graduated with a B.A. in English. Currently, she resides in Bronxville, New York. She writes every day.

Jessica Magers is a graduate of Billings Central High School, 1996. She studied Spanish and French, and traveled with Close Up to Washington, D.C. She writes poetry and hopes to someday publish a book of poems. She also anticipates furthering her education. Jessica can be reached at 1245 Rimrock Road, Billings, MT 59102.

Nailah Malik is a multicultural storyteller, literacy advocate and young-adult librarian of the Los Angeles Public Library. Having triumphed over formidable personal challenges, she brings a warmth and passion to her presentations that inspire and empower others. Her emphasis on stories that have practical applications for learning and living has made her a highly sought-after trainer and weaver of tales, and a powerful motivational speaker for students and educators of grade schools, colleges and universities in California. She has earned a B.A. in drama and an M.L.S. from the University of Southern California, and a B.A. in Economics from the University of California, Santa Barbara. Nailah can be reached at P.O. Box 6026-282, Sherman Oaks, CA 91413, or by calling 213-857-8089.

James Malinchak, age 27, is the author of two books for students: *Teenagers Tips for Success* and *From College to the Real World.* He specializes in motivational and inspirational presentations for teenagers and college students worldwide and is being called "America's #1 Teen Motivator." For information on his talks or books, contact him at P.O. Box 3944, Beverly Hills, CA 90212, or call 954-796-1925, or e-mail JamesMal@aol.com.

Paula McDonald has sold over one million copies of her books on relationships, and has won numerous awards worldwide as a columnist, inspirational feature writer and photojournalist. She writes regularly for *Reader's Digest* and other magazines, and has been a guest on many major U.S. television shows, such as *The Today Show* and *Larry King Live.* For Paula, life is an endless adventure to be lived to the fullest. She resides happily on the beach in Rosarito, Mexico. Paula is available as a speaker or writer, and can be contacted through Creative Consultants, 417 W. San Ysidro Blvd., Suite L724, San Ysidro, CA 92173, phone/fax: 011-52-66-313173, e-mail: 102526.356@compuserve.com.

Rick Metzger is a nationally recognized speaker who focuses on how to be the best using the abilities and talents that we each possess. From professional athletics to his current world and national power lifting championships, he understands motivation and setting goals and shares messages with millions. He can be reached at 33 N. Melody Lane, Waterville, OH 43566, or at 1-800-215-TALK (8255).

Chick Moorman is the director of the Institute for Personal Power, a consulting firm dedicated to providing high-quality professional development activities for educators and parents. His latest book, *Where the Heart Is: Stories of Home and Family,* celebrates family strength, love, tolerance, hope and commitment. It can be ordered for $14.95 from Personal Power Press, P.O. Box 5985, Saginaw, MI 48603, or by calling 1-800-797-4133.

Brooke Mueller is 17 years old and has been a resident of Anchorage, Alaska, all her life. At age eight, she began writing, along with her other hobbies of drawing and playing the piano. She also enjoys the many experiences life in Alaska has to offer, such as moose and caribou hunting, fishing, and skiing.

David Naster is a nationally known comedian. His numerous major television appearances and national tours reflect his uncanny ability to share his humor with people of all types and ages. David travels throughout the world sharing his "Your Sense of Humor Will Get You Through It" keynote speeches. Writing children's stories is David's latest passion. Please feel free to contact him at 12317 W. 79th Place, Lenexa, KS 66215, phone: 913-438-4722.

Kent Nerburn is an author, sculptor and educator who has been deeply involved in Native American issues and education. He has served as project director for two books of oral history, *To Walk the Red Road* and *We Choose to Remember.* He has also edited three highly acclaimed books on Native American subjects. Kent won the Minnesota Book Award in 1995 for his book *Neither Wolf Nor Dog: On Forgotten Roads.* The story *Like People First* appeared in Kent's book *Letters to My Son.* Kent holds a Ph.D. in Theology and Art and lives with his family in Bemidju, Minnesota.

Nicole Nero is 15 years old and a sophomore at Saranac High School. An honor-roll student, Nicole plays in the school band. She enjoys spending time with her friends, reading and listening to music.

Tony Overman is a nationally known motivational youth speaker. He founded the National Youth I Care Hotline and produced *Teen Talk,* a nine-part video series. Tony conducts training workshops for teachers and motivational assemblies for schools. He can be reached at 18965 F.M. 2252, Garden Ridge, TX 78266, phone: 800-487-8464.

Theresa Peterson is a high school student and an active member of her church. He spare time is spent reading, writing and having fun with her friends. She is a warmhearted person whose loyalty to her friends and family is admirable. She can be reached at P.O. Box 366, Woodstown, NJ 08098.

John Powell, S.J., is a professor at Loyola University in Chicago. He is a popular lecturer, teacher and bestselling author who effectively brings together psychology and religion in a unified approach to personal growth and spiritual development. For more information about any of John Powell's books, please call Thomas More Customer Service at 1-800-822-6701.

Daphna Renan is currently a freshman at Yale College. She moved six times before she entered sixth grade, and it was during these early years that she learned the significance of deep and enduring friendships. Daphna would like to thank those who have filled her life with love, laughter and learning.

Sheila K. Reyman is a certified community college instructor. The consultant/trainer for a family child care program, Sheila presents workshops throughout the state. She has also been invited to speak with teens regarding goal-setting and positive attitudes. She can be reached at P.O. Box 20987, Mesa, AZ 85277, or by calling 602-807-1965.

Jennifer Rosenfeld is a career counselor and is currently authoring *Building Your Yellow Brick Road: Real Women Create Extraordinary Career Paths.* She would love to hear more inspiring career profiles and can be reached at 212-794-6050.

Bill Sanders makes a dynamic impact on the lives of teenagers through his nationwide speaking ministry. He is the author of 13 books and numerous cassette programs, and currently writes two books each year. Bill Sanders and his family live in Kalamazoo, Michigan.

Jack Schlatter is a well-known speaker, writer and recording personality. A frequent contributor to *Chicken Soup for the Soul* books, he can be seen and heard on the video and audio versions of the *Chicken Soup for the Soul* series. He stars in the bestselling *Gifts by the Side of the Road* by Career Track. Jack is listed in *Who's Who Among Teachers in America,* and his talks are filled with humor, wisdom and inspiration. He can be contacted at P.O. Box 577, Cypress, CA 90630, phone: 714-879-7271, e-mail: jackschlatter@themailnet.

Harley Schwadron is based in Ann Arbor, Michigan. He has been a professional cartoonist for more than 20 years. His cartoons appear in *Barron's,* the *Wall Street Journal, Harvard Business Review, National Law Journal, Medical Economics* and other periodicals. Previously, he worked as a newspaper reporter and PR editor, but he always aspired to be a cartoonist. He can be reached at P.O. Box 1347, Ann Arbor, MI 48106, phone: 313-426-8433.

Veronica A. Shoffstall is a member of the Baha'i faith, which teaches that all people are from one race and have been created noble by one God. She has been trying to make sense of the world through words all her life. Now in her mid-40s, she is trying to recapture the wisdom of her youth and learn the lessons expressed in her poem *After a While,* which she wrote at the age of 19. She can be reached at 229 East 25th Street, #4D, New York, NY 10010.

Mark E. Smith is an author and sought-after inspirational speaker. He shares the priceless lessons he's learned from living with cerebral palsy with thousands each year. For Mark's autobiography ($11.95 + $3 S&H), or to inquire about having him speak at your function, write: 27 Goree, Martinez, CA 94553, or call 510-228-8928.

Jason Summey is a 14-year-old high school freshman who handles himself in front of audiences like a 40-year-old pro. He speaks regularly about his "Be Cool, Stay in School" program and is currently completing a book on the subject. He can be reached at P.O. Box 16844, Asheville, NC 28816, or by calling 704-252-3573.

Andrew Tertes authors enchanting books, stories and poetry intended to inspire passion for one's own personal journey. For news on Andrew's upcoming books for adults and children, write to Unicorn News, P.O. Box 3164, San Rafael, CA 94901, or call 888-434-6789.

Terri Vandermark graduated from Johnson City High School in 1983. She spent her first five years after graduation as a PCA for the elderly and continues to enjoy helping others. Today she works full-time as parts crib attendant for Felchar Mfg., a division of Shop Vac Corp. She enjoys writing, reading *Chicken Soup for the Soul,* being in love with Randy and spending time with her special friend, Tonya. Her latest dream has come true—getting her story published in *Chicken Soup for the Teenage Soul.*

Glenn Van Ekeren is a dynamic speaker and trainer dedicated to helping people and organizations maximize their potential. Glenn is the author of *The Speaker's Sourcebook, The Speaker's Sourcebook II* and the popular *Potential*

Newsletter. Glenn has a wide variety of written publications and audio and video presentations available. He can be reached at People Building Institute, 330 Village Circle, Sheldon, IA 51201, or by calling 1-800-899-4878.

Jennifer Vetter is a student at Sentinel High School. She enjoys playing the cello in the orchestra and playing tennis. She likes to read, write poetry and spend time with her friends. She can be reached at 1740 Cyprus Ct., Missoula, MT 59801.

Sarah Vogt was born and raised in Columbus, Indiana. Currently, she resides in South Florida and works as a PC/network analyst for a major corporation. Sarah has an undergraduate degree in business administration from Florida Atlantic University. Computers are her hobby and livelihood; writing is her passion. She can be reached at 2050 Spectrum Blvd., Fort Lauderdale, FL 33309.

Jane Watkins is an artist, masseuse and poet residing in Santa Monica with her daughter Lia. She continues on a journey of self-discovery which began at Esalen in the 1960s and continues today in her affiliation with the Sterling Institute of Relationship.

Mary Jane West-Delgado is a physical therapist and author of short stories and cartoons. She is president of Toe Bumpers, Inc., creating fun and decorative safety products for the home. You can reach Mary Jane at 805-688-1372 or by e-mail at delgado@terminus.com.

Sharon Whitley is a former bilingual grade-school teacher who has also taught high-school special education. Her work has appeared in *Reader's Digest* (including 18 international editions), *Los Angeles Times Magazine, Guideposts* and the *San Diego Union-Tribune.* She can be reached at 5666 Meredith Ave., San Diego, CA 92120, phone: 619-583-7346.

Amy Yerkes is currently a student at University of Maryland, College Park. She is planning a career in public relations and enjoys writing poetry in her spare time. She can be reached at 50 Rainbow Trail, Denville, NJ 07834, or by calling 201-625-2690.

Bettie B. Youngs, Ph.D., is one of the nation's most respected voices in youth and parent education. She is the author of 14 books published in 30 languages, including *Values From the Heartland, Gifts of the Heart: Stories That Celebrate Life's Defining Moments* and *You and Self-Esteem: A Book for Young People,* from which this piece is excerpted. Contact Dr. Youngs at 3060 Racetrack View Dr., Del Mar, CA 92014.

Permissions *(continued from page iv)*

Losing the "Us." Reprinted by permission of Lia Gay. ©1996 Lia Gay.

After a While. Reprinted by permission of Veronica A. Shoffstall. ©1971 Veronica A. Shoffstall.

Soul Mates. Reprinted by permission of Fran Leb. ©1996 Fran Leb.

The Miss of a Great "Miss." Reprinted by permission of Jack Schlatter. ©1996 Jack Schlatter.

My First Kiss, and Then Some. Reprinted by permission of Mary Jane West-Delgado. ©1996 Mary Jane West-Delgado.

Changes in Life. Reprinted by permission of Sheila K. Reyman. ©1996 Sheila K. Reyman.

First Love. Reprinted by permission of Mary Ellen Klee. ©1996 Mary Ellen Klee.

A High School Love Not Forgotten and *Mrs. Virginia DeView, Where Are You?* Reprinted by permission of Diana L. Chapman. ©1996 Diana L. Chapman.

Betty Ann and *Anne.* Reprinted by permission of William Morrow & Company, Inc. Excerpted from *A Prayer for Children* by Ina J. Hughes. ©1995 by Ina J. Hughes.

A Simple Christmas Card. Reprinted by permission of Theresa Peterson. ©1996 Theresa Peterson.

She Told Me It Was Okay to Cry. Reprinted by permission of Daphna Renan. ©1996 Daphna Renan.

Lessons in Friendship. Reprinted by permission of A. J. Langer. ©1996 A. J. Langer.

The Days of Cardboard Boxes. Reprinted by permission of Eva Burke. ©1996 Eva Burke.

She Didn't Give Up on Me. Reprinted by permission of Sharon Whitley. ©1994 Sharon Whitley. Excerpted from *Woman's World Magazine.*

Mama's Hands. Reprinted by permission of Warner Books, Inc. From *Girl Power* by Hilary Carlip. ©1996. All rights reserved.

Unconditional Mom. Reprinted by permission of Sarah J. Vogt. ©1996 Sarah J. Vogt.

The Birthday. Reprinted by permission of Melissa Esposito. ©1996 Melissa Esposito.

The Home Run. Reprinted by permission of Terri Vandermark. ©1996 Terri Vandermark.

My Big Brother. Reprinted by permission of Lisa Gumenick. ©1996 Lisa Gumenick.

A Brother's Voice. Reprinted by permission of James Malinchak. ©1996 James Malinchak.

Daddy Weirdest. Reprinted by permission of Rebecca Barry. ©1994 Rebecca Barry. *Daddy Weirdest* first appeared in *Seventeen.*

A Famous Father. Excerpted from *Moments for Teens* by Robert Strand. ©1996 New Leaf Press. All rights reserved.

Lessons in Baseball. Reprinted by permission of Chick Moorman. ©1996 Chick Moorman.

The Champ. Reprinted by permission of Nailah Malik. ©1996 Nailah Malik.

I Love You, Dad. Reprinted by permission of Nick Curry III. ©1996 Nick Curry III.

I Am Home. Reprinted by permission of Jennie Garth. ©1996 Jennie Garth.

Tigress. Reprinted by permission of Judith S. Johnessee. ©1996 Judith S. Johnessee.

Bright Heart. Reprinted by permission of Jennifer Love Hewitt. ©1996 Jennifer Love Hewitt.

The Secret of Happiness and *From Crutches to a World-Class Runner.* Reprinted by permission of Glenn Van Ekeren. ©1994 Glenn Van Ekeren.

Reaching Out to a Stranger and *Courage in a Fire.* Excerpted from *Kids with Courage: True Stories About Young People Making a Difference* by Barbara A. Lewis. ©1992. Used with permission from Free Spirit Publishing Inc., Minneapolis, MN; 800-735-7323. ALL RIGHTS RESERVED.

Smile. Reprinted by permission of Barbara Hauck. ©1996 Barbara Hauck.

Mrs. Link. Reprinted by permission of Susan Daniels Adams. ©1996 Susan Daniels Adams.

The Mirror and *Adulthood.* Excerpted from *It Was on Fire When I Lay Down on It* by Robert Fulghum. ©1988, 1989 by Robert Fulghum. Reprinted by permission of Villard Books, a division of Random House, Inc.

A Gift for Two. Reprinted by permission of Andrea Hensley. ©1996 Andrea Hensley.

Life Just Isn't. Reprinted by permission of Katie Leicht. ©1996 Katie Leicht.

Tell the World for Me. Reprinted by permission of John Powell, S.J. ©1996 John Powell, S.J.

Like People First. Reprinted by permission of Kent Nerburn. ©1995 Kent Nerburn.

Lilacs Bloom Every Spring. Reprinted by permission of *blue jean magazine.* ©1996 *blue jean magazine.*

Paint Brush. Reprinted by permission of Bettie B. Youngs. Excerpted from *You and Self-Esteem: A Book For Young People.* ©1996 Bettie B. Youngs.

A Long Walk Home. Reprinted by permission of Jason Bocarro. ©1996 Jason Bocarro.

The Cost of Gratefulness. Reprinted by permission of Randal Jones. ©1996 Randal Jones.

The Eternal Gifts. Reprinted by permission of Jack Schlatter. ©1996 Jack Schlatter.

Socrates. Reprinted by permission of Eric Saperston. ©1996 Eric Saperston.

Challenge Days. Reprinted by permission of Andrew Tertes. ©1996 Andrew Tertes.

I Am . . . Reprinted by permission of Amy Yerkes. ©1996 Amy Yerkes.

Sparky. Reprinted by permission of *Bits & Pieces.* The Economics Press, Inc., Fairfield, N.J. 07004. 800-526-2554.

Detention Can Be Fun. Reprinted by permission of the Putnam Publishing Group from *CHILDHOOD* by Bill Cosby. ©1991 by William H. Cosby, Jr.

Eleven. From *Woman Hollering Creek.* ©1991 by Sandra Cisneros. Published by Vintage Books, a division of Random House, Inc., New York, and originally in hardcover by Random House, Inc.

I'll Always Be with You. Reprinted by permission of Dale and Dar Emme. ©1996 Dale and Dar Emme.

Somebody Should Have Taught Him. Reprinted by permission of Jane Watkins. ©1996 Jane Watkins.

Just One Drink. Reprinted by permission of Chris Laddish. ©1996 Chris Laddish.

The Premonition. Reprinted by permission of Bruce Burch. Excerpted from *Songs That Changed Our Lives* by Bruce Burch. ©1996 Bruce Burch.

Dead at 17. Reprinted by permission of John Berrio. ©1967 John Berrio.

I'll Be Looking for You, Ace. Reprinted with permission from *Guideposts* magazine. ©1987 by Guideposts, Carmel, NY 10512.

My Story. Reprinted by permission of Lia Gay. ©1996 Lia Gay.

"Gabby, You're Sooo Skinny." Reprinted by permission of Gabriella Tortes. ©1996 Gabriella Tortes.

Last Wish. Reprinted with permission from *Guideposts* magazine. ©1996 by Guideposts, Carmel, NY 10512.

Gold-Medal Winner. Reprinted by permission of Rick Metzger. ©1996 Rick Metzger.

Desiderata. Reprinted by permission of Robert L. Bell. ©1927 Max Ehrman.

Be Cool . . . Stay in School! Reprinted by permission of Jason Summey. ©1996 Jason Summey.

The Leader. Reprinted by permission of Tony Overman. ©1996 Tony Overman.

Courage in Action. Reprinted by permission of Fleming H. Revell, a division of Baker Book House Co. Excerpted from *Goalposts: Devotions for Girls* by Bill Sanders. ©1995 Bill Sanders.

Turning Up Your Light. Reprinted by permission of Eric Allenbaugh. ©1995 Eric Allenbaugh. Excerpted from *Wake-Up Calls: You Don't Have to Sleepwalk Through Your Life, Love or Career.*

Broken Wing. Reprinted by permission of Jim Hullihan. ©1996 Jim Hullihan.

Passing the Dream. Reprinted by permission of Penny Caldwell. ©1996 Penny Caldwell.

The Girl Next Door. Reprinted by permission of Amanda Dykstra. ©1996 Amanda Dykstra.

I'll Be Back. Reprinted by permission of Jack Cavanaugh. ©1992 Jack Cavanaugh. Also, reprinted by permission of the February 1992 *Reader's Digest.*

Just Me. Reprinted by permission of Tom Krause. ©1996 Tom Krause.

True Height. Reprinted by permission of David Naster. ©1995 David Naster.

The Gravediggers of Parkview Junior High. Reprinted by permission of Kif Anderson. ©1996 Kif Anderson.

Teenagers' Bill of Rights. Reprinted by permission of Lia Gay, Jamie Yellin, Lisa Gumenick, Hana Ivanhoe, Bree Able and Lisa Rothbard.

The Boy Who Talked with Dolphins. Reprinted by permissions of Paula McDonald. Also reprinted with permission from the April 1996 *Reader's Digest.*

To Track Down My Dream. Reprinted by permission of Ashley Hodgeson. ©1996 Ashley Hodgeson.

No-Hair Day. Reprinted by permission of Jennifer Rosenfeld and Alison Lambert. ©1995 Jennifer Rosenfeld and Alison Lambert.

I Did It! Reprinted by permission of Mark E. Smith. ©1995. Excerpted from *Growing Up with Cerebral Palsy* by Mark E. Smith.

Growing. Reprinted by permission of Brooke Mueller. ©1996 Brooke Mueller.

New Beginnings. Reprinted by permission of Paula (Bachleda) Koskey. ©1996 Paula (Bachleda) Koskey.

Sudden Inspiration

For the first time ever, you can enjoy a batch of new "short" stories—each one no more than two pages long. This delectable gem is chock-full of insightful cartoons, inspirations and uplifting messages. **#4215—$8.95**

The very best short stories from *Chicken Soup for the Soul, A 2nd Helping* and *A 3rd Serving* are right at your fingertips. This single-serving volume is filled with morsels of wisdom, teaspoons of love and sweet pinches of heartwarming goodness. **#4142—$8.95**

This personal journal provides you with a unique place to create your own magic. Neatly lined blank pages are interspersed with words of encouragement giving you a special place to record your day's activities, plans, goals and dreams. **#4843, hardcover—$10.95**

Available in bookstores everywhere or call **1-800-441-5569** for Visa or MasterCard orders. Prices do not include shipping and handling. Your response code is **CCS**.